ONE MORE
FOR THE
WHITE RAT

ONE MORE
FOR THE
WHITE RAT

The 1987 St. Louis Cardinals
Chase the Pennant

DOUG FELDMANN

Foreword by Ricky Horton

University of Nebraska Press | LINCOLN

The University of Nebraska Press is part of a land-grant institution with campuses and programs on the past, present, and future homelands of the Pawnee, Ponca, Otoe-Missouria, Omaha, Dakota, Lakota, Kaw, Cheyenne, and Arapaho Peoples, as well as those of the relocated Ho-Chunk, Sac and Fox, and Iowa Peoples.

Library of Congress Cataloging-in-Publication Data
Names: Feldmann, Doug, 1970– author.
Title: One more for the white rat: the 1987 St. Louis Cardinals chase the pennant / Doug Feldmann; foreword by Ricky Horton.
Description: Lincoln: University of Nebraska Press, 2025. | Includes bibliographical references and index.
Identifiers: LCCN 2024038727 (print) | LCCN 2024038728 (ebook)
ISBN 9781496241405 (hardcover)
ISBN 9781496242440 (epub)
ISBN 9781496242457 (pdf)
Subjects: LCSH: St. Louis Cardinals (Baseball team)—History—20th century. | Major League Baseball (Organization)—History—20th century. | World Series (Baseball) (1987) | BISAC: SPORTS & RECREATION / Baseball / General | HISTORY / United States / State & Local / Midwest (IA, IL, IN, KS, MI, MN, MO, ND, NE, OH, SD, WI)
Classification: LCC GV875.S3 F464 2025 (print) | LCC GV875.S3 (ebook) | DDC 796.357/640977866—dc23/eng/20250107
LC record available at https://lccn.loc.gov/2024038727
LC ebook record available at https://lccn.loc.gov/2024038728

Designed and set in Questa by K. Andresen.

To every player who wore the Birds on the Bat and electrified the turf of Busch Stadium during the magical years of the 1980s.

I'm forever getting on first base because of a walk or a single, and hearing first basemen on other teams second-guess their managers. You hear it all over baseball—guys saying this or that about their managers. But that's one thing we don't have here.

I'm not saying he doesn't have an ego, because he does, and it's not a small ego. And it's not that all of his moves work. It's just that we all feel Whitey's got a couple of things going for him that other managers don't. He always keeps you in a position to win a ballgame, and you always feel that in a close game you're not going to get outmanaged.

—TOM HERR

Contents

Illustrations

Foreword

Ricky Horton

HAVING BEEN CONNECTED TO CARDINAL BASEBALL FOR PARTS of five decades, I have grown to appreciate the great pageantry and celebration of past teams. Opening day is such a meaningful experience at Busch Stadium, and Cardinal fans seem to embrace the wonderful history of the organization—during a time when history seems to be unimportant to so many people. Baseball has a way of connecting us to this history, and I am appreciative of Doug's desire and his work to bring us back to 1987, a season that I certainly remember. So many players from that team are still great friends, and so many moments are etched in my memory of a team that achieved so much. Tudor, Cox, McGee, Dayley, Herr, Pendleton, Worrell, Lawless, Clark, Forsch, Smith, and many others come to mind—big names to Cardinal fans, but lifelong friends of mine. I have great joy remembering a Willie McGee triple, an Ozzie Smith acrobatic play, a John Tudor masterpiece.

I HOPE YOU HAVE GREAT JOY READING DOUG'S BOOK ABOUT a team that was absolutely a *team*. Whitey Herzog was the mastermind of a group of men that cared about each other, cared about winning, and loved the ride. I hope that you enjoy the ride as well.

Acknowledgments

A SPECIAL WORD OF THANKS GOES TO THE FORMER PLAYERS who contributed interviews for this book, especially Ricky Horton, Howard Johnson, Jim Lindeman, Joe Magrane, Greg Mathews, Roger McDowell, John Morris, and Mookie Wilson, in addition to Larry State of the Cardinals and Jay Horwitz of the New York Mets, who provided great assistance in procuring research. Finally, I thank my editor at the University of Nebraska Press, Rob Taylor; his assistant Taylor Martin; and copy editor Joseph Webb for their encouragement and expertise.

1

Met with Disaster—after a Meltdown in KC

I very seldom take a ballgame home with me. I usually go home, have something to eat, watch a little television, and hit the sack. I'm asleep in five minutes. But I took the sixth game [of the 1985 World Series] home with me, [and] sat up late talking about it with Mary Lou and the kids. I knew we had had it.

—Whitey Herzog

AT 10:00 P.M. ON OCTOBER 26, 1985, TWO FRIENDS WERE nearing the end of a chess game in Kansas City. They were employed in the same line of work, had once worked for the same company, and at one point had even lived in the same subdivision. They stared at each other from across the table and then turned their eyes back to the chessboard. Because of the late stage of the game, the men realized they had only a few remaining pieces left to play.

One of the men, St. Louis Cardinals manager Whitey Herzog, got ready to slide one his pawns. With his team holding a slim 1–0 lead in the ninth inning of Game Six of the World Series, Herzog stood in the third base dugout at Royals Stadium and directed his left-handed relief pitcher Ken Dayley out to the mound for a second inning of work. Only three outs stood between the Cardinals and their tenth championship.

The other chess player, Kansas City Royals manager Dick Howser, leaned against the railing in the home dugout on the first base side—the place from which Herzog himself had directed the

Royals from 1975 to 1979. After watching Dayley emerge, Howser motioned to his bench for the right-handed-batting Darryl Motley to pinch-hit for the left-handed Pat Sheridan.

As soon as Motley was introduced by the public-address announcer, Herzog countered. Warming up in the bullpen was his precocious closer, Todd Worrell, a right-hander with a blazing fastball and a devastating slider.

Howser volleyed back. He then replaced Motley with another left-handed batter, thirty-four-year-old Jorge Orta. A decade earlier, Orta had been known for his running speed; but with his career now in its twilight, he had slowed a step and was hitless in his only two plate appearances in the series, also occurring in pinch-hitting roles.

Despite the tense situation, the young Worrell showed no hesitation. He aggressively went after the veteran with fastballs, getting ahead in the count at 0-2, as Orta took one pitch for a strike on the outside corner and then fouled two more off.

The fourth pitch was another fastball that sailed high and outside and that Orta, going against the tenets of hitting, attempted to pull. In doing so, he dribbled a weak grounder that Cardinals' first baseman Jack Clark dashed forward to retrieve. Worrell raced over to cover the bag, as pitchers are taught to do on any ground ball hit to the right side of the field.

In the next instant, the actions of a veteran umpire for whom Herzog held the utmost respect precipitated a rapid demise of the nine St. Louis players on the field, a freefall that would carry over into the following night.

"Here's Donny Denkinger, a guy I've known for years and a guy I regard as one of the top five or six umpires in the major leagues," the St. Louis skipper recalled.[1]

Clark flipped the ball to the six-foot-five-inch Worrell, who was able to keep his foot on first base while fully outstretched in reaching for the throw.

Describing the play on the nationwide broadcast for CBS Radio was Jack Buck, the Cardinals' legendary voice, who was paired with renowned Cincinnati Reds and Detroit Tigers manager Sparky Anderson to cover the series.

"Sparky, did he have his foot on the bag?"

"Yep."

"Did he have the ball?"

"Yep."

"Was the batter's foot still above the base?"

"Yep."

"He's out, right?"

"Well, that depends."[2]

Orta, after making a final lunge for the bag, was called safe by Denkinger despite the baseball already being in Worrell's glove. Television replays—employed merely for entertaining second looks in 1985 and not for overturning calls on the field—exposed the arbiter's error to the world in no uncertain terms. Herzog stormed off the bench as Denkinger absorbed his protests, in addition to those of the entire Cardinals infield.

When play resumed, Worrell appeared to have quickly reversed the momentum back to St. Louis. His next pitch induced the power-hitting Steve Balboni to slice a foul pop-up near the first base dugout. But when Clark misplayed the ball and let it fall to the ground, the batter took advantage of the new life and promptly singled Orta to second base. Onix Concepcion was then inserted by Howser to run for the girthy Balboni.

Worrell, for a third time, composed himself and did his part. He smoothly fielded a sacrifice bunt off the bat of Jim Sundberg and was able to force Orta at third. But a passed ball by catcher Darrell Porter subsequently put the tying run on third base in the person of Concepcion, with Sundberg the potential winning run on second.

"And here's the Cardinals," Herzog continued in his recollection of the evening, "a team that hasn't lost a game in the ninth inning all year. And in our 174th game of the year, it catches up with us."

With first base now open, Herzog decided to load the bases with an intentional walk to Hal McRae, and Howser then moved his final chess piece. It was another left-handed pinch hitter, who happened to be a former St. Louis hero and a trusted late-inning bat for Herzog himself in years past.

"And then here comes Dane Iorg, one of my favorite people, a guy who hit .529 for the Cardinals in the 1982 World Series. He flares a ball to right field that scores two runs. We lose the game, and deep in my heart, I knew we lost the World Series," said Herzog.

After nearly four decades in professional baseball as a player, scout, front office man, assistant coach, general manager, and manager, a discouraging battle on the field had finally penetrated the stoic mind of the cool White Rat. "I very seldom take a ball game home with me. I usually go home, have something to eat, watch a little television, and hit the sack. I'm asleep in five minutes. But I took the sixth game home with me, [and] sat up late talking about it with Mary Lou and the kids. I knew we had had it."[3]

HERZOG'S PREMONITION WAS ACCURATE. THE LISTLESS Redbirds traipsed onto the field the following evening as a beaten team before the first pitch was thrown.

Precisely twenty-four hours after Iorg's game-winning hit, the Cardinals' Andy Van Slyke swung and lofted a long fly ball toward the right-field wall at 10:11 p.m. on October 27. Motley ran under it and made the catch, which ended the game and the 1985 baseball season. The result of the contest, however—and the entire World Series—had already become a foregone conclusion an hour earlier.

Crafty and unflappable St. Louis left-hander John Tudor, one of the best pitchers in baseball in 1985, who had lost only once in the regular season since the end of May, staked the Royals to a 5–0 lead in Game Seven before the third inning was over. Three more Cardinals hurlers went to the mound after Tudor—who smashed his hand in frustration on an electric fan in the dugout upon being removed from the game by Herzog, causing severe lacerations—as the deficit expanded to 9–0 by the fifth inning. In desperation, Herzog was compelled to call upon his most volatile player, who, in contrast to Tudor's incredible success in the second half of the season, had been victorious only once since August 23.

Joaquín Andújar was "the only pitcher I had left in the bullpen with any life in his arm," the manager asserted. "He had told me he was ready to pitch if I needed him."[4] Known for his Dizzy Dean-like utterances and playful antics, Andújar enjoyed "six-gunning" the batter with his thumb and finger like a Colt pistol after a strike-out and, on occasion, remaining in his uniform when showering after a game. One time, a writer had asked Andújar how he would pitch to himself. "I'd throw me a fastball right down the middle," he answered, giving the person an incredulous look. "What do you think, I'm going to try to get myself out?"[5]

But Andújar's temper was equally famous.

After running the count full, Andújar gave up a line drive to Frank White, just over the reach of the leaping Terry Pendleton at third base, scoring Willie Wilson for the 10th Kansas City run.

Batting next was Sundberg, an outstanding defensive catcher but generally modest hitter over the course of his twelve years in the Majors at that point in 1985. On the first pitch, Andújar got the benefit of a borderline strike call at the knees on the outside edge from Denkinger, who in the normal umpire rotation was now behind home plate for the seventh game.

The next pitch ran inside on Sundberg and was called a ball, but Andújar felt it had caught the corner. He gestured demonstratively in the direction of home plate, which Herzog and others on the Cardinals' bench merely interpreted as a request by the pitcher for Porter to come to the mound for a meeting. But to untrained eyes watching in the stadium and around the globe on television, it was seen as an angry motion toward the umpire.

Sundberg fouled off the next pitch, bringing the count to 1-2. The fourth pitch was a carbon copy of the second, the ball again narrowly missing the inside corner as Andújar slammed his glove in disgust while turning his back on Denkinger.

After Sundberg fouled off another, the sixth pitch again came inside. But despite being closer to the corner than the other two, it was again called a ball. Andújar sprung forward off the mound and charged toward the plate. Denkinger, finishing his twenty-seventh year in the big leagues, met him halfway.

By the time the two were nose-to-nose, Herzog was already across the foul line. He nudged his pitcher aside while taking over the conversation and, a moment later, became the first manager ejected from a World Series game since the Yankees' Billy Martin nine years earlier.

Things had not calmed down by the time Herzog retreated down the dugout steps. Even with the manager gone, Andújar and a swarm of other Cardinals continued to cluster around Denkinger as the pitcher became more enraged. Herzog, looking back over his shoulder and noticing the escalation, did a 180 and, despite his ejection, returned to the field in an effort to protect his player.

The trouble seemed to subside after Herzog left the premises a second time, as his pitching coach Mike Roarke and the St. Louis infielders gathered with Andújar at the mound for a normal meeting. After his teammates had dispersed back to their positions, Andújar was once again by himself on the hill. The TV cameras caught the pitcher drawing a deep breath, adjusting his cap, and going back to work on Sundberg with a full count. Denkinger pointed at the Cardinal right-hander in ordering the game to restart.

But then the lid came off for Andújar, who was stewing over the 10–0 deficit and just-finished combative interlude. For the fourth time in Sundberg's at bat, a pitch barely missed the inside corner yet again, sending Sundberg down to first base with a walk. Andújar again stomped toward the plate, both of his hands flailing in the air in protest. For the final thirty feet, it turned into a dead sprint toward Denkinger.

The pitcher had to be restrained by Pendleton, Roarke, and assistant coach Nick Leyva. All five of the other umpires (with two extras working the foul lines for the World Series) rushed toward home plate as well, getting in between their colleague and the men in the gray uniforms. Roarke, though a large man, struggled to physically remove Andújar from the scene, subduing the Dominican in a makeshift full nelson and walking him off the field, where he joined his manager in the clubhouse as the first player thrown out of a World Series game in fifteen years.

Bob Forsch, one of the most decorated pitchers in team history, was forced to undertake a thankless task. On his first offering, he uncorked a fifty-foot slider to Balboni, a wild pitch that plated George Brett for an 11–0 Kansas City advantage.

The margin stood as the final score four innings later when Van Slyke's fly ball landed in Motley's glove. As the Royals leapt into each other's arms and commenced their victory celebration in the Battle of Missouri, Van Slyke's out meant the Cardinals' final team batting average for the series had fallen to a paltry .185, the lowest mark ever for in a seven-game championship set. Without the .360 performance of backup outfielder Tito Landrum—subbing for the injured Vince Coleman and likely the Most Valuable Player of the series if the Cards had triumphed—the club's ledger would have read .162. "Thirteen runs in seven games is almost a disgrace," Herzog summarized afterwards of his team's offensive output.[6]

NONETHELESS, TO THOSE WHO REMEMBER THE ENTIRETY OF the spring, summer, and early fall of 1985, it was a season of spectacular and surprising success for the Cardinals. After being predicted to finish last in the National League's Eastern Division, they rode stellar pitching, a galloping defense, and the best offense in the league (747 runs scored and a .264 team average, both NL highs) to 101 regular season wins as the team's relentless style of play left an indelible mark on baseball.

It was their unbridled running game, however, that stoked horror in opponents. With five switch-hitters in the lineup, the 314 stolen bases by the Cardinals was the second-most in the Majors since 1912. Over a third of that total came solely from Coleman, a rookie who did not even come north with the team from spring training at the end of March. By the All-Star break, it seemed as if Herzog's men were trying to steal third base as often as second, and the immense pressure they were putting on pitchers, catchers, and managers caused dread for teams having to visit the hot Astroturf of Busch Stadium. As each errant offering from a jittered pitcher got them closer to a walk, Coleman, Van Slyke, Willie McGee, and the other jackrabbits would stand menacingly at the plate as the noise and energy from the fans in Busch would gradually rise in a frenzy of anticipation of what was to come on the basepaths.

When fans looked toward 1986, therefore, only some fine-tuning of the roster appeared necessary for a return to the postseason. And with the conclusion of the World Series, the Cardinals moved quickly to discard two prominent figures.

In December, Andújar—a 20-game winner in each of the previous two seasons in St. Louis—was traded to the Oakland A's. Just hours before the deal was finalized, the Boston Red Sox had nixed a Cardinals proposal to send Andújar and fellow pitchers Rick Ownbey and Jeff Lahti to Boston for Bruce Hurst, who was quickly becoming one of the steadiest starting pitchers in the American League. Andújar's services for any team, however, would be delayed.

Due to the incident in Kansas City, he was required to serve a ten-game suspension at the beginning of the 1986 season, a punishment handed down from the office of Major League Baseball Commissioner Peter Ueberroth. (The penalty was ultimately reduced to four games.)

Even in advance of his World Series troubles, Andújar had already worn his welcome out in St. Louis. After refusing to pitch in the 1985 All-Star Game after National League manager Dick Williams decided Andújar would not be the starter, he lost five of six decisions during the Cardinals' final pennant charge in September while simultaneously seeing his name surface in the ongoing inquiry Ueberroth was conducting into cocaine use by Major League players.

Although Andújar's unraveling on national television in the World Series had already gotten him convicted in the court of public opinion, Cardinals general manager Dal Maxvill insisted the trade was not a punitive measure mandated from the team's ownership. "I was not told to move anybody," Maxvill assured the press in the wake of the transaction. "I've never had it come down from above. And we did not decide as soon as the season was over that we trade this guy or that guy."[7] The field manager was blunter, however, and saw it for what it was. "The brewery was embarrassed," Herzog said plainly of the fallout passing through the boardroom at the Anheuser-Busch headquarters. "It's been reported that Maxvill and I were ordered to trade Joaquin, and I won't deny that."[8]

From Oakland, the Cardinals received what they considered to be a couple of versatile players in the classic Herzog mold. One was left-handed pitcher Tim Conroy, who, just weeks after graduating high school in 1978, became the twentieth overall pick in the amateur draft, skipped the Minors after signing his contract, and started a game for the A's that June at the age of 18, becoming the first player born in the 1960s to appear in the Major Leagues. With the potential to fill any slot on the staff from starter to long reliever to short reliever, Conroy also impressed Herzog with his natural hitting ability despite never coming to the plate in an American League game. "The best hitting pitcher I've had around here," he would say after watching the new acquisition take some swings.[9]

MET WITH DISASTER

Herzog even considered sending Conroy to the Instructional League over the winter, where he could work as a designated hitter, with the idea of being another left-handed bat off the bench come 1986.

The other player in the Andújar deal was Mike Heath, a strong-armed catcher who possessed an adequate bat and, with his diverse defensive skills, could play nearly anywhere on the field. But Heath's primary glove strength was envisioned to be behind the plate, and he had been specifically targeted to replace the enigmatic St. Louis catcher of the past five seasons.

"Darrell Porter has surely played his last game in a Cardinals uniform," *St. Louis Post-Dispatch* beat writer Rick Hummel penned just three days after the World Series loss to the Royals. "Club officials have been disappointed not only in his failure to hit but by his passive style of play." The frustration with Porter was recently fueled by his critical passed ball in the ninth inning of Game Six after the Denkinger debacle. "The Cardinals paid Porter about $750,000 a year for the last five years," Hummel noted, "but probably wouldn't even consider paying half that now, even for a one-year contract."[10] Therefore, on November 14, the man named the MVP of both the 1982 National League Championship Series and World Series but judged to have otherwise underperformed was placed on waivers.

WITH THE OFF-SEASON UPON HIM, HERZOG TURNED TO HIS beloved autumn fishing regimen. Nipping at his heels for the entire summer of 1985 had been the improving New York Mets, a balanced team with blossoming young superstars Dwight Gooden and Darryl Strawberry and steady veterans such as Gary Carter and former Cardinal Keith Hernandez. Another war was thus primed between the two clubs for Eastern Division honors in the National League for 1986, with the fleet Redbirds looking to complete their unfinished business and the rising Mets seeking to ascend to the Fall Classic themselves. "They had what we wanted," the Mets' Howard Johnson said in 2023. "We wanted a championship. There was such a deep rivalry. It's a shame it's not like that anymore. It was always so much fun."[11]

Driven by Herzog's desire to vindicate his club after the October swoon, the 1986 Cardinals initially reclaimed their magic from the previous season. The team stood at 7-1 on April 19 after grinding out a 9–6 win in seventeen innings at Montreal, with Conroy getting his first victory in relief—but also with Heath going 0-8 at the plate, a troubling harbinger of things to come for himself as well as the entire club.

Tudor bounced back from his difficulties in Game Seven of the World Series and had earned 3 of the 7 wins. But due to the numerous rainouts the team encountered early in the schedule, Herzog had been able to throw him more often than usual. Such a pace was not sustainable for the southpaw, and the coaching staff knew that another pitcher would have to emerge as a leader in the absence of Andújar.

Then, as quickly as the bats had resurfaced, they went back into hiding in the second week of the season, the tipping point of a long-term plunge that was reminiscent of the World Series.

After the marathon game against Montreal, the Cardinals were blanked the following afternoon by Jay Tibbs of the Expos, 2–0. It was one of five times in the next ten days St. Louis would be shut out during a seven-game losing streak, something a Herzog team had not done in two full years, as the Cardinals and their manager were about to embark upon one of the most frustrating and inexplicable summers in franchise history. "Of the thirty-seven years I've been in professional baseball," Herzog would reflect, "the 1986 season with the Cardinals was the strangest."[12] Another losing streak of five games sank the Cardinals into last place in the National League East for the first time since April of the previous year, a string punctuated by being shut out again on May 3 by Fernando Valenzuela and the Los Angeles Dodgers.

The upstart Mets, meanwhile, did not lose a game in the second half of April, storming to the top of the standings with an eleven-game winning streak.

As the battle lines were drawn, one advantage that Herzog counted on having over New York in 1986 was a deeper bullpen, but during a four-game sweep by the Mets in Busch Stadium at the close of the season's first month, the injury ax started to fall upon the relief corps. Lahti, who had risen to lead the team with 19 saves in 1985 after the departure of ace closer Bruce Sutter, came in to face Carter in the eighth inning on the night of April 24. Permitting an RBI single, Lahti had to leave the game with soreness in his shoulder after facing the lone batter. "It was a weak fastball," Lahti said of the meager offering to the Mets' All-Star catcher. "[The hit] went by me like a bullet. I knew I was in trouble. When you're throwing 90 and all of a sudden 83 is all you can get, you know something's wrong."[13] With the appearance being only his fourth of the young season, Lahti underwent surgery two weeks later.

With the Cardinals losing twelve of thirteen games in the middle of May, the team's hitting had become so abysmal that the scoreboard operator at Busch Stadium was ordered to halt the display of batting averages for public view. After a 5–3 loss to the Reds at home on May 20 had dropped the Redbirds to a 13-21 record, Herzog was rumored to be leaving the Cardinals to replace the retiring Chub Feeney as president of the National League. "The St. Louis Cardinals' loss [would be] the National League's gain," wrote Bob Verdi in *The Sporting News* of the proposed scenario— one that Herzog vehemently denied.[14]

In addition to their woes at the plate, another albatross for the Cardinals was their inability to simply execute the basics, an area in which they had excelled so consistently the previous year. Herzog pointed to his reigning National League Rookie of the Year as an example. "[Vince] Coleman suddenly has decided he's got the greatest arm in baseball," the manager scribbled in his personal journal that month, "and is trying to throw everyone out at the plate instead of throwing the ball into second base to keep the double play in order." Coleman's trouble was but one example, as Herzog labeled the entire team as complicit. "We're missing signs, swinging at balls over our heads, not getting the bunt down when we need it, generally playing stupid baseball. We're the kind of team that has to do the fundamental things right because we don't have the long-ball hitters to make up for our mistakes. . . . We [have] veteran players—some of the biggest stars in the game—who seemed to forget how the game is supposed to be played."[15]

McGee, the league's MVP a year earlier, was letting multiple fly balls go over his head in center field; Clark, the lone power threat in the batting order, did not come to the plate with the bases loaded until the thirty-seventh game of the season; and second baseman Tom Herr had to fight to *raise* his average to .170 by the end of May, yet he was barely outperformed by the third baseman Pendleton, who was yearning to reach the .200 mark himself. And the new catcher Heath ended April with an .080 performance, posting a scant 4 hits in 50 at bats. "He hasn't hit anything, he isn't throwing well, and he can't even catch the ball," was Herzog's evaluation of Heath's early performance. Bad luck could not be pinned as a scapegoat for the lack of offense, as hitting coach Johnny Lewis noticed the batters were making very few hard outs on line drives.

It was as if the entire National League had exposed the Cardinals as a paper tiger, with their 1985 outburst nothing more than a fluke. "The Royals' staff did it to us in the World Series, and now the word is out all over baseball," the manager continued in jotting down his thoughts about the nightmare season. "'Throw the Cardinals high fastballs and don't worry about it because Clark is the only one who can take you deep. Everybody else has warning-track power.'"[16]

Herzog, one of the most resilient men the sport has ever seen, described the month of May 1986 as

the longest I've ever spent in baseball. The fact that we won only nine games all month was bad enough, but there were things going on with our club that publicly I can't talk about and privately I didn't know what to do about. . . . I will say that we had some deep divisions on our club, personal animosities that had nothing to do with baseball. . . . I couldn't believe that some of our players were acting the way they did. We had guys who weren't talking to each other, guys who wouldn't even carry other guys' gloves and hats out to them between innings. They were almost like a bunch of little kids, pouting out there.

I met with the people in the front office about it, told them the problems we were having, and offered to resign if they thought it would do any good.[17]

In the second week of June, Herzog was at his wit's end. "It's about got me to the point where I don't want to manage the damn club anymore," he put in his diary. "I halfway wish [owner] Gussie [Busch] would call me up and tell me he's decided to make a change, so I could get the hell out of here, get off to the mountains and go fishing. Then I wouldn't have to watch this bullshit night after night."

Between the performance of those on the Major League roster and the perceived lack of talent in the Minor Leagues, the personnel issues were in such disarray that simply putting nine competitive players on the field became a challenge for one of baseball's greatest thinkers. "In a way, it was kind of fun trying to come up with a lineup every night which might have a chance of winning."[18]

Herzog tapped further into his creativity, which enabled the team to muster a six-game winning streak at the end of June. But in another discouraging downturn, his main run-producing bat became unavailable.

On the twenty-fourth, Clark broke his thumb while sliding into third base, a mishap more aggravating to Herzog because Clark should not have been heading there in the first place with two men out on the play. The manager had no idea how he would fill the slugger's shoes. "Jack is really the one guy we can't replace. We can replace all the other Punch-and-Judy hitters in the lineup because we've got a lot of them in the organization. But we don't have anybody who can drive the ball like Jack can."[19] The injury prompted the manager to throw up his hands and unofficially capitulate to the New York club, which was now eight games in front of the second-place Expos and fifteen-and-a-half ahead of the fourth-place Cardinals. "There isn't going to be any race. The Mets are a shoo-in," Herzog told Hummel.[20]

Naturally, the win-loss records of the St. Louis pitching staff were tainted by the lack of run support. After his 3-0 start to the season, Tudor regressed to 6-4 by Independence Day; Danny Cox, an 18-game winner in 1985, was 2-7 after spending the first month of the season on the disabled list from chipping his right ankle while jumping off a sea wall during a fishing trip in Florida; and the man who had been expected to at least partially fill Andújar's absence, Conroy, was victorious only three times. Hope emerged in the form of rookie left-hander Greg Mathews, who since being summoned from the Minors at the beginning of June had won four times in five decisions. And holding his own was the thirty-six-year-old veteran Forsch, with a strong 2.49 ERA to go along with his even 6-6 mark. "It ought to be 12-4," Herzog lamented. "It's a shame what he and Tudor have to show [in wins and losses] for what they've done."[21]

A 1–0 loss to the Dodgers in Los Angeles on July 7 was the tenth shutout inflicted upon the Cardinals' offense for the season and the tenth defeat in their last eleven contests, dropping their record to 33-47 and only a half game from last place. In those first eighty games of 1986, they had been held to three or fewer runs in fifty-three of the contests that had gone nine innings.

More bad news on the injury front struck in the middle of July. Dayley, another member of the bullpen by committee that had been so successful in replacing Sutter in 1985, went down with elbow problems and became the fifth Cardinals pitcher to land on the disabled list. "There were times," the exasperated Herzog would reflect, "when I thought we'd be the first team ever to win 100 games one year and lose 100 the next."[22]

Yet, despite their continued anemic performance at the plate, the Cardinals willed their way back to the .500 mark and to third place in the East at the end of August, with a 19-12 record for the month. Just eight days after Heath had finally surmounted the .200 mark for the year in nearly 200 at bats, Maxvill shipped him back to the American League and the Tigers on August 10, as Herzog handed the everyday catcher's job to Mike LaValliere. For support at the position, backup catcher Steve Lake was acquired from the Chicago Cubs, while Herzog was also hoping to get former Cardinal Terry Kennedy back to St. Louis from San Diego.

On Labor Day, the Redbirds crept over the break-even mark at 66-65 but still stood a distant twenty-two games behind the rampaging Mets, with the second-place Philadelphia Phillies barely any closer. "They [the Mets] have led the Eastern Division since April 23, a span of 117 days," Ross Newhan of the *Los Angeles Times* had pointed out two weeks earlier, "a lead that has been as many as 19 games and no fewer than ten since July 1 which prompted a demoralized Whitey Herzog, who manages the league's defending champions, the St. Louis Cardinals, to concede by June—or was it May?"[23] By the season's end in early October, the gulf between St. Louis and New York landed at a whopping twenty-eight-and-a-half games.

Flipping their statistical dominance from just the previous year in two important categories, the 1986 Cardinals finished last in the Major Leagues in runs scored with 601 and in team batting average at .236—the latter of which was easily outdistanced by the next highest club, the Chicago White Sox, at .247. In keeping with the trend they set in the first half of the decade, the Cardinals once again hit fewest home runs in baseball, but in 1986, it occurred without the usual array of singles, doubles, triples, stolen bases, double steals, perfectly executed hit-and-run plays, squeeze bunts, and other weapons that normally accompanied their lack of power.

In August, Herzog predicted that "it's entirely possible that we as a club won't hit as many home runs this year as Roger Maris did all by himself in 1961."[24] He was correct with room to spare. The team's 58 round-trippers in 1986 were barely half as many as the next highest club, the Expos (110), and threatened the record for the fewest in the era of the 162-game schedule by the 1979 Houston Astros (49). Additionally, the Cardinals played 116 games in which they failed to hit a home run, which was the most homerless contests in a season since the 1952 Washington Senators. Coleman and star shortstop Ozzie Smith became the first teammates in either league to each have 500 at bats in a season without a homer, as Ozzie's last trot around the bases had been his famous playoff shot against the Dodgers in 1985. "We hit six home runs in August," Herzog noted—before recalling another tally that he had been counting. "We only hit 22 in batting practice, and I was giving the guys $1 for every home run they hit in BP."[25]

In the wake of the disappointing performance, Herzog took some measure of satisfaction in seeing one of his protégés go to the postseason. After being an assistant coach in St. Louis for five years, Hal Lanier had beaten out ninety other candidates for the Astros' head job at the beginning of 1986. He proceeded to earn the National League Manager of the Year award, improving Houston a full 13 games with 96 wins and taking the Western Division crown to secure a playoff appearance against the Mets. "A lot of things we've accomplished this season I would have to attribute directly to my years under Whitey," Lanier said, having crafted an athletic roster around a spacious ballpark and making certain to have plenty of arms in the bullpen, which his mentor always emphasized. "I would have been cheating myself and the team if I hadn't used the things I learned from him."[26]

But the Mets, with their 108-win regular season behind them, disposed of Lanier's Astros in six games and then the Red Sox in seven for the World Series title, positioning them as the club to beat in the National League heading into 1987. If the Cardinals were to return to the top, they certainly had their work cut out for them.

"Boys, go home and relax—give yourselves a break," Herzog told the team in the visitors' locker room at Wrigley Field on October 5 as the tiresome season finally concluded with an 8–1 loss to the Cubs. "But after the football bowl games are over on New Year's Day, you'd better get your asses back in shape."[27]

2

Seeking Answers in Saint Petersburg

*I don't think I've ever had a team with as many important ques-
tion marks.*
                                    —Whitey Herzog, March 22, 1987

ALONG WITH LEAVING PLENTY OF TIME FOR BASS FISHING
and hunting each fall, Whitey Herzog also looked forward to early
December on the off-season calendar. During the second week of
that month, he annually weaved spells on the personnel direc-
tors of other teams at Major League Baseball's Winter Meetings,
where his wheeling and dealing sent him back home with bargains
having value that exceeded the sum of their parts. Perhaps his most
famous horse-trading took place at the 1980 gathering in Dallas,
when Herzog moved twenty-three players over six days, some of
whom had been fan favorites and sacred cows in St. Louis, such
as catcher Ted Simmons and third baseman Ken Reitz. In return,
he regularly harvested a crop of nondescript individuals in addition to established veterans—all of whom he needed as important
parts in his blueprint for a championship.

At the 1985 version just before Christmas, Herzog had cornered
the Oakland A's executives at the Town and Country Hotel in San
Diego, where he unloaded the Joaquín Andújar baggage from the
Cardinals. He made the sale despite the hotel not having a lobby,
the place where many trade conversations at the Winter Meetings
were often initiated. But when the game's power brokers met at

the Diplomat Hotel in Hollywood, Florida in December 1986 for their yearly negotiations toward strengthening their rosters, most of them became gun-shy upon arrival.

After the kickoff address by Ueberroth on Sunday night December 7, the hotel conference rooms—normally filled with team representatives crouched over tables and holding briefcases full of notes—were empty. Sportswriters did not hurry back to their rooms to make phone calls to their editors as they usually did. And despite a spacious foyer available to the attendees this year, there was not the typical noisy conversation and traffic going through it. "The Diplomat's football-sized lobby offered a better atmosphere in which to conduct business," one writer observed in comparison to the prior year's event. "It did not help. The 1986 Winter Meetings turned into the slowest in history with a record low of seven trades involving 21 major-league players."[1]

Undeterred from the lack of activity early in the week, Herzog stayed the course and kept his ears open in Florida. With his proven history for providing a mutual benefit for his trading counterparts, Herzog remained confident he would ultimately get something done. "Some of these general managers who've never won a damned thing always think we're trying to screw them," he complained of the inactive reps present. "I tell them, 'Look at the teams I've dealt with. Milwaukee won the pennant. San Diego won a pennant. What the hell are you waiting for?'"[2]

In particular, he was seeking another catcher or a strong right-handed bat—or maybe both, in someone like Pittsburgh's Tony Peña or Detroit's Lance Parrish. Peña was his preferred choice, but Herzog was afraid the Pirates were never going to put him on the market. "Syd doesn't move that fast," Whitey said of Pittsburgh general manager Syd Thrift, as he tapped his pen on the desk of his room at the Diplomat while pondering which angle he might take with the Pirates' GM. "It took him nine months to trade Rick Rhoden. I saw him this morning and I said, 'Let's start talking now. I may be fired by the time we do it.'"[3] Herzog echoed the comments of Bruce Keidan of the *Pittsburgh Post-Gazette*, who wrote, "It takes Thrift nine months to decide how he wants his eggs." Keidan was implicitly advising Thrift to get things in motion, suggesting that another year with Peña would be detrimental in the long run to a Pirates team that finished in last place in 1986 with 98 losses. "Although he is one of baseball's premier catchers, Pena is a diminishing asset. Ten months from now, he will be a free agent, free to sell his services to the highest bidder. And it is most unlikely that the Pirates have the financial wherewithal to be the highest bidder."[4]

Other notable players were available by the time the clubs met in Hollywood, such as pitcher Jack Morris (Parrish's teammate in Detroit) and a pair of accomplished Montreal outfielders in Andre Dawson and Tim Raines. Dawson, a multiple All-Star and Gold Glove winner, turned down a guaranteed two-year, $2 million contract to go on the market and find a stadium with natural grass for his aching knees, while Raines had just won the National League batting title while also posting his sixth-straight season of at least 70 stolen bases. But for the second year in a row, the lack of meaningful pursuit of any free agents at the Winter Meetings suggested to the Major League Baseball Players Association that the owners were colluding, with players before forced to re-sign their existing contracts for less money. "Winning is not the number one priority anymore," Jack Clark, another unsigned player, said in his blunt summary of baseball's twenty-six teams. "Sticking it to us *is*."[5]

Still, Herzog waited patiently for someone to approach him with something—anything—that would open the door to conversation. No one did. Six days passed without the Cardinals being involved in a single significant move. "I have never gone to as many meetings as we did and accomplished nothing," Herzog muttered upon leaving at the end of the week.[6]

It was nothing like the good old days of the Winter Meetings, he recalled fondly, when the off-season interleague trading deadline always fell on the Friday of that week, before interleague trading could resume on February 15, followed by the in-season July 31 deadline. "People stayed around until late Friday night to see what would happen," Herzog said of past versions of the December conference. "People used to run out and get the papers on Saturday morning to see what trades were made before the deadline. I don't think many people are going to come off the [golf] links this Saturday to see what happened."[7]

Now, in essence, there was no deadline at all. "There's no use coming here if no one is going to do anything. I liked the deadline. Now you hear people say, 'There's no hurry.'" The Cardinals' manager put forth the idea of future Winter Meetings taking place the week before spring training with the trading deadline inserted around March 1, which he believed would prod the teams into making more deals.

ONE NOTABLE TRANSACTION WHICH *HAD* TAKEN PLACE AT the Diplomat Hotel, however, impacted the fortunes of the St. Louis club directly. Uncertain that the center fielder McGee would fully return from a serious knee injury, the Cardinals had offered the 1985 MVP and batting champion to the San Diego Padres for slugging outfielder Kevin McReynolds. But the Padres' general manager Jack McKeon, with whom Herzog had struck multiple deals over the years, was simultaneously entertaining an offer for McReynolds from the Mets—and he took the opportunity to tease both suitors. "Put him [McReynolds] in the Cardinals' lineup with all those rabbits in front of him getting on base," McKeon suggested in November, "and he might drive in 150 runs. Put him with the Mets in that lineup with Carter, Hernandez, and Strawberry, [and there's] no telling what he'd do.

"I've told clubs that I don't really want to trade him, but I've also told them, 'If you really want to overwhelm me with an offer, I'll consider it.'"[8]

Maxvill and Herzog were willing to throw a pitcher into the deal along with McGee. But in the late hours of Thursday night, December 11, the Mets—winners of two-thirds of their games in 1986 on their way to the World Series championship—appeared to empower themselves even further for 1987 in emerging as McKeon's choice.

In a massive eight-player swap that was the culmination of McKeon and Mets assistant general manager Joe McIlvaine speaking daily at the meetings since Monday, New York added McReynolds to the middle of their stacked lineup. In doing so, they had to part with several of their best young prospects, including outfielders Kevin Mitchell (a key bat for them against left-handers in their 1986 title charge) and Shawn Abner (the top overall selection in the 1984 draft).

For the next forty-eight hours, the word *dynasty* pervaded the discussions on the streets of Queens, Brooklyn, and Manhattan when people spoke of the Mets. But as the Winter Meetings were ending on Saturday, December 13, the momentum was dashed.

The elite pitcher Gooden was arrested that night in his hometown of Tampa after fighting with police officers in the wake of a traffic stop. "According to the police, one officer was kicked in the head and another was kneed in the groin," reported the *New York Times*. "Witnesses said Mr. Gooden was beaten to the ground with nightsticks and flashlights before being handcuffed and shackled. Neither Mr. Gooden, his companions—including his nephew, Gary Sheffield, the top 1986 draft choice of the Milwaukee Brewers—nor the officers were seriously injured, according to the police."[9] Mets' followers were hoping that the matter and its aftershock would be resolved quickly, and that Gooden—perhaps trying to be more inconspicuous going forward, exemplified by soon replacing his signature golden front tooth with a plain white cap—and the team would prepare for spring training with an appetite to repeat as champions.

While leaving the meetings with nothing to show for it, Herzog nonetheless took heart in knowing his pennant-winning club from 1985 was largely still intact. Yet, even for the manager, there was uncertainty about the Cardinals' true colors for 1987. Which version would surface—the one predicted for last place but unexpectedly earned the pennant, or the one that fell flat the following year? "I don't think I've ever had a team with as many important question marks," Herzog pondered. "I'm talking about a guy like McGee—he not only had a knee injury, he had an off year. Tommy [Herr] is coming off his worst year in the big leagues. Vince [Coleman], we still don't know what he can do because he hasn't been here that long. Clark's coming off the thumb . . . and at this point we really don't know about Dayley and Lahti, and they're important people to this club."[10] A semblance of doubt also hovered over third base, where Pendleton had seen his batting average decline to .240 and .239 over the past two seasons after a breakout rookie year in 1984 with a .324 mark in limited duty.

Nonetheless, there were also bright spots to be salvaged from an otherwise dismal 1986. Coleman stole 107 bases to become the first player ever to swipe over 100 bases in each of his first two years and was also the first National League player to steal 100 bases twice. While Herzog was despondent about Coleman's lack of hitting over the latter part of the season, the left fielder had been nearing the .300 mark by the first week of June before a prolonged 0-37 slump.

Additionally, the rookie left-hander Mathews won 11 games in little more than half a season of work after being promoted from the team's Triple-A farm club at Louisville; Ozzie Smith won his seventh straight Gold Glove at shortstop, and McGee, though struggling at times in center, won the third of his career; LaValliere emerged as a better catching prospect than the scouts had surmised; Forsch had shown resilience in providing needed stability during his thirteenth Major League season; and Van Slyke and Herr powered their way through early-season struggles to perform well in the second half of the schedule. And through it all, the fans remained faithful as the Cardinals reached the two million mark in attendance for the fifth consecutive year.

But perhaps the most pleasant surprise was the emergence of Worrell as a dominant force in relief, the latest iteration of Herzog's mantra that "great closers shorten games."

With men such as Worrell, Sutter, and others coming out of the bullpen during the 1980s, a Cardinals' lead heading into the ninth inning—or sometimes the eighth, if the closer was needed earlier—had usually become permanent. After being elevated to the Majors in the final month of the 1985 season, contributing to the Cardinals' victory over the Los Angeles Dodgers in the National League Championship Series, and saving Game One of the World Series in Kansas City, Worrell followed Coleman's 1985 selection as the National League Rookie of the Year by being so honored in 1986. Worrell had also been the first rookie pitcher to lead the league in saves, and the first to be selected as the National League Relief Pitcher of the Year.

With the nightmare of 1986 fading in the rearview mirror, the healing power of time allowed for winter introspection, mental resurgence, physical strengthening, and solution-seeking. Proven veterans such as Clark and the second baseman Herr were aware of the friction in the clubhouse early in the previous season, which

Herzog had cited, but also knew that better things were on the horizon. "When we went through adversity in the first half [of 1986], we pulled apart a little bit," said Herr, who in 1987 had attained the second-longest tenure by an active Cardinal after Forsch. "We didn't stick together. We started playing so badly that no one was worrying about the team anymore. It was, 'Worry about myself and put some good statistics up for myself.'

"That attitude is very easily detectible and it creeps into things. You have a lot of bickering and finger-pointing. You're never going to turn a team around that way. But after the All-Star break, it was a cleansing process."[11]

Others such as Forsch, who signed with the organization in 1968 and was preparing for his nineteenth professional spring training (and sixteenth in the Major League camp), did not notice any malignant presence. "Losing will do that to you, but I don't know if it was as bad as everybody made it out to be. . . . I found out about it [the team's poor attitude] by reading it in the papers."[12] Ozzie Smith agreed and downplayed such stories. "There wasn't a whole lot of it [disharmony]. People from the outside can start that and, before you know it, you get caught up in it."[13]

The vast majority of the Cardinals showed up in shape to Al Lang Stadium in Saint Petersburg in February. Even the manager himself arrived in a healthier state, having lost thirty-two pounds since New Year's Day, which put him near the two hundred mark. "I was out quail hunting, and I got short-winded," Herzog revealed. "I've never been short-winded. I thought, 'I'd better do something.'"[14] The formula for his success? "I'm not drinking. I went to a diet center and got some vitamins. I'm eating fruit and cottage cheese and all the salad I want and I have nine ounces of protein a day."[15]

The eager Herr and Clark were the first position players to come through the door at the Cardinals' spring facility in Florida. The latter reported having no recent trouble with his thumb, aside from not being able to fully grip the ball when attempting to throw. "I'm not having any problems, and I didn't think I would. I really want to do everything normal and not think about it."[16] Herr, like his manager, had also lost weight. "I'm 14 or 15 pounds lighter than when I ended last season," he noted in being four years removed from three knee operations, as Herr knew well the benefit of lugging less encumbrance. "It should be a lot less strain on my legs as the season progresses."[17]

On the contrary, Herr's double play partner Smith showed up at camp 19 pounds *heavier* due to a strenuous off-season weightlifting program and was swinging a bat that weighed more than the one Clark used (thirty-four ounces to thirty-one). Backup outfielders Landrum and John Morris participated in a similar weight-training regimen, and Coleman had also bulked up—in addition to having shaved his head for a new look on top as well. "It's not like I'm going to hit 50 home runs," Coleman said of his increased strength while also being contrite about his sophomore slump in 1986. "But I want to be strong enough for when that fatigue sets in about the sixth or seventh inning when it's 130 degrees. I'm looking at it like it's my first year. I have to redeem myself."[18] Additionally, Coleman set a personal goal to bunt at least once per game in 1987, a strategy that he largely ignored in 1986.

The lanky, left-handed-hitting and -throwing Morris, whom the Cards had received in a trade with the Royals for Lonnie Smith in 1985, looked to build upon his initial Major League experience from the previous season. In the traditional Herzog realm, he knew he had to embrace what the manager expected of him:

In '86, I got some playing time at the end of the year when the Mets were running away with the division and found that I had more success coming off the bench than I did when I was a starter. When spring training for 1987 began, Whitey pulled me aside and said, "John, you seem to do more with one at bat than you do with four. You're really something when you come off the bench, but when you start, I don't know what the hell happens." He was gauging my response to see if I was going to be on board with being a reserve player or if I was going to fight it. And I figured I'd rather be on board with it in the big leagues in a part-time role than back in the Minors playing every day.

I'm grateful for it, because I actually learned a lot sitting on the bench for the first six innings of the game, watching Whitey manage and trying to anticipate how he would line up the pinch hitters and bullpen, and that was fascinating to watch. It got to the point where, after a year, I knew when he was going to use me, and I knew who I would be hitting against. I would anticipate double-switches, when I would pinch-run or spot start. It was just a great education in playing for Whitey, who in my mind was one of the greatest managers ever.[19]

When the slimmed-down Herzog emerged from the locker room at Al Lang in his No. 24 jersey for the first full-squad practice, the White Rat looked around at his new gym rats and could hardly recognize much of the team. "I've got a strange club here. Willie [McGee] comes in with curls in his hair. Vince [Coleman] comes in with *no* hair and Ozzie has muscles he never had before."[20]

Nagging injuries to other Cardinals, however, provided uncertainties. In addition to the ailing knee of McGee—who reiterated Coleman's approach in saying "I have to prove myself all over again"—Tudor's immediate status remained unknown, as he had missed the last three weeks of the 1986 season with a tender pitching shoulder. The timeline for Clark to fully permit his broken thumb to heal was also indefinite, and key relief pitchers Dayley and Lahti were held out of initial exercises. In addition to his recovery from shoulder surgery a year earlier, Lahti had suffered a broken foot over the winter when he fell down some stairs while moving boxes at his home, which occurred just as he was restarting his throwing program.

The second-year left-hander Mathews was considered to have one of the best changeups to enter the Majors in several years, and he believed he had improved his throwing motion over the winter—along with his velocity—by working out at Maryville University in St. Louis with Steve Carlton, the legendary Cardinal and Phillie who had been released by Philadelphia the past June before playing later in the season for the Giants and the White Sox. As Mathews was landing with the Redbirds in Saint Petersburg, Carlton was over in the Phillies' camp in Clearwater seeking to make the team as a nonroster free agent, but after throwing fourteen spring innings in which he permitted 13 hits, 6 walks, and 11 runs, Carlton would be released again on March 21. Meanwhile, at the Oakland A's complex out in Arizona, Andújar followed suit with his previous Februaries with the Cardinals by arriving ten days late—before promptly hurting his arm at his first workout while throwing the ball to first base during pitchers' fielding practice.

In the wake of Mathews' promising debut in the second half of 1986, an even newer Cardinals southpaw was also figuring into Herzog's plans for 1987 and was the manager's choice to start the 1987 exhibition opener on March 7 against the Mets. While growing up in eastern Kentucky where his father was a professor at Morehead State University, 6-foot-6-inch Joe Magrane was so big he was permitted to pitch high school ball while in the seventh grade, the first year his family moved to town. "Because my dad taught there, we just walked everywhere around campus," Magrane recalled of those days. "There were some outstanding athletic role models at Morehead, such as Phil Simms, who was the quarterback at MSU when I was in the eighth grade. On occasion, my dad would take me over to Cincinnati, and I could watch my idol Steve Carlton go head-to-head with Tom Seaver."[21]

Herzog's first impressions of the young lefty were positive. "He's got a nice, smooth delivery—I like him."[22] Magrane was two years removed from being the Cardinals' number-one draft pick out of the University of Arizona, where in 1984 he had fired a no-hitter against the eventual College World Series victor Cal State Fullerton, which had posted 66 wins on the season. Scouting him at the game was the Cardinals' director of player development Lee Thomas, who decided to stick around an extra day and watch the Fullerton pitcher who was finishing the series on Sunday—a senior southpaw named Greg Mathews. On his way back to St. Louis, Thomas decided that the Redbirds should go after both men.

Magrane did not disappoint in his debut. He threw three scoreless innings, permitting a lone hit and one walk, as the Cardinals beat New York in a rain-shortened spring opener, 5–1. In the first inning, Magrane struck out Hernandez and Carter in succession—prompting McIlvaine to suggest the Cards might have a third straight Rookie of the Year on their hands. But then came Strawberry in the slugger's first preseason at bat. "I was trying to make the ballclub and throwing as hard as I could—almost with my eyes closed," Magrane recalled. "The first pitch

Straw saw that spring got away from me, and it hit him square in the middle of the back."[23]

More encouragement followed later in the game, as prodigal son Dave LaPoint fired three effective innings himself. LaPoint, who helped the Cardinals to the World Series title as a rookie in 1982, was back in the organization after a two-year hiatus spread across stints in Detroit, San Diego, and San Francisco—the latter where he was sent, with others, in a 1985 trade for Jack Clark, who on the same day as LaPoint's return to the spring training mound saw his first live pitching since the previous June. "We had a chance to pick somebody up who'd pitched well in the past, had pitched well for Whitey Herzog, and had pitched well in our park," a pleased Maxvill said of LaPoint. "I see him competing for a fifth starting spot right out of the chute."[24]

The bats seemed to quickly reawaken to their 1985 form. In their second spring game on Sunday, March 8, the Cardinals roughed up Gooden, who was regrouping from his legal troubles and who had dominated the National League for the past three years (beginning as a nineteen-year-old in 1984). He was Herzog's choice to start the 1986 All-Star Game. The Redbirds posted 9 runs in the first inning in Saint Petersburg on their way to an 11–4 win over the Mets. "The Cardinals have been playing the Grapefruit League schedule as if it were midseason," an impressed Bill Conlin wrote in *The Sporting News*. "Herr has been the same pesky number three hitter he was in 1985 and appears primed for a big comeback season. Equally impressive has been Andy Van Slyke, brilliant both at bat and in the field."[25]

While the victories were pleasant, Herzog never wished to have an exceedingly impressive spring training record nor a terrible one, as the former tends to set unreasonable expectations while the latter incites unreasonable panic. What was his prediction, then, for how the team would sit at the end of March? "We'll have about eight wins and 22 losses and everyone will be wondering what the hell is wrong."[26]

Wins and losses notwithstanding, Herr noticed a different attitude on the team from the start, a businesslike disposition that he and the other veterans had been hoping to establish. From the second baseman's perspective, the manager had sharpened his own tactics as well. "Most of the starting lineup has gone on every trip," Herr said of the many bus rides that are part the exhibition circuit. "In the past, Whitey was a lot more lax about the regulars playing a lot, especially in spring training. [Now] I get three at-bats every day. It's obvious he's taken a new approach, and it's a sound theory. We may not like it down here, but at least we're going to be ready when the season starts."[27] His partner around the keystone also wanted the folks in St. Louis to know that the team was determined to improve. "If we win it all again or not, guys have really worked hard to make things better," Smith said. "We've got to do something different—even if it's wrong."[28]

One of Herzog's primary goals was to find more help against left-handed pitching for Clark (who hit his first homer of the spring on March 13) and get him under contract, especially in the absence of any such acquisitions over the winter. "What we have to do now is get Clark re-signed and then find a righthanded hitter to hit behind him. And I mean a good righthanded hitter, someone who can drive the ball and get a runner in from first base. I don't care if he's an outfielder or a catcher or an infielder, I'll find a place for him to play if he can hit. If we do that, we'll be good again."[29]

Getting the first crack at the job was Jim Lindeman, the Cardinals' top draft pick in 1983. After his first Major League spring training in March 1986, the muscular Lindeman socked 20 home runs with 96 RBIs at Triple-A Louisville over the summer before being summoned for a nineteen-game trial with the Major League club in September, during which he batted .255 with a homer while spending the vast majority of his defensive time at first base. Herzog had also inserted him to play a couple of innings at third, and after Lindeman enjoyed further success at that position in winter ball under Leyva in Puerto Rico, rumors began flying that deals were imminent to send Pendleton out of town, in light of the incumbent third baseman's hitting struggles over the past two seasons. The first of these scenarios predicted Pendleton going to the Cubs for outfielder Keith Moreland and, later, to the Expos along with Mathews for Tim Wallach. Herzog, however, assured Pendleton on the first day of camp that the gossip was unfounded. "It bothered me," Pendleton, who started 153 games at third for the Cardinals

SEEKING ANSWERS

in 1986, said of the trade rumors. "My wife and parents were more unnerved. I like St. Louis and I want to stay in St. Louis. He [Herzog] said they hadn't talked to Montreal in a month, and that as far as he was concerned, I was his third baseman."[30] Like several other Cardinals, Pendleton spent the winter recovering from a physical setback with his arm sitting in a sling from hyperextending an elbow while playing golf. As a result, he spent much of the off-season watching videotape of his at bats from 1986 instead of taking actual swings.

Lindeman's performance in Florida, however, forced the Cardinals to play him as the Grapefruit schedule wore on. He doubled off Hal Lanier's 1986 Cy Young Award winner Mike Scott of the Astros in Kissimmee on March 16, as Lindeman's spring average soared to .391 while being tied for the club lead in homers (3) with Clark, Van Slyke, and Landrum—and while keeping six different gloves in his locker for all the possible positions he could be playing. "I would be very surprised," an impressed Herzog predicted, "if by the end of the year he wasn't a very good candidate for Rookie of the Year."[31] Each day, Maxvill was fielding more calls from other general managers who were inquiring about the rookie slugger.

If he was to come north with the Major League team, Lindeman's job would be explained by the manager in no uncertain terms. It was a yearly practice for Herzog to go around to the final roster of twenty-five players at the end of spring training and tell each man exactly what was needed from him. If a player was likely to get no more than a hundred at bats during the year, Herzog would be honest and tell him so, believing it was a disservice to give a backup player the false hope that he might have larger role down the road. Over the years, Herzog had found individuals who were willing to sacrifice their egos and playing time for the overall strength of the team—men such as Landrum, Iorg, Steve Braun, and Mike Ramsey. "The players understand that Whitey is in charge," as Herr would say. "You do it his way if you want to remain a Cardinal."[32]

Now, in 1987, he was once again auditioning relative unknowns in camp for some of those positions. Among them was the versatile Tom Lawless, who had seen big league action as far back as 1982 with the Reds but had yet to land full-time work in the Majors. Lawless held the distinction of being the only man ever traded for

Pete Rose in an Expos-to-Reds swap in 1984. With running speed comparable to the other electric Cardinals (evidenced by his 289 stolen bases in the Minors), Lawless was improving his chances of making the big league club by agreeing to work as the third or "emergency" catcher in addition to his usual infield spots. "I think I've got the mechanics down," he said of catching after being behind the plate for a 4–0 combined shutout by Tudor and reliever Scott Arnold in a B game versus the Phillies in Saint Petersburg. "The hardest part is throwing, and that's a matter of footwork. I try to rely on my quickness rather than on the strength of my arm. Other than that, you just have to catch the ball every time. Sounds simple, but it's not."[33]

Another candidate for a utility job, infielder José Oquendo, had batted .297 in a back-up role for the Cardinals in the previous year. With a batting stance remarkably similar to that of Rod Carew, Oquendo was asked if he had patterned his form after the great hitter whose jersey No. 29 would be retired by the Minnesota Twins during the 1987 season. "No, Cecil Cooper, actually," Oquendo responded with a laugh in citing the Milwaukee Brewers' home run–hitting first baseman who was entering his seventeenth and final season in the Majors. "I'm Rod Carew with power."[34] Signing into professional ball out of Puerto Rico at the age of fifteen, Oquendo had mostly been a center fielder as a youth in his home country. He switched to shortstop upon his arrival in the Minor Leagues and gradually showed the ability to play anywhere on the field. His versatility, however, was not an indication that he lacked skills. "There's not a better arm in the league than his," Herzog would go so far to say.[35]

Some considered Oquendo the second-best defensive shortstop in baseball behind Smith, even though he had been a reserve in St. Louis; thus, he garnered interest as a potential starter from other teams, including the New York Yankees and Chicago White Sox. Maxvill, however, recognized Oquendo's value and refused to move him unless he received a substantial offer. Therefore, back in December, the general manager instead dealt another desirable infield prospect, Fred Manrique, to the White Sox. In return, Maxvill bolstered the Cardinals' bullpen with right-handed reliever Bill

Dawley from Chicago, a former Houston Astro whom Herzog had selected for the 1983 National League All-Star Game when Whitey managed the team. Dawley, though talented, had snuck under the radar of other potential suitors because of his off-season elbow surgery. "It's not going to shock the baseball world," Herzog said of the acquisition, "but it's a step in the right direction." Regarding Dawley's penchant for challenging hitters in the strike zone, Maxvill said, "He is big and strong and he might want to pitch in a big ballpark."[36]

The manager was hoping Dawley (and Ray Soff, who had contributed valuable innings from the right-handed side during the previous season) would keep him from having to use Worrell in seventy-four games, as had been the case in 1986, especially with the uncertain status of Lahti—although the injured reliever had been cleared by team physician Stan London to resume throwing on March 11. "I'm up to 55 miles per hour," Lahti joked four days later. "All changeups."[37]

Yet, by the end of March, Lahti would fail to pitch in a single exhibition game and was put on the sixty-day disabled list, being left behind in Florida to recover in the baseball purgatory known as extended spring training. After another setback in April, he would never pitch again.

Also working alongside position players Lawless and Oquendo on the back fields of Saint Petersburg had been the other convalescing member of the bullpen, Ken Dayley, whom the Cardinals had quietly released in December while he healed from elbow surgery. On January 19 (the same day that the Cardinals reacquired LaPoint), Dayley re-signed for a base salary of $75,000 with the possibility of making as much as $300,000 if he met certain appearance benchmarks during the 1987 season, which included bonuses of $75,000 each time he passed the milestones of twenty-two, twenty-eight, and thirty-five games pitched. On March 25, he did his first off-the-mound throwing since the previous July, as he tossed a simulated game against some of his teammates. Having pitched a perfect final two innings of Game Seven of the 1985 World Series, Dayley had authored twelve scoreless innings that postseason. Now, he was shooting for a May return to the active roster, if not before. "Dayley was the best lefthanded relief pitcher in the league in '85," Herzog stated. "He was better than [Jesse] Orosco, [John] Franco, all of them."[38]

Also gaining strength in his left arm was Tudor, who had permitted just 2 earned runs in sixteen innings of spring work and reported no problems with his shoulder. His best pitch, a changeup that he threw with his index, middle, and ring fingers like a palm ball (rather than with the last three fingers, known as a circle change, which had become popular among pitchers), appeared to be already operating at midseason form.

Following Magrane's stellar debut against the Mets, he was roughed up by the Toronto Blue Jays five days later but then righted himself in baffling the Astros' bats in Kissimmee on March 16, as Lindeman was teeing off against Scott. But after Maxvill suggested near the end of March that Magrane might be returned to Louisville to get some starts instead of being stuck in a limited relief role in the Majors, Tudor opined it would be better if the rookie was placed in the St. Louis bullpen as a left-handed complement to Worrell, especially with Dayley out of the picture for the time being. "If the kid is ready to pitch in the big leagues, he's ready to pitch in the big leagues," the veteran said plainly. "It sure wouldn't hurt to have him in the bullpen for a couple days the first week. I'm sure he'd be able to pitch from there unless Maxvill knows something I don't know."[39]

Along with Magrane and LaPoint, the return of Mathews and Conroy, and the trio of Dayley, Pat Perry, and the versatile Ricky Horton in the bullpen (the three of which together had added 10 saves to Worrell's 36 in 1986), the Cardinals' pitching staff was suddenly loaded with left-handers. "I don't care how many lefties we have as long as we improve the quality of those we have," Maxvill said.[40] Horton, entering his fourth season with the club, recognized the importance of stepping up and guiding the young hurlers. "It's amazing in baseball how you go from a rookie to having more seniority in a heartbeat," he reflected in 2023. "I remember toward the end of 1986, Terry Pendleton and I kind of challenged one another to take on more of a leadership role on the team. You get old fast in the game of baseball. I think winning and going to the World Series get you old fast and give you extra years of experience."[41]

Despite Lahti's regression, there was also good news from the right-handed side, as the starter Cox sparkled throughout the exhibition schedule with an 0.56 ERA—though he was somewhat disgruntled in having lost $275,000 in salary in an arbitration hearing against the front office.

At the end of camp, Dayley was put on the fifteen-day disabled list with the understanding he would be elevated to the Major League club before long. In the interim, Horton would thus be asked to take a heavier load in the bullpen as Magrane (with spring totals of 10 walks in 20 innings and a 4.79 ERA) and Conroy were sent to Louisville for further seasoning. Conroy, because of his previous Major League service time, had the right to refuse the assignment. In one of his final Grapefruit League outings on March 21, Conroy had walked 6 batters in one inning, a stint that included 13 straight pitched balls at one point.

With the slots on the pitching staff having become clear, Herzog and his staff turned their attention to filling the holes in the batting order. The excessive rain that had hit Florida in March 1987—ultimately shortening the Cardinals' exhibition schedule by nearly a third, from thirty-one games down to twenty-three— had hampered McGee's return from his knee injury. By the end of the month, he had not played an inning in the field and had not even slid into the bases once during practices. "Until he does," Herzog said of the noticeable hesitation on the part of the center fielder's play, "there's going to be some doubt in his mind."[42] It was not until March 25 that McGee would take an at bat in an exhibition game, as he grounded into a double play against the Blue Jays. Nonetheless, like Dayley, his time on the sidelines was expected to be relatively brief. Whenever McGee was fully ready, it was the manager's plan to move him from his typical second slot in the batting order down to fifth to give Clark more protection in the cleanup spot. "If he can drive in 82 runs batting second," the manager reasoned, "Why can't he drive in a hundred batting fifth?"[43] Herzog's additional logic was that McGee, in the process of gradually testing the knee at full throttle, would likely not show an initial inclination to steal very often and thus would be more useful in the middle of the lineup.

Therefore, with McGee not slated to be set for opening day, Herzog announced on March 30 that Van Slyke would shift over to center field, Coleman would stay in left, and Lindeman was his right fielder. The revelation was shared with the media just after the rookie hit a 475-foot home run off the Mets' Ron Darling that afternoon, Lindeman's fourth of the exhibition schedule. The Bradley University product would finish the spring with a .350 average and a team-leading 15 RBIS. "I'll start him every day and give him an all-out chance," Herzog said. "I've been very impressed with him."[44] Time, however, would tell for sure. "The flowers that bloom in the spring sometimes wilt in the summer and die in the fall," Whitey warned.[45]

WHEN THE CARDINALS' PITCHERS AND CATCHERS HAD reported to St. Petersburg back on February 23, those of the Kansas City Royals further down the Gulf Coast in Fort Myers had already been at work for three days. On that date, Dick Howser, having undergone two surgeries over the past seven months for a malignant brain tumor, announced he was stepping down as the Royals' manager. "I'm going to have to give it up this year," he told the press. Howser had not been in the dugout since managing the American League in the 1986 All-Star Game against Herzog's National League squad, after which he turned the Royals over to assistant coach Mike Ferraro for the remainder of the season. "I pushed and I pushed and I pushed, but it didn't happen for me."[46] Billy Gardner, who had led the Minnesota Twins from 1981 to 1985 and who was hired by the Royals over the winter as their third base coach, took over as the interim manager for 1987.

During his absence from spring training, Howser was thus unable to witness the development of one the game's newest stars. On March 22 the Cardinals faced the Royals in Saint Petersburg and watched young outfielder Bo Jackson go 2-4 and score two runs in helping Kansas City to an 8–2 win. Jackson, having made his MLB debut the prior September, had won the 1985 Heisman Trophy at Auburn University and was subsequently the first pick in the NFL draft the following spring. Gardner was hoping that

Jackson would be ready to claim the starting right-field spot on opening day in Kansas City, where he had gotten a twenty-three-game trial in 1986. "He's not the kind of player who can sit on the bench," the new Royals' leader said. "He has to play every day because he hasn't played much baseball to begin with. We just want to see how he progresses in the next week before we make our final cut."[47]

IN SPITE OF LINDEMAN'S DEVELOPMENT, HERZOG STILL DID not have the proven, veteran right-handed hitter he had sought for the lineup to help Clark (who wound up re-signing with the team for his same 1986 salary of $1.2 million instead of opting for free agency, which he instead was considering pursuing at the end of 1987). But before the team left Florida, one was found.

With six days left before the regular season was to begin, the Cardinals were preparing to play one of their final preseason games in Florida on Wednesday, April 1. When Herzog posted the batting order on the dugout wall at Al Lang Stadium, the catcher LaValliere noticed he was not in the starting lineup as he normally was against a right-handed pitcher. Van Slyke, another left-handed hitter who was enjoying an excellent spring at a .390 clip, also expected to see his name written alongside his new center field spot, but when he scanned the batting order and then the entire roster card, he did not even see himself listed among the substitutes at the bottom. "That's when I knew," Van Slyke said, "that the two of us were going north to a town other than St. Louis."[48]

Looking for the defense-first catcher he always craved but also one with a potent bat, Herzog sent LaValliere, Van Slyke, and pitcher Mike Dunne—the Cardinals' 1984 first-round draft pick and a United States Olympian that year, as well as a senior at Bradley when Lindeman was a freshman—to the Pirates for Tony Peña, considered to possess baseball's deadliest arm behind the plate, which he used to fire pickoffs at any base, any time. "Mechanically, he throws as well as anybody in the game," Herzog said, "maybe better than anybody."[49] Peña, with an infectious enthusiasm that always seemed to have him smiling, was also the most unorthodox catcher to come into professional baseball in decades. To facilitate his quick release of the baseball, he utilized a glove that was an inch smaller than a typical catcher's mitt while squatting in nearly a splits position, like a gymnast, with no runners on base, in order to offer the pitcher a low target. While some had questioned Peña's ability to handle a pitching staff, Maxvill noted that Pittsburgh's hurlers had crafted a league-best 3.11 ERA in 1983 despite the team finishing in last place—a testament to the work that Peña had done with them, the Cardinals' GM believed.

After being unable to seize neither Peña nor Lance Parrish four months earlier at the Winter Meetings, the Cardinals had gradually backed off on their pursuit of Parrish after the dedicated weightlifter was diagnosed with chronic back problems. His latest setback ended his 1986 season in July, prompting the Tigers to pick up Heath two weeks later from the Cardinals. "Our doctors looked at the X-rays and all the medical reports on Parrish and advised us it would be a great risk to sign him," Herzog said. "I'm not a doctor, but I'd say that Lance has a lot of slippage in that back."[50] The Phillies, however, were amenable to the gamble and signed Parrish as a free agent on March 13.

Peña was not the prolific run-producer that Herzog and Maxvill had ideally been wishing to acquire, especially with the catcher's position being paramount in that regard with no designated hitter in the National League at that time. But Herzog pointed out that Peña's RBIS, averaging a modest 64 per season for the past five years, always seemed to come at opportune moments. "Managing against him, I always hated seeing him coming up in the clutch. He always got his rips and he always hit the ball hard. RBIS come in bunches. It depends a lot who's on base when you hit."[51] Like Lindeman and Van Slyke, Peña had enjoyed a strong spring, batting .356; with his decent speed (despite having led the National League in grounding into double plays in 1986 with 21), he would allow Herzog to avoid having to pinch-run for the catcher's spot in the late innings as he was forced to do with his slow-footed ones in LaValliere and Lake. In 1984 Peña had set the Pirates' season record for stolen bases by a catcher with 12, a total he duplicated the following year.

The trade was not welcomed among certain individuals in St. Louis. The outspoken Tudor felt that a full-scale pursuit of the powerful yet damaged Detroit catcher would have been more beneficial. "Apparently, we don't need Parrish," the pitcher scoffed—pointing to the fact that, within the division, the Cubs had picked up Andre Dawson. He continued:

> It's hard to figure out what they're [the Cardinals' front office] trying to do. Apparently last year didn't teach them anything. You can't win by hoping you get 15 hits a game. We had games last year where we got 15 hits and two runs. . . . We're going to be better offensively than we were [in 1986], but I really don't think we can be as good as we were in 1985. That's hard to expect for a team that doesn't hit home runs.[52]

Maxvill respected Tudor's opinion but stood by his choice. "If Stan London would have come down with a glowing report—or an average report—we would have been in on it [the bidding for Parrish]. Not that I'm in complete disagreement with John, but I look to three positions on our offense to give us a little better contribution. Everybody on our club didn't have a career year in 1985."[53] Regarding the acquisition of needed power at the plate, the quick rise of the Cardinals' hottest rookie made the Peña deal more understandable. "We probably could not have done it if Lindeman had not emerged as a hitter," Herzog said. Some other Cardinals players had also questioned the recent commitment of the ownership toward spending the necessary money for quality talent, but the fact that Peña would be making about twice as much as Van Slyke put that topic to rest for the time being. "With a player like this coming available, there was no hesitation on that front," Maxvill added regarding the financial necessities of the deal.[54]

At the Pirates' spring training facility in Bradenton, the catcher gave an emotional farewell after his seven years with Pittsburgh. "Pena stood there, tears running down his cheeks," beat writer Bob Hertzel wrote of the scene. "[Manager] Jim Leyland's lower lip was quivering. Tears were not far behind. He grabbed Pena and hugged him. Then he said goodbye."[55]

Peña participated in the few remaining Cardinals exhibition games while donning the No. 5 on the back of his new St. Louis jersey, the numeral most recently worn by the failed experiment at the position in Heath. Peña's familiar No. 6 he had worn with the Pirates was unavailable, as it had been retired in St. Louis at the conclusion of Stan Musial's career. (Peña would ultimately settle for No. 26.) Shortly after the trade, the Cardinals also acquired twenty-six-year-old pitcher Lee Tunnell from the Pirates and assigned him to Louisville. Tunnell had been released after a disastrous 1986 season at Pittsburgh's Triple-A club but had previously shown flashes of potential at the big league level.

Darrell Porter, meanwhile, had signed a second-consecutive one-year contract with the Texas Rangers—who fired their payroll director Jean Connelly when she authorized an erroneous overpayment of $17,000 on one of Porter's first 1987 checks. "If overpaying Darrell Porter is a crime," offered Kevin Horrigan in the *Post-Dispatch*, "then the entire Cardinals front office should be in jail."[56]

The insertion of Peña into the St. Louis lineup did little to sway National League prognosticators in their forecasts of the 1987 season. In the wake of the Mets gaining McReynolds, the experts were ready to hand a second-consecutive pennant to New York without much of a fight. But Herzog, despite his midseason deference to the Mets in 1986, refused to get on the bandwagon. "This business about the Mets being one of the great teams of all time—can we hold off on that? Can we please keep them out of the archives until they earn it?"[57] He pointed to New York's defunct 1986 platoon system in left and center field, which had garnered 29 home runs, 56 stolen bases, and a .288 batting average from three players (in addition to the contributions of veteran George Foster, who had been released in August), and wondered why that success had been abandoned so quickly. "I don't know if they're going to be better. What did they get out of [Kevin] Mitchell and [Lenny] Dykstra and [Mookie] Wilson? What's McReynolds going to do that they didn't do? If Mitchell plays every day, he might do what McReynolds did."

Tom Herr was bolder, taking a jab directly at the Mets' new acquisition. "I've always questioned his desire to play," he stated about McReynolds, echoing a concern regularly raised in recent seasons by former San Diego manager Dick Williams. "It kind of looked like he didn't want to be out there. The fans in New York aren't going to let him get away with that. They'll bury him."[58]

Trouble was also swirling around their incumbent right fielder. Strawberry, the 1983 Rookie of the Year and an All-Star outfielder in the three seasons that followed, nearly got into a fight on March 14 with Red Sox pitcher Al Nipper (the man off whom Strawberry had homered in the eighth inning of Game Seven of the 1986 World Series), overslept and thereby missed team workouts on March 21, and completely walked out on the team the following day after he was fined $1,500 by Manager Davey Johnson. "He overslept?" an incredulous Gary Carter wondered about the explanation. "Can't he afford an alarm clock? I have one and I get up in the morning. But then, I go to bed at night."[59] Keith Hernandez added that "Darryl's not wet behind the ears. He's an established veteran who should know what's expected of him." Ron Darling, meanwhile, spared none of his anger. "He has a responsibility not only to his employer, the New York Mets, but also to his teammates. Hopefully, one day he'll turn around and recognize that responsibility. It's your job. You get paid a lot of money. The least you can do is show up. It's just incomprehensible to me."[60]

But whatever uncertainties lingered for the Mets' outfield in 1987, they paled in comparison to the jarring hits they would absorb on their pitching staff—both toward the end of spring training and as the regular season was about to begin. On March 29 it was announced that their premier reliever, Roger McDowell, had entered the hospital for an emergency hernia operation and would miss the first six to eight weeks of the regular season. Five days later, a larger bombshell dropped. Gooden tested positive for cocaine use, which was a violation of his parole from a no-contest plea to his December charges in Florida. To avoid being suspended by Ueberroth, the ace of the Mets' staff immediately entered the Smithers Alcoholism Treatment Center of St. Luke's–Roosevelt Hospital on April 1. Gooden was required to stay a minimum stay of twenty-eight days, but the duration was envisioned to more likely be two months, or, perhaps, the entire 1987 season. "Gooden said he had used cocaine two days before the Mets had tested him," reported the *New York Times*, "and he was shocked when the results came back positive."[61]

Some within the Mets' front office, however, believed that Gooden *wanted* to be caught. "Four or five days before the test, we informed him we were going to take it," General Manager Frank Cashen said. "We allowed him the opportunity to reschedule it if he wanted. He did not. He knew the consequences. We discussed it for some time, and it was voluntary. He had plenty of time to back out and say no.

"He never had a chance to grow up in a normal way," Cashen noted about Gooden's meteoric rise to the Major Leagues as a teenager. "It may be the best thing to happen to this young man that it was identified at this time."[62]

In an attempt to mitigate the situation, the Mets acquired twenty-four-year-old Kansas City native David Cone from the Royals in the days prior to the Gooden situation being made public.

CONTRARY TO HERZOG'S LATE FEBRUARY "PREDICTION" ABOUT the Cardinals' final spring training record, his team broke camp with the best preseason mark in baseball (17-6). They also left Florida with, as expected, more left-handed pitchers than at any time in recent memory—which was fine with the manager. "If you don't walk people, any lefthander with any brains at all will be good in our ballpark, because you've got Ozzie Smith, Terry Pendleton, Vince Coleman, and Willie McGee in the field. It was the same way in Baltimore when they had [Mike] Cuellar and [Dave] McNally. They had [Mark] Belanger and [Brooks] Robinson on the left side and they'd just slop that little slow curve up there."[63]

After beating their in-state rival Royals 8–2 in a final exhibition game in Memphis on Sunday, April 5, the Cardinals prepared for the April 7 season opener in Wrigley Field, the place where they had finished their brutal 1986 campaign. Wrigley housed yet another team looking to get back atop the National League East, the Cubs, which, like the '85 Cardinals, had made an unlikely charge to the division title a year earlier in 1984.

In consideration of the stark difference between the 1985 and 1986 St. Louis teams, which one would show up at Clark and Addison in Chicago? "When the National Anthem is played the first day, everyone feels it is going to be the best year they ever had," the veteran Forsch warned. "For some, it is. And for some, it isn't. You really can't tell what kind of team you have until you've been playing for a couple months."[64]

Herr agreed that time was needed to make an accurate assessment. "Because of that, no one quite knows what to expect. But the anticipation is there in this clubhouse that we're going to have the ability to be an explosive ballclub and win. I wouldn't be surprised to see us do that."[65]

Hernandez, having played next to Herr for four years but being an enemy for the last four, agreed. He knew well the dangers that lurked for opponents under the Gateway Arch. "As long as Whitey's in their dugout, you can never count the Cardinals out. They'll be tough to beat."[66]

3

The First Showdown

They're going into the season assuming it's going to be easy again. That's human nature. They're on top of the world. But your approach can be affected and your work habits suffer. They may not get as hungry as they were.

—Tom Herr on the New York Mets, December 13, 1986

THE FALLOUT FROM GOODEN'S COCAINE ISSUE NOT ONLY hovered over the Mets as they broke camp but also stayed in the minds of many around baseball. The issue had tainted the positive image the players were attempting to rebuild after the sport's repeated scandals with illicit substances over the past decade. "It happened at a real bad time," said Jack Clark, "a time when I think people are getting tired of this drug stuff. I know as a player I'm getting tired of playing with these guys. They're costing all of us in the long run." Added Danny Cox, "Here we're trying to overcome a bad public image because a couple of people ruined things, yet we can't do it. Now we're going back to Step One. People are saying, 'Is *everyone* doing it?' because we don't have mandatory testing."[1]

With Gooden off to rehab, Davey Johnson handed the starting assignment for opening day—which Gooden had performed the past two years—to left-hander Bob Ojeda, as the Mets sought stability in launching the season at home in Shea Stadium against Van Slyke and the Pirates. Having lost both their top starter and reliever for at least several weeks, Johnson's club was counting on the batting order to make up the difference, which, in addition to McReynolds, included a new third baseman. Postseason hero Ray Knight batted .391 against the Red Sox to take home the World Series MVP award but had departed in November via free agency for Baltimore, where he would become the twenty-seventh Oriole to patrol the hot corner since the retirement of Brooks Robinson in 1977. In Knight's place went Howard Johnson, a switch hitter who possessed both power and speed. With the rest of the team relatively in place from the World Series winner, the Mets were hoping that Strawberry would behave, McReynolds would fit in, Carter would stave off the twilight of his career, and there would be no more bad surprises within the ranks of the pitching staff.

Having been winless in all eight of their previous regular season openers at Wrigley Field, the Cardinals arrived in Chicago with a few minor bumps and bruises. Lindeman was nursing a sore back after making a diving catch against the Mets in the Cardinals' final Florida preseason game on April 4, while Herr was trying to reduce the swelling on his elbow due to an errant batting-practice pitch from Leyva. Both men, however, were in the starting lineup—as was the healed Tudor, who took the mound against the Cubs' Rick Sutcliffe in a rematch of the 1986 season opener at Busch, a pitcher's duel in which Tudor went the distance in prevailing 2–1.

As kids around the Chicago area rushed home from school and adults ditched work early to catch as much of the game as they could, a legendary voice was missing for those tuning into WGN Television. Seventy-three-year-old announcer Harry Caray was slowly recovering from a mild stroke he had suffered on February 17 at his off-season residence in Palm Springs. "He is a little difficult to understand at times," Caray's physician said of his slurred speech a few weeks after the incident, "but I'm sure his fans will be sympathetic."[2] Caray would miss the first several weeks of the season, as local and national celebrities—most of whom had no experience behind a microphone—took turns in the booth as guest broadcasters of the Cubs games.

A brisk game-time temperature of 56 degrees along the Chicago lakefront was abated with a warm, hearty cheer from the home crowd for Dawson, who jogged out to right field ten years after his Rookie of the Year season with the Expos. One of sport's true five-tool talents since entering baseball, Dawson had beaten teams over the past decade with his running speed and throwing arm in addition to his powerful bat, and Chicago fans were looking forward to more of the same. When free agency had finally gotten moving over the winter after the alleged stalling by the owners, Dawson and his agent were quickly sold on what the Cubs had to offer. "We talked about Atlanta, because that is closer to my home in Florida, but Chicago is where I really wanted to be," the player decided. "There's the natural turf, which is kinder to my knees, but the real reason is that I really like this city. It's a baseball city where the fans really support the team."[3] The ligaments in Dawson's knees had first been torn and repaired during his high school days, which temporarily prevented him from being drafted into pro ball as he instead paid his own way to study and play at Florida A&M University. Since 1977 his legs had constantly pounded upon the hard Astroturf of Olympic Stadium in Montreal, where the wear-and-tear ultimately necessitated the Expos shifting him from center field to right field. Instead of the $1 million for each of the next two years he could have gotten from Montreal, Dawson would be playing the 1987 season for the Cubs for half that amount—plus a $150,000 bonus if he did not appear on the disabled list by the All-Star break.

While some Chicagoans were heading to the polls on election day to choose between incumbent mayor Harold Washington and Alderman Ed Vrdolyak, over thirty-eight thousand other city dwellers and their suburban neighbors huddled together inside Wrigley Field to watch Coleman, Herr, and Smith be retired easily in order by Sutcliffe in the top of the first.

As the Cardinals' defense took the field, McGee watched from the bench. But unlike Dawson, he held no lingering reservations about his own knee and was ready to go if Herzog needed him. As McGee looked on, a new right fielder was heading out for the visiting team as well, and, as with Dawson, some of the home fans cheered for the Cardinal running out to the spot.

Departing the dugout for the outfield was Lindeman, inspired by the presence and support of twenty-eight friends and relatives on hand from his nearby hometown of Des Plaines, Illinois, just northwest of Chicago. The previous night, Lindeman was granted permission by Herzog to leave the team hotel and sleep at his parents' house to help ease some of the tension. And although Dawson had patrolled the right field of Wrigley for many years with the Expos, Lindeman was getting his first introduction to the dreaded sun-field portion of the ballpark—although he had started the final two games of the 1986 season in left field and at first base against the Cubs in Chicago. "As luck would have it, I was in right field for opening day in Wrigley Field," Lindeman fondly recalled in 2023. "I remember being introduced, going out and standing on the line, hitting behind Jack Clark. That was a great moment for me and my family, to be on the field for opening day against a team I always rooted for in the Cubs."[4]

Dawson would go hitless in his Chicago unveiling, which included popping out with runners on first and third and two out in the fourth inning. In the second inning, Dawson had struck out with the bases loaded and two out after nearly missing a grand slam as he "hit one [foul] into the bicuspids of a Lake Michigan gale," observed Horrigan on the scene for the *Post-Dispatch*. "The ball curved foul at the last moment."[5]

Instead, it was the play of the rookie opponent, both in the field and at the plate, that would have the patrons at Wrigley lean forward in their chilly seats in interest. In the bottom of the second with the Cubs already having jumped on Tudor for a 2–0 advantage, Chicago's Brian Dayett rocketed a double down the left-field line. Next was former Cardinal Leon Durham, who lofted a lazy fly to Lindeman in right, which nearly drifted to the warning track. Lindeman was able to retreat in time to get behind the ball before unleashing a powerful, one-hop throw to Pendleton at third to double up Dayett trying to advance. "Boy, that made me feel good," Lindeman said after the game. "I'm still pretty uncomfortable out there. I just need more experience. I've only played about 20 games in my life in right field. [But] I'd rather play where I'm uncomfortable than sit on the bench."[6] Coupled with Dawson's bases-loaded strikeout to end the inning, the throw by Lindeman kept the score at 3–0 and prevented the game from possibly becoming a blowout by the Cubs.

The Cards immediately seized the momentum off the rookie's accomplishment. Five of the eleven St. Louis batters in the top of third scored, as Sutcliffe did not make it out of the inning. The 1984 Cy Young Award winner, normally a fan favorite in Chicago, was booed off the field as he was replaced by rookie Greg Maddux, who, like Lindeman, had gotten a brief taste of the Majors at the end of the 1986 campaign.

The visitors' assault resumed in the seventh with 4 more runs, which included Peña notching the first Cardinal stolen base of the season. It was not without precedent for the honor to go to an unexpected candidate, as Andújar had stolen the first of the team's 314 bases in 1985 (off Gooden and Gary Carter), while Heath, another catcher, had swiped the first of 262 for the team in 1986. Tudor was lifted in the sixth inning after throwing 91 pitches, giving way to Dawley for the final four in shutting down the Cubs for a 9–3 win. Whiteyball had returned, as the 9 runs had been scored on 11 singles, reminiscent of the Cardinals' 1985 crisply executed philosophy of "Get 'em on, get 'em over, get 'em in."

Even so, Herzog did not hide his disdain for the Chicago ballpark and the impact its elements had on his moves. "You can't manage at Wrigley—not with the wind blowing out. You just worry that you don't ruin your pitching staff for the next few days by using too many pitchers. You don't run a lot because the wind's blowing out. And you can't hit and run, because you can't hit a ball through the infield because the grass is so high."[7] Moreover, there was the dreaded three o'clock starting time that the National League would occasionally issue for games at Wrigley, when the third base upper deck casted a treacherous shadow halfway between the pitcher's mound and home plate. "I'm surprised someone hasn't gotten killed in those conditions," Whitey continued. "It changes the entire game around. Get the lead, get the shadows, and get out of there."[8]

The Cards shared victory on the day with Harold Washington, who would return to the Chicago mayor's office by soundly beating Vrdolyak with 54 percent of the vote.

In the second game of the series two days later, Pendleton nearly decapitated Lindeman when he missed the sign for a squeeze play as the rookie barreled in from third. But Terry redeemed himself by slugging a two-run homer in the sixth, the margin of victory in a 4–2 win for Cox, as Coleman stole 4 bases in twice nabbing second and third base (two of thirteen times he would do so in

1987). Peña had also stolen another, suggesting he was more than ready to join the cast of roadrunners.

It was now off to Pittsburgh for a reunion with Van Slyke and a homecoming for the new Cardinals catcher. "I'll have a good time," Peña remarked as the team left Chicago and headed for his former place of work. "I have a good time every day."[9] Like the Cardinals, the Pirates had also opened the year on the road, as Peña's catching counterpart Carter had posted the 1,000th RBI of his career for the Mets in their 4–2 win over the Bucs in New York.

Converging at Three Rivers Stadium on the night of April 10 for the Pirates' home opener was a Pittsburgh baseball record of 52,119 spectators. Whether the figure suggested a renaissance of the sport in the city (which had been the epicenter of baseball's cocaine dilemma two years earlier) or a visceral excitement for Peña's return, a standing ovation greeted the catcher on his first trip to the plate in the top of the second inning. The applause lasted so long that Peña, observably emotional, had to step out of the batter's box twice to acknowledge it. "The sooner I get this series over, [the] better," Peña had said before the game. "Then, I can relax a little bit more. Right now, I'm thinking about everything."[10]

With the Cardinals behind 3–1 heading into the top of the ninth, Peña was leading off the inning once again. Most of the cheers had by now died down, as Peña was an enemy. The Pirates needed to retire him to keep the potential tying run from coming to the plate.

Many of those around Pittsburgh who were watching on television and listening on the radio were planning on coming to the stadium for one of the three remaining games in the series, intent on seeing the former Pirate great in person. They would be disappointed, as would the Cardinals, whose plans for the season took a sudden hit—and potentially, a catastrophic one. On the first pitch from the Pirates' Brian Fisher, Peña was hit on the thumb.

Shaking off the impact, Peña stayed in the game and went down to first base before advancing to third on a Pendleton double. But as Peña's finger continued to throb, Herzog decided to remove him despite the catcher's protests, with Steve Lake inserted as a pinch runner. Peña insisted the injury would not impact his catching and had wanted to finish the game but was advised by team trainer Gene Gieselmann that doing so would make it worse.

After McGee struck out, third-year reserve outfielder Curt Ford came to the plate. Back in 1985, Ford delivered a game-winning RBI single in his first Major League at bat against Lee Smith of the Cubs in the tenth inning on June 22, which put the Cardinals in first place for the first time that season. In 1987, however, Ford had endured a horrible spring and did not appear in the two-game set in Chicago. He took advantage of the opportunity by delivering a two-run double to tie the game. LaPoint subsequently collapsed in the ninth for the first Cardinals loss of the year, 4–3, but just as Ford had risen to the occasion, another "no-namer" from whom contributions would be needed in 1987 followed suit the next afternoon.

The Cardinal players had given a rousing endorsement in the newspapers about Steve Lake as an able replacement behind the plate; he had very quietly led the team in hitting in spring training with a .421 mark to go along with 12 RBIS, which trailed only Lindeman. Lake responded to Peña's absence by going 2-4 in his first start while Lindeman belted 2 home runs in a 6–3 St. Louis win. McGee, far ahead of schedule in his recovery, also made his first start, and despite only going 1-5 at the plate, he reported no pain in his knee, as the Cardinals and Pirates split the four-game set. Few were there to see it, however, as an average of only 6,200 fans wandered into Three Rivers Stadium for the final three games that were played without Peña after a standing-room-only crowd had been present for the season opener.

Before Peña flew back to St. Louis by himself for treatment, it was estimated by Gieselmann that his thumb would have to remain in a cast for four weeks, followed by a minimum of two weeks of therapy. The inactivity quickly became unbearable for the high-strung catcher, who had averaged playing in 147 games per season for the previous four years, in addition to a full slate of games he typically elected to play each winter in the Dominican League. "I'm getting crazy already," he muttered only a few days later. "I know it's going to be the longest six weeks of my life. I never take six weeks off. I was sitting there in my TV room [watching the Cardinals games] and seeing my teammates, and there was nothing I could do about it. But who knows? I might come out of all of this on June 1 and maybe win the MVP."

While Peña healed, Dr. London permitted him to continue throwing, running, riding a stationary bicycle, and even taking some swings in batting practice. "I'm trying to keep my body in good condition. When I come out of the cast, I can step in right away. I'm going to be in good shape. I'll already have my rest in."[11] But both Peña and the Cardinals knew that the biggest long-term problem with the injury would be his delay in getting familiar with the pitching staff.

FINALLY ARRIVING IN ST. LOUIS FOR THEIR HOME OPENER BY way of Florida, Memphis, Chicago, and Pittsburgh, the Cardinals' first six games on the road had produced 8 home runs, which already surpassed their output from all of April 1986 and helped them to a 4-2 start. With the sun setting and game time approaching for the inaugural at Busch Stadium on the night of April 14, the wagon gates behind the left-field wall suddenly opened. Back behind home plate and near the press box high above the field, Ernie Hays stretched his fingers and pressed four quick notes on the Yamaha organ, the prelude to his playing of "Here Comes the King." As the familiar tune echoed throughout the massive circular ballpark, the Budweiser Clydesdales rolled onto the Astroturf with Gussie Busch in tow, a sight that lifted the joyous patrons to their feet. Shortly thereafter, the entire rosters of the Cardinals and the winless 0-5 Expos were introduced as they took their places along the foul lines. Seated behind the first base dugout was Rachel Robinson, the widow of Jackie Robinson, who threw out the first pitch on the eve of the fortieth anniversary of Jackie breaking the color barrier.

Mathews, making his second start, opened strongly by fanning the first two Expos hitters, Alonzo Powell and Mitch Webster, on called strikes. But he was chased from the mound quickly thereafter, as the Cardinals' 9–4 loss would have been a shutout if not for a ninth inning rally that only around four thousand of the original forty-eight thousand–plus remained on site to see. They fell again two days later by a 4–3 score, as McGee, struggling to regain his timing and form, missed three flies in the outfield that he ordinarily would have caught. "I'm just tired of coming in on balls and looking behind me and finding somebody else picking the ball up,"

THE FIRST SHOWDOWN

he said while shaking his head afterward.[12] Also suddenly struggling was his outfield partner Coleman, who sat out the contest with blurred vision and was ordered by Herzog to receive an eye test. The downturn dashed the team's initial momentum it had established on the road in the first week of the season, just as the Cardinals' arch-enemy arrived in town.

When Gooden was arrested the night of December 13, Tom Herr had spoken to the media only hours earlier about the potential complacency that might haunt the New York Mets heading into 1987. "They're going into the season assuming it's going to be easy again. That's human nature," the Cardinals' second baseman noted. "They're on top of the world. But your approach can be affected and your work habits suffer. They may not get as hungry as they were."[13]

Although the events of the preceding months might have suggested that the Mets were losing their focus, Davey Johnson appeared to have successfully deflected the majority of the off-season distractions. Having opened the season with six victories in eight games, Johnson had his team ready to play when it entered Busch Stadium on April 17. The power-laden Mets had homered in all eight contests, which included five by the rededicated Strawberry, who after four solid but unspectacular seasons finally appeared destined for a year that would match his much-hyped potential.

As usual, the St. Louis skipper was in the home clubhouse several hours before game time, thoroughly preparing for the imminent battle with the Mets, as he did for every series. "The best show in town is the Cardinals' manager's office from 4 p.m. to 5 p.m. on game days, when Herzog hunkers down with his hitting charts and his mail," wrote Tom Wheatley in the *Post-Dispatch*. "He pulls the charts on the opposing lineup and studies each hitter. He has charts on anyone who waved a bat at his pitchers in either league. He still has files on deceased hitters, such as Thurman Munson and Lyman Bostock. 'If they ever come back,' Herzog says, 'I'll be ready for them.'"[14]

Shortly before the first pitch, Wheatley left the locker room and went up to join Hummel, Joseph Durso of the *New York Times*, and the scores of other scribes jamming the press box for the greatly anticipated early-season battle. They would see three up-and-three-down, roller-coaster games, emblematic of what was to follow in the summerlong feud between the two clubs. "When the Mets returned to the scene tonight [Busch Stadium]," Durso wrote, "they were greeted by a crowd of 43,699 fans, mostly hostile, and by the Cardinals, entirely hostile."[15]

In the first game, Tudor went up against Ojeda, his former Red Sox teammate. Out behind the St. Louis left-hander was Coleman, having returned to the field with confirmation of twenty-twenty vision, and he rebounded with a stolen base and a sprinting catch that robbed Strawberry of extra bases. Later in the evening, Tudor was rescued by Horton with three innings of shutout relief, as the Cards held on to take the opening round by a 4–3 score. The hostility was growing between the combatants; the following night, April 18, would be recorded for posterity as a landmark date on the Cardinals' 1987 calendar.

As the sellout crowd got comfortable upon the free seat cushions given away at the gates, a palpable tension simmered down on the field—and even between former teammates. When Ozzie Smith appeared as the second hitter in the bottom of the first inning, he dribbled a foul grounder in the general direction of Hernandez at first base. Instead of grabbing the ball with his glove, the former Cardinal stood upright, timed his steps toward the ball like a field goal kicker, and defiantly booted it ninety degrees toward the home dugout. Whether it was intended with humor or purposeful inso-lence, it was taken as affront by the St. Louis club.

Pendleton, relaxing on the bench while waiting for his turn in the seventh spot in the batting order, went over and picked up the ball and hurled it back onto the field in Hernandez's direction. Watching outside the batter's box was Smith, who was miffed at the New York player's actions. "What kind of sense is it to do that? You're just asking for trouble. There's no need for stuff like that. Just pick the ball up and throw it back to the pitcher."[16]

There was little doubt that Hernandez, despite all the individ-ual and team laurels he had already achieved in his career, greatly wished to succeed against St. Louis. "Keith was a former Cardinal and had extra incentive," Roger McDowell recalled. "Here is our leader who is a former Cardinal. We looked to him for direction and leadership. And when you have this guy who wanted to beat them as badly as he did, I think we fell in line with that."[17]

A back-and-forth struggle ensued, with four lead changes transpiring over the course of the night. After the Cards had tied the game in the ninth inning, the Mets appeared to take command once again in the tenth as a wild pitch from the struggling LaPoint sent home reserve rookie infielder Al Pedrique, who was appearing in his second big league game, for the latest New York advantage at 8–7.

Nonetheless, the situation was merely the next challenge and opportunity for yet another untested talent to come to the forefront and contribute for Herzog. "On a night that will haunt their memories," Durso wrote in his column for New York readers the next day, "the Mets blew a five-run lead in the fourth inning and a pair of one-run leads in the ninth and tenth innings.

"And then they blew the entire evening."[18]

The newest protagonist in the emerging plot was Tom Pagnozzi, who back in early 1986 appeared destined to share the catching job in St. Louis with LaValliere by the end of the season. Having batted and defended well at every level of the Cardinals' farm system for three years, Pagnozzi had been on the fast track to the Major Leagues after being the team's eighth-round pick out of the University of Arkansas in 1983. But thirty games into the 1986 Minor League schedule, Pagnozzi's progress was stunted when he broke his wrist on a foul tip at Louisville. After working his way back to full health by the fall, discouragement struck again when the organization acquired Peña, as Pagnozzi figured he would be mired at Triple-A for another year. "'I'm never going to play in the big leagues'—that's what I thought," he admitted when he heard about the trade for the Pittsburgh catcher.[19]

But the young backstop was reminded that in life, things can—and will—change. Less than a week into the season, Peña's injury to his own hand necessitated Pagnozzi's elevation to the Cardinals.

With runners on first and second and one out in the bottom of the tenth, the right-handed-hitting rookie was sent in by Herzog to pinch-hit for Ford against the gritty southpaw reliever Jesse Orosco. Pagnozzi kept his hands back patiently and went with an outside pitch, punching a single through the hole on the right side for his first big league hit, as Pendleton dashed around third and to the plate, tying the game yet again.

After a Coleman groundout, Smith walked to load the bases, with Herr due up. Despite Orosco now being far into his second inning of work (in facing his eleventh hitter) and Herr having batted over a hundred points higher from the right side than the left in 1986 (.315 as opposed to .212), Johnson decided to leave the left-hander in the game.

Knowing that his run meant nothing, Pagnozzi stood close to the bag at second. He wound up scoring unexpectedly anyway.

Herr turned on a belt-high fastball from Orosco and launched it into the first row of the left-field bleachers for a grand slam, which instantly tied him with Strawberry for the league lead in RBIs with 15—a figure that the St. Louis second baseman did not reach in 1986 until the fifty-first game of the season.

A few feet away from where the home run ball had landed, a delirious fan in the bleachers, consumed with euphoria, flung his free seat cushion upward in celebration. The white square cut through the St. Louis night sky like a deformed frisbee, ultimately landing upon the turf in left-center field. It was soon followed by hundreds of others—one of which Herr himself grabbed after circling the bases as he threw it into the air to join the fun. It made for a breathtaking 12–8 victory after the Mets had built a 5–0 advantage in the fourth inning, the first time in three years New York had blown any five-run lead.

As the team converged on home plate to celebrate, Herzog first embraced not Herr but Pagnozzi, putting his arm around in the rookie in appreciation of the key role he played in the rally.

"As if that weren't enough for one night," grumbled Durso further, "the Mets also suffered another injury that could haunt them." McReynolds, who had taken part in the Mets' home run barrage during the first week of the season with two of his own, sprained a ligament in his right foot while trying to score in the top of the ninth. "Their new power-hitting left fielder had to be helped off the field. No broken bones were detected on the early X-rays, but the Mets said they had no idea how long McReynolds might be lost."[20]

To give Lake a breather from his new role as the number-one catcher, Pagnozzi was rewarded as the starter for the following game on Easter Sunday afternoon of April 19, in yet another critical early-season matchup against New York. Meanwhile, the affable Hernandez apologized for the foul-ball incident from the previous night and assured his former team that there was no ill will. Intent to instead focus upon his struggles at the plate, Hernandez had arrived at Busch early in the morning for extra batting practice to address a 7-38 stint (.184) he was suffering to start the season.

When the afternoon concluded, the Cardinals had claimed another triumph to take all three games, Coleman had swiped 2 more bases to run his season total to 10 (and was now successful on all 18 of his attempts against the Mets in his career), and McGee homered and notched his 1st stolen base of the year to suggest all is well with his knee. "Talk about the unthinkable," Durso continued in his report of the most unusual trio of days. "The Mets, who arrived here this weekend in first place with a three-game winning streak, left today in second place with a three-game losing streak. They took a 4–2 tumble to the St. Louis Cardinals, who completed a sweep of the series just when the Mets were beginning to 'send a message' to the rest of the National League. The only message they seemed to be sending was that they were human, vulnerable, and even beatable."[21]

The victory, however, was pyrrhic for St. Louis. In a season already filled with ups and downs that would continue through its end, the St. Louis celebration was diminished by a freak accident that threatened to shatter all the Cardinals had worked for since climbing up from their 1986 downfall. "But how's this for unthinkable," Durso ended his narrative. "The Cardinals, at their moment of cheer, suffered an ironic and devastating blow to their long-range chances of displacing the Mets as champions."[22]

The calamity occurred under what had seemingly been safe circumstances. In the bottom of the third, Clark, who doubled in his first at bat off the top of the center-field wall, nearly missing a home run, lifted a foul pop fly near the Cardinals' bench. Chasing after it in only his third Major League start was the Mets' rookie catcher Barry Lyons. With his shin guards flapping and his head tilted upward while staring into the glare of a midwestern afternoon,

Lyons sprinted after the ball at a maximum gallop, unaware of his closing proximity to the dugout. No railing, warning track, or any other visual or physical barrier had been installed in front of the dugout steps at Busch Stadium to that time, as architects had considered such an addition problematic for the football games that the ballpark also hosted.

In finally realizing his surroundings at the last moment, Lyons—still going full speed—attempted to stop his progress by sliding late, and a couple St. Louis players tried to slow him up. One of them was John Tudor, whose kneecap was impacted by Lyons's foot.

After collapsing to the dugout floor, Tudor was helped up a moment later by Cox and Lawless. They placed the pitcher's arms around their shoulders as he limped down the corridor toward the clubhouse.

In a trivial yet bitter irony, the hard-charging Lyons wound up having no chance to catch the ball, as it landed three rows deep in the stands. "I was yelling, 'No play, no play,'" said Herr, who was standing next to Tudor in the dugout. "Lyons was coming full tilt. Everybody was yelling, 'No play.' I don't know what he was thinking. I got out of the way. Self-preservation took over, I guess."[23] Lyons explained his thinking afterward: "The ball was kind of in the sun. I thought I had a play all the way. I knew I was getting close to the dugout, so I went into my slide. The next thing I knew, I was *in* the dugout."[24]

An inning later, Pagnozzi drove his first Major League home run out of Busch Stadium for the fourth and final Cardinals' run in the 4–2 win.

Despite the sweep, all thoughts were on Tudor. His tibia had been shattered just below the knee; the devastating blow was expected to keep him out of action until at least August. Herzog, however, warned that the date was a most optimistic timetable, for even if Tudor's leg healed soon enough for him to be able to contribute later in the season, the danger existed of him hurting his arm if he returned to the mound too quickly without his entire body being back in shape.

It was a solemn ending to Easter, the same holiday on which Cox had broken his ankle in 1986. "We're not scheduled on Easter of next year," Herzog later announced in disgusted humor, despite knowing they of course would be. "I'm going to take the team to Menard Prison on Saturday night and lock them up. We'll celebrate Easter with the wardens."[25] With television viewers getting their first glimpse of *The Simpsons* that Sunday night as part of *The Tracey Ullman Show*, the Cardinals' skipper went home to Mary Lou while trying to decipher an answer to the continuous cartoon reel of injuries that would not leave his team alone.

For the rest of the pitching staff, the injury meant stepping up. Taking Tudor's place was Conroy, recalled from Triple-A, where he had rebounded from his problems in spring training and would start against the Cubs on Tuesday, April 21. Also waiting in the wings was Magrane, who had authored a shutout against Omaha the same day as Tudor's injury and had not been scored upon in his last eighteen innings at Louisville.

Conroy and Pagnozzi were not the only fresh faces from whom contributions would be needed, as the injury bug devastated the team further. Four days after the Lyons-Tudor incident, Herr pulled his groin muscle in the finale of the Cubs series and was placed on the twenty-one-day disabled list, while McGee, Clark, and Lindeman were all dealing with nagging hamstring issues. Jumping in as replacements were Oquendo at second base, Ford in center field (where his eight putouts in his first-ever start at the position on April 23 would fall four short of the Major League single-game record in center), and Tom Lawless, with his first career start in right field and only his second-ever start in the outfield. John Morris (hitting .325 at Louisville) and infielder Rod Booker (.362) would soon follow, while hot on the heels of Pagnozzi was Todd Zeile, another catching prospect coming up through the system, who hit 5 home runs in the Midwest League during the third week of April.

With every regular except Pendleton having already missed action on the young season, the Cardinals had not fielded their normal starting lineup since Clark had broken his thumb on June 24 of the previous summer. When the sportswriters had finally asked one too many times about the disabled list, Herzog issued his summary of the team's frustrating injury report. "Willie is day-to-day. Tommy is week-to-week. Pena is month-to-month. Lahti is year-to-year."[26]

Despite the medical malaise, the Cardinals were determined to continue to right the ship for 1987, and the experienced novices filling in were among the most undeterred. With another three-game series with the Mets to begin in New York on April 24, reinforcements continued to arrive. After Mathews dropped a tough 2–1 decision in the opener, it was Magrane's turn to finally be elevated to the Major League level to face the same formidable team against which he had first taken the mound in spring training.

Unable to sleep in the team hotel the night before his debut, Magrane channeled his restlessness in his room by studying the flight patterns of planes zooming overhead from nearby LaGuardia Airport and the distractions they might cause the next evening in Shea Stadium. The pensive young left-hander calmly pushed fear aside and did his job, striking out seven batters in six innings of work and beating the champs by a 3–2 count, aided by the 4th save from Horton, who had become the leader of the relief corps with Worrell struggling to the tune of a 10.00 ERA by early May. "We kind of mixed and matched there for a while," Horton recalled of the bullpen situation in the first portion of 1987, "and I wound up having a fair number of saves in the early part of the year. But obviously, closing was a new thing for me. Several of the games I closed out were three-inning appearances."[27]

Herzog felt good about putting the multitalented Horton on the mound in any situation. "He really has a good knowledge of how to pitch. I have a lot of confidence in him. He's an intelligent guy." Horton—recently named in a poll of managers as having the best pickoff move in the National League—used both his physical and mental skills to be effective. "People say I quietly do some things on the mound, and that's right," he told the writers after saving the game for Magrane. "I try not to throw 30 pitches an inning. I try to throw strikes, utilize the defense and get out of an inning on eight to 10 pitches. That's not as impressive an inning as somebody who's out there throwing 20 pitches and striking out the side."[28] Horton knew, however, that his position in the closer's role was likely to be temporary. "I view this as an aberration, a short-term phenomenon. I'm enjoying it, of course, but I'm not going to be surprised if I give up a hit and Gary Carter's coming up and Todd comes in."[29]

Former Cardinals reliever and third-year St. Louis television analyst Al Hrabosky thought he had figured out the core of Worrell's problems:

> The worst thing that happens to Worrell is when he is 0-and-2 [on the batter]. Guys have different mental makeups, and Todd has never thrown inside. Guys know that, and they're over the plate looking for him to waste something. I think he's going to work himself out of it. But before that, I think he's going to hit several guys. Not because he's trying to, but they're going to hit themselves. If he had that killer instinct—or should I say, effectively wild—when you've got that little fear in there for the hitters, that makes a difference.[30]

Magrane's first Major League win was also the 1,000th for Herzog as a big league manager—the thirty-seventh man to attain the mark—and it came in the 999th game he had piloted for the Cardinals. After the milestone victory, Whitey was seen drinking from a congratulatory $90 bottle of Dom Perignon purchased for him by Leyva, Gieselmann, and equipment manager Buddy Bates. The manager, in turn, took the game ball he had been awarded from the team and gave it to Magrane, who sent it to his father back in Kentucky.

The rookie's effort inspired the club to another important victory the next day, the 145th win in the career of Bob Forsch, which placed him fourth on the Cardinals' all-time list. Helping relay the action that day to the folks back home in St. Louis was eighteen-year-old Joe Buck, who took over the microphone on KMOX Radio for the play-by-play in the sixth inning after celebrating his birthday in New York the prior evening with his father Jack.

Exactly one year after the 1986 campaign started going sour in an April series against the Mets, the bruised and battered Cardinals had thus taken five of six games from Davey Johnson's club before a month had expired in the new season. Coleman stole 4 more bases in the latest three games, running his season total to 16 and continuing a perfect 22-22 ledger in his career attempts against the Mets. "It wasn't a hateful rivalry with the Mets, just an intense competition," the New York native John Morris explained in 2023. "They were extremely talented. They probably had the best players in the division, but they probably weren't as fundamentally sound as us, especially on defense, and I say that out of respect. They had great pitching and power, but they didn't always make the routine play or throw to the correct base, which played right into our hands—because we were masterful at turning ground ball singles into doubles or triples."[31]

One of those usually masterful men and one of the lone healthy starters, Ozzie Smith, endured a brutal April at the plate with a .185 mark (12-65) and ended the Mets series in a 2-32 slump, but Herzog planned on keeping him in the number-two spot in the batting order. The Mets' team ERA ballooned to 4.56 for the month, and among the enemies most responsible for the crooked figure were the men from St. Louis, as the Cardinals had almost doubled their run output from April 1986 (59 to 102). Herzog snickered when hearing a report that some Mets pitchers were not required by Davey Johnson to be in the dugout during games. "I have a rule that my pitchers have to be in the dugout, although maybe I shouldn't have with Tudor," said Whitey, who in one of his first acts after taking over as manager in 1980 had removed the television from the Cardinals' locker room. "It seems to me that a starting pitcher wants everybody to bust their butts and root for him when he's pitching, so he ought to be out there rooting for them."[32] In the rare occasions when the St. Louis starting pitchers had tried to duck out of sight early, Herzog applied the simple solution of locking the clubhouse door from the outside.

The Redbirds closed out April with a 5–4 win over the Padres in Busch Stadium, as Coleman stole his league-leading 17th base, about twice as many as the second-place Eric Davis of the Reds. Coleman, however, was also caught at second base for the first time on the year by the dazzling rookie San Diego catcher Benito Santiago, who had thrown out 57 percent of potential stealers (13 of 23) so far on the season and emulated Peña in throwing from his knees to anywhere on the field.

WHEN NEWSPAPER READERS OPENED UP THEIR MAY 1 ISSUES, the Cardinals were shown to be a game in front of the Mets for the top spot in the National League East—the first time a new month displayed a team other than New York leading the way since the fall of 1985.

THE FIRST SHOWDOWN

4

Powering Through

*They know what they're doing. They're all good hitters. They get
a lot of good games out of their extra people. But you can talk all
you want about the Cardinals' offense. They win because of their
infield defense and their pitchers' abilities to get ground balls.*

—Mike Schmidt, June 1987

THE CARDINALS STARTED THE NEW MONTH BY HOSTING THE
Dodgers, whose leader retained a bitter taste in his mouth nearly
two years after they had been defeated by St. Louis in the 1985
National League Championship Series. "People thought that ballclub was great to watch," Los Angeles manager Tommy Lasorda
mentioned back in spring training, classifying the '85 version of
the Redbirds as an anomaly and the faltered '86 club as its true
self. "The Cardinals won 101 games, and people said they were so
exciting and that they would be great for years."[1] As for Lanier's
Astros, who had the audacity to wrest the National League West
title away from his team, Lasorda warned the Houston manager
that "the lease was about up"—implying that the Astros had merely
been renting first place temporarily.

Lasorda's point—at least at the time—was not without merit,
as the early evidence in 1987 suggested Herzog's team was indeed
evolving from the flash-and-dash form taken by its last pennant
winner into something else. While its running speed was still apparent, the Cardinals appeared to have moved away from their other

trademarks of defensive and pitching prowess and, like the Mets, were now relying upon outscoring their opponents. The days of the starting pitchers going deep into ballgames seemed gone, as Cox was the only one to log a complete game through the first week of May, while in the bullpen, Horton and his fellow left-hander Perry had cooled off from their hot April beginnings. Worrell continued to stumble, while the newcomer Dawley possessed an 0-3 record and a 6.11 ERA before being sent to Florida to tend to a resurfacing elbow problem after his off-season surgery.

But as had been already witnessed with the hitters, the 1987 Cardinals' pitching staff also saw fresh faces rise to the challenge. As the team started a West Coast trip in San Diego on May 6 with no travel day beforehand (and thus no rest for the beleaguered relief corps), the rookie Magrane posted another victory by blanking the Padres 3–0, despite Santiago nailing Coleman once again at second base, now making the rookie San Diego catcher 15-29. Magrane was able to induce 17 outs on ground balls, as he logged the first complete-game shutout by a Cardinals pitcher since Tudor in September 1985. The young lefty had baffled everyone in the San Diego lineup—including Tony Gwynn, who was on his way to leading the National League in hits for the third time in four seasons. "A lot of us had never seen him before," Gwynn said after the game. "He kept me off stride all night. He didn't get into any trouble."[2] While displaying some unusual habits in the southpaw tradition (such as his examination of the flight schedules at LaGuardia), there was no doubt that Magrane was all business about his craft. "I really like to relax the next day after a game and then the next day, when I throw on the side. But as I get closer to my next start, I get more serious and internalize [sic] on things as I prepare to pitch. There's no excuse to go out on the mound and not be prepared."[3]

Magrane was also learning to ignore the slings and arrows of the media, which began taking more of an interest in the rookie as his success continued. Six days later, he notched his 3rd win in as many decisions and lowered his ERA to 1.74 in beating the San Francisco Giants. He did so after being disparaged by a Bay Area reporter who scribbled that, from his view, the soft-throwing left-hander might be able to get little leaguers out and nothing more.

The pitcher took it as a compliment. "I've always done well against little leaguers," Magrane responded.[4]

Aware that his team was 20 homers ahead of its 1986 pace and, more important, was leading the National League in runs scored at 5.5 per game, Herzog nonetheless lamented his team's familiar and relative lack of power as he gazed at the Sunday papers in his hotel room on the morning of May 10. "I see we're last in the league in home runs again," he quipped.[5] The home run production would have been greater if not for the falloff of Lindeman, who had proven himself as a sturdy player in the Minors but was suddenly enduring myriad injuries as well as an 0-22 slump at the plate that included ten strikeouts, in addition to being tentative on defense. "He's not going after the ball," the manager said of Lindeman's difficulties in the outfield. "Ford has played much better defensively. I can wait for hitting, but I can't wait for defense. He's just pressing. He's afraid to make a mistake."[6]

Years later, Lindeman had time to reflect on what had happened. "Everything was going smoothly," he said in thinking of the early months of 1987. "I got off to a pretty good start. And then one day during batting practice at Dodger Stadium, I bent over to pick up a ball, and I hurt my back somehow. I was very fortunate that Whitey always stood behind me and had confidence in me, and I appreciated that. I had never been hurt before in my life; I played every day of every sport I ever played."[7]

The difficulties earned him a trip to Louisville, along with an equally besieged Mathews and his 6.62 ERA after permitting 5 runs in five innings in Dodger Stadium in a game that the Cardinals' bullpen ultimately lost in the eighth. Herzog held a private meeting with Mathews before the young pitcher was sent to Triple-A. "He understands it will be easier for him to get it back together there than to have him here and struggling," Herzog told the press after meeting with the pitcher in his office. "He's just hesitant to throw an off-speed pitch. That was his success. He thinks he's a power pitcher, that he's going to smoke them. He's pitched 35 innings and had 63 baserunners."[8]

The moves opened up a roster spot for Herr to be activated, as Mathews responded to the challenge by hurling a 4-hit shutout with 11 strikeouts against Nashville four days later. Meanwhile, another Mathews with one *t*—seventeen-year-old T. J. Mathews of nearby Columbia, Illinois—pitched a no-hitter for Columbia High School in its regional playoff game in the Illinois High School tournament. At the plate, Mathews, a junior, also singled, tripled, and homered in the game.

With the Cardinals having come from behind in 11 of their first 19 wins on the season, the middle of May brought to St. Louis the first visit of the team many thought to be the biggest threat to the Dodgers and Astros in the National League West.

Back in spring training, Herzog had favored neither Los Angeles nor Houston in that division but the Cincinnati Reds, which Whitey thought would have an easier time winning the West than the Mets would have repeating in the East. Pete Rose had taken his final at bat in the previous August as a player-manager at the age of forty-five but remained on in 1987 as the skipper, and he had at his disposal the five-tool talent Davis emerging as an elite player in center field and a twenty-three-year-old prodigy named Barry Larkin at shortstop in his first full Major League season. "I like their young kids, and they've got a good blend of veterans," Herzog assessed Rose's outfit.[9] The talented Reds were capitalizing on their potential, leading the West by a game over the Giants, with the Astros and Dodgers tailing behind in third and fourth, respectively. Yet, in the fourth inning of the opener in St. Louis, it looked as if their pennant drive had been derailed.

Davis, the reigning National League Player of the Month for April (an honor he would duplicate in May) and the Major League leader in home runs and RBIs, sustained a shoulder injury when making a diving catch of a Pendleton live drive, robbing the Cardinal third baseman of a double or perhaps a triple. Pendleton was in the midst of hitting safely in 23 of 24 games, his lone hitless effort occurring on May 2 when another diving play was made against him by Steve Sax of the Dodgers. "That catch might have saved the game for us—he didn't bat anymore," joked Herzog respectfully about Davis's spectacular grab in center field, referring to the fact that the Reds' star had already doubled twice in two trips to the plate before having to leave the contest.[10] Davis missed the remainder of the series but would return to the lineup when the Reds moved on to Chicago to play the Cubs.

Davis was being closely pursued in the home run chase by Jack Clark, who surpassed his 1986 total by connecting off Cincinnati ace Mario Soto in the middle contest, as the Cardinals swept all three games, capped by a 10–2 triumph on Sunday, May 17. In the battle of first-place clubs, the series against the Reds drew 140,508 fans to Busch Stadium, the second most ever for a three-game set at the ballpark and just missing the 141,263 that had attended a series against the Mets during the pennant drive of 1985. Lee Tunnell had been summoned from Triple-A to make his first start in the finale, as the former Pirate had found new life in the Cardinals' system in having been named the American Association Pitcher of the Month for April at Louisville with a 3-1 record and a 2.74 ERA. He was supported by Pagnozzi's 410-foot grand slam to straightaway center field off Guy Hoffman as the forty-seven-thousand-plus crowd at Busch kept roaring until he reemerged from the bench for a curtain call. "When I got back to the dugout, I was shaking," the rookie said of the ovation.[11]

The euphoria for the young catcher, however, would be short-lived—and perhaps expectedly so. After an off-day on Monday the 18th as the Cardinals prepared to go on the road, Peña, after catching five innings in Nashville for the Louisville club in a reha-bilitation assignment, was activated off the disabled list. Pagnozzi was returned to the Minors, having batted only .212 in his first taste of the Majors but also providing a much-needed bridge with Lake, who was now able to return to his backup role. Herzog made it clear that the move was no indictment of Pagnozzi's performance or his potential, but, rather, an opportunity for him to play every day once again. "If I didn't think he had a chance to be a pretty good player, I wouldn't have sent him out. I just feel he has to catch right now."[12]

When Peña showed up at Herzog's office the following day, the manager felt like he had to get to know him all over again.

"Do you hit righthanded or lefthanded?"[13]

Peña laughed in reply. "I've had a lot of opening days this year."[14]

His teammates welcomed the return of his attitude and sense of humor. "Tony had this really gravelly voice and was kind of hard to understand," Ricky Horton recalled. "He was from the Dominican, so of course his first language was Spanish. When he would come out to the mound to talk to me, he would talk to me in English, and I would talk to him in Spanish. I'm not sure we really knew what each other was saying, but when it comes to that, it's really kind of the unspoken words that count anyway."[15]

While the catcher's reappearance was a boost to the team's morale, another round of injuries once again cast a pall over the season. Just as Worrell was starting to improve and Peña and Dayley returned to the team, Magrane had to leave a start early in Atlanta on May 19 due to pain in his pitching elbow.

It seemed like 1986 all over again, as one player after another visited the infirmary and prevented Herzog from making any semblance of permanent plans. The outfield was as much of a problem as the pitching staff, as Lindeman was still struggling with his sore back and Landrum had fouled a ball off his foot in batting practice on May 1, which sidelined him for the entire month. "When I sat at my desk and filled out the lineup card," the St. Louis manager said, "I couldn't just use one—I needed three or four. Somebody would get hurt, somebody would get the flu—there's just no end to it."[16]

Unlike in 1986, however, there continued to be many saving graces among the new faces. Thrust into a starting role, Jose Oquendo responding by getting on base in half of his first 38 at bats and hitting .433 during that stretch. It became Oquendo's routine to check with Herzog when he got to the ballpark several hours before game time to see if he was starting at one position or another; if not, he would run a couple miles to stay in shape, before getting into his uniform. Ford was 10 for his first 23, and Lake had batted .333 in addition to a .500 mark with men in scoring position. The infielder Booker, who had spent the better part of a decade in "the bushes" before getting his first taste of Major League action on April 29, had also contributed greatly, hitting at a .450 clip when Magrane went down in Atlanta. "Whitey told me I'd probably be up anywhere from ten to 21 days, however long it takes Tommy [Herr] to come back," Booker said. "After spending seven years in the minor leagues, I'm going to try to change their minds."[17]

Thanks to its depth, the team was able to win ten of eleven games from May 12 to 24, allowing it to reclaim the top spot in the East from the resurgent Cubs, while the Mets fell three games under the .500 mark at 19-22, only a game and a half out of last place. Davey Johnson had fined Strawberry again, this time $250 for being late to the clubhouse. The Cards' hot streak was capped on May 24 with a grand slam by Clark in the Astrodome (as he took home the National League Player of the Week honors), which was hotly contested by Lanier as clearly being a foul ball and which Houston writers complained was five feet left of the pole according to the replays. It was part of a frustrating month for Lanier, who not only saw his defending Western Division champion Astros slip to fourth place by the time they visited St. Louis on May 29 but also had his room at the Marriott Pavilion Hotel get robbed while the Cardinals were beating the Astros 8–2 across the street at Busch Stadium. "He lost two suits, his wife lost most of the clothes she had brought with her, and the thief also took Lanier's briefcase containing his credit cards and his scouting reports on the Chicago Cubs and the Pittsburgh Pirates," read a report after the incident.[18]

The Cardinals' bench players had performed so well that some had actually played their way into a starting role—a rarity for a Herzog-managed team. When Lindeman returned from his injury on May 29 (the same day as Mathews, who had posted another shutout for Louisville on May 27 against Omaha), he pulled a hamstring in his very first game back in the sixth inning against the Astros at Busch Stadium. "Here is a kid who has never been hurt," a bewildered Herzog muttered in shaking his head, unable to understand the bad luck haunting the rookie.[19] The misfortune for Lindeman opened the door for Ford, more of a prototype Cardinals hitter with his speed and contact, who was inserted as the everyday right fielder indefinitely instead of platooning against right-handers only. By the end of the month, Ford led the league in triples with 4. And when Coleman went down temporarily as well, even Peña got a start in the outfield on May 30—something he had not done in twelve years of professional ball but, according to him, had performed "hundreds of times" in the winter leagues.[20]

By the end of May, the Cardinals (29-17) had posted eighteen come-from-behind victories and were batting .287 as a team, 63 points higher than at the same juncture the previous season. Clark finished the month with a total of 44 RBIs for the young season to lead all of baseball. The production had been sorely needed, as a 17-9 record for the month had been achieved despite a pitching staff ERA of 4.76. Yet, with Clark's emergence as a club leader and his open desire to stay with the Cardinals for the long term, he put his house in St. Louis County up for sale while the team was in town for a brief homestand at the end of May, explaining it as an act of self-protection against the collusion he felt was still being propagated by the owners. "It's better to be safe than sorry," he said. "I don't want to be caught with my hands tied behind my back and have to do something real quick if I'm not around. Business is business with the owners, and it's the same with me. I can't wait for answers and timing and contracts and politics. . . . I have three kids, and I think I should know where they're starting school."[21]

Only the superhuman feats of his power-hitting rival, Eric Davis, could halt Clark's hot streak at the plate. In two consecutive games in Cincinnati at the beginning of June, the long-limbed Davis leapt over the center-field wall at Riverfront Stadium and snatched home runs away from the slugger.

Herzog's club held a two-game lead over the Cubs heading into the new month, while the Mets (24-23) were struggling to stay above .500. But with one day off in the upcoming thirty-five days on the schedule starting on May 24, the Cardinals' bullpen needed to step to the forefront.

From Cincinnati, the Cardinals moved on to their second visit to Wrigley Field, where, two weeks earlier, Harry Caray had resumed his place in the broadcast booth after recovering from the stroke he suffered over the winter. He did not have time for sympathy, health concerns, or phone calls from luminaries; his only care was getting back to baseball. "Having shed 41 pounds, tanned and bubbly," Bob Verdi reported the good vibes for *The Sporting News*, "Caray ambled into Wrigley Field like nothing happened. Banners in the bleachers heralded his return, and Governor James Thompson proclaimed it 'Harry Caray Day' in Illinois. And from the White House, President Reagan placed a telephone call during the first inning—but Harry was all wrapped up in the game, describing a bunt."[22]

The Cards took three out of four from the Cubs without the services of Magrane, sidelined for three weeks with his sore elbow.

Unfortunately for Herzog, the rash of recent hotel burglaries committed against baseball managers continued while he was in Chicago. Whitey was robbed of $1,600 at the Westin, while a couple of weeks later, Pirates' manager Jim Leyland lost $4,400 from the very same room—which Leyland was going to use to buy plane tickets for his assistant coaches and their wives for an off-season trip to Las Vegas. Both men were later reimbursed by the hotel. "Thank God Leyland got robbed," Whitey chuckled in retrospect a few days later. "I wouldn't have gotten anything back if he hadn't got robbed. But they sent him a check and then they had to send me one." Later in the season, thieves would strike at the Westin once again. In early August, veteran outfielder Juan Beníquez reported having $13,000 in cash and jewelry stolen while staying at the hotel as a member of the Toronto Blue Jays.[23] A few days later, Whitey received a measure of monetary security, as both he and Maxvill received contract extensions from Gussie Busch, with Herzog reportedly going from the $350,000 he had been making to closer to the $500,000 that Chuck Tanner was getting from the Atlanta Braves.

Besides Caray, another figure long absent from the baseball scene resurfaced during the first week of June. On the fifth, Gooden had completed his drug-therapy obligations and returned to the mound for the Mets. "Everywhere Dwight Gooden turned last night, the camera crews were sure to follow," reported Peter Alfano on the emotional pregame scene at Shea Stadium for the *New York Times*, "from the dugout to the batting cage and back again, peering over his shoulder as he sipped from the water fountain before disappearing down the runway to the locker room." Gooden showed few ill effects from his hiatus, pitching all the way into the seventh and crowned as the victor in a 5–1 decision over Mike Dunne and the Pirates. "If there's a start of good things, it happened tonight," said his catcher Gary Carter.[24]

On June 8 the Cardinals met the Phillies for the first time on the season and their new catcher whose abilities Herzog likened to Carter. "With [Lance] Parrish, that's a better lineup than the Mets," the Cards' leader had said back in March when Parrish signed with Philadelphia. "I would think if he's healthy, they have a hell of a chance to win it, because he gives you a catcher like the

Mets have got."[25] Davey Johnson agreed before the season began that Philadelphia posed a strong threat to his team's chances to repeat as division champs. "The Cardinals may have deeper pitching, but they don't have the explosive power of the Phillies, who can break out at any time."[26] Despite having rebounded slightly in the succeeding weeks, a poor April for Parrish (a .188 batting mark) left the former Tigers star hitting at .219 while throwing out only eleven of the sixty-three runners against him, which elicited furor from the relentless Philadelphia crowds. The arrival of Herzog's speed-laden team to Veterans Stadium did nothing to help Parrish's numbers.

With Coleman tying a career high with 4 stolen bases while also reaching base in his thirty-eighth consecutive game, the Cardinals' 12–8 victory in the opener in Philadelphia—secured by Horton with his four innings of relief—put them fourteen games over the .500 mark for the first time since the end of the 1985 season. "Very impressive," Parrish said of his first glimpse of the Cardinals' running game. By this time, Coleman and Smith had developed their own private sign for a hit-and-run play when one was on base and the other was at the plate. "I was geared up," the new Phillies' catcher revealed. "I knew exactly what I was in for. I was just glad nobody else decided to run besides Coleman."[27] Coleman's performance on the evening kept him perfect on stolen base attempts in his career against Philadelphia (38-38), while he also continued to be unblemished against the Mets (22-22).

Parrish, however, was not the only catcher in the series who was struggling with his new team. Through the middle of June, the healing Peña was still finding his footing, only having thrown out an uncharacteristic four out of twenty-four base stealers against him. The data did not concern Herzog, who was sure the veteran would eventually find his way. "He's really only missed one runner he should have had. When the pitching staff starts going bad, they start concentrating so much on the hitter that they forget about the runners."[28]

On Friday, June 12—as Reagan met with General Secretary Mikhail Gorbachev and urged the Soviet leader to tear down the Berlin Wall—the Cardinals began their longest homestand of the season, a full two-week stretch of fourteen games in as many days.

It began most appropriately with another clash with the enemy from up north on Interstate 55, the Cubs, and with record heat bearing down on Busch Stadium for the weekend. After Forsch got help from a revitalized Worrell (now having notched 15 saves) for a victory in the opener on Friday night, a temperature of 102 degrees was registered in downtown St. Louis the following afternoon, with 110 recorded on the searing surface of the stadium. In a blow to the Cubs' hopes of staying with the Cardinals at the top of the standings, their star second baseman Ryne Sandberg was lost in the third inning after attempting to beat out a tapper to Pendleton at third. While trying to avoid a collision with Clark at first base, Sandberg severely sprained his ankle and had to be carried from the field. "It was the worst pain I ever felt," the 1984 National League MVP said the following day, adding that the discomfort kept him awake until four in the morning as the ankle was placed in a pressurized cast.[29] He would not return to the Chicago lineup until mid-July.

The loss of Sandberg demoralized the Cubs, as a 9–2 Cards win on Saturday was followed by Cox taking a 3–2 lead into the ninth in the series finale, which was preserved by Worrell. The three-game sweep permitted the Cards to open up a six-game lead over Chicago, six and a half over Montreal, and seven and a half over New York.

When *Post-Dispatch* readers had picked up their copies earlier that Sunday morning, they may have noticed in a nondescript corner of the sports page that the Cardinals had signed former Reds first baseman Dan Driessen to a Minor League contract. Driessen, a thirty-six-year-old veteran and contributor to two World Series–winning teams in Cincinnati, had been sitting at home since being released by the Astros in spring training after being on the roster (but not appearing) for Houston in the 1986 National League playoffs. Though the addition aroused little interest in the sports world, Lee Thomas saw value in the move: "It's nice to have him there in case we get a couple of guys hurt. I think he can still hit and play in the big leagues."[30]

While the baseball news continued to be favorable in the eastern part of Missouri with the resurgence of the Cardinals, those in the western portion of the state were dealt a sad blow on June 17.

Howser, the leader of the 1985 champion Royals team who began his playing career in Kansas City as an All-Star rookie with the Athletics in 1961, passed away after his battle with brain cancer at Saint Luke's Hospital in the city, less than four months after relinquishing his managerial duties before the start of spring training. "In October I played a few holes of golf with him," Herzog recalled sadly of the previous autumn. "He tried to act like everything was all right." Then, thinking of his 1986 matchup in the All-Star Game against his friend, Whitey added, "He managed his last game against me. Maybe it's right he went out a winner."[31] Television broadcasters during the All-Star Game had noticed Howser was messing up his signals when attempting to change pitchers, and Howser later admitted he had felt sick before the contest. It was the last game he would manage in the Major Leagues.

After a moment of silence offered for Howser at Busch Stadium before the Cardinals game with the Pirates that night, the Cardinals took the field with Oquendo running out to first base to give Clark a rest. It was already the sixth position at which the man whom Herzog was calling his "secret weapon" had appeared thus far on the season. Oquendo had also been 5-7 as a pinch-hitter, part of a team pinch-hitting rate standing at .353 after the Cardinals had posted a .194 mark in 1986—an improvement that Herzog credited to the reserves getting ample and meaningful at bats in starting assignments due to the number of injuries to the starters. The sustained quality play of subs like Oquendo had also allowed wounded regulars such as Herr to heal properly, as Herr had batted a consistent .288, .293, and .308 in April, May, and June of 1987, respectively, a complete turnaround from his poor start to the 1986 season.

Like Lindeman, Oquendo had any glove ready to go at any time. And as the series continued with the Pirates the following night of June 18, Jose had to grab yet another from his locker.

Pendleton—the lone iron man among the Cardinal starters to date—sat out his first game of the year, which gave Oquendo a start at third, already giving him a 1987 appearance at every position except pitcher and catcher. Moving to shortstop later in the game to replace Smith as part of a double-switch, Oquendo helped the Cardinals to an extra-inning victory, their 40th win of the season—more than a month earlier than they had won their 40th in 1986.

Since the start of spring training in February, Herzog had pointed to the necessity of Coleman rebounding from his 1986 batting average of .232 and on-base average of .301 in order for the Cardinals to be successful. In 1987 an irrefutable correlation had emerged. Heading into the opener of a series with the Phillies at Busch Stadium on June 23, the left fielder boasted a .294 batting mark and 36 walks. Coleman had also reached base via a hit or a walk in sixty-one of the sixty-two games in which he had played to date, having been denied only on April 22 against the Cubs. The revival of Coleman and the rest of the Cardinals had impressed the legendary Philadelphia third baseman Mike Schmidt, who in the middle game of the series belted the 512th home run of his career high off the left-field foul pole at Busch. The long ball tied him with Eddie Mathews and Ernie Banks for eleventh on the all-time list, and with Banks for fourth in National League annals. While in town, Schmidt extolled several aspects of the 1987 version of the Cardinals but especially their depth, as St. Louis took two of the three games and stole another four bases off Parrish in the finale, a 3–0 complete-game shutout for Mathews, who had the Phillies' batters beating the ball into the infield turf all night long. "Speed. On-base percentage. They know what they're doing," the Philadelphia star affirmed. "They're all good hitters. They get a lot of good games out of their extra people. But you can talk all you want about the Cardinals' offense. They win because of their infield defense and their pitchers' abilities to get ground balls."[32]

The evidence clearly showed that Herzog's pitching staff was starting to solidify. Magrane returned on June 21 to gather another win (followed by his first Major League loss on June 26) while on June 28, Dayley picked up his first victory in two years in the eleventh inning in Montreal. Coupled with the improvement on the mound, the offense had not taken its foot off the gas. With his 23 home runs by the end of June, Clark had already gone deep against every club in the National League except for his former team, the Giants, while his 72 RBIS had passed the Reds' Davis for tops in the circuit—with McGee's 56 (including 30 in a twenty-nine-game stretch) closing in. Even Ozzie Smith, recovering from his bumpy start, ultimately had flourished while batting second in the order behind Coleman and posted 42 RBIS by the close of the month—which was more than the injured Sandberg, Van Slyke, and other noted hitters around baseball had been able to produce. With his arm not as strong as it had been earlier in his career due to a rotator cuff injury, Smith, approaching his thirty-third birthday, had started the habit of making more throws on the run rather than planting his feet, so as to take some stress off his shoulder.

All of the offensive and defensive cylinders were therefore firing when the Cardinals ventured to New York to confront the vaunted Mets on June 29, the first meeting between the two rivals since St. Louis had taken five of six from Davey Johnson's team in April. Except for Gooden (who was 4-1 with a 2.15 ERA since his return), Johnson was still seeking to stabilize his inconsistent starting pitching staff. To help, he turned to a franchise legend.

Splitting the 1986 season between the White Sox and Red Sox, forty-one-year-old Tom Seaver—with 311 wins and over 3,600 strikeouts in his career—had been ineffective with Boston and was released on November 12. Picked up by New York after having been granted free agency, Seaver was in Johnson's plans to make a spot start against the Phillies in New York on June 20. The experiment failed, as the future Hall of Famer was hit hard in two scrimmages against the Mets' Triple-A team, and the owner of three Cy Young Awards and twelve All-Star Game appearances hung up his glove for good. When asked a few days later who the toughest hitter was whom he ever had to face in his career, "Seaver replied without hesitation that it was Barry Lyons, a Cardinal favorite," Hummel reported. "Lyons was six for six with a home run off Seaver in the last 'simulated game' he tried to pitch for the Mets."[33]

Instead of relics from the glory days of Shea Stadium, such as Seaver, Johnson was obliged to manage a new generation of Mets; as a result, he had to balance all of the egotistical spinning plates on his fingers. This included Strawberry, who was still having difficulty in simply getting to work on time.

Strawberry's latest tardiness occurred when he was supposed to join his teammates at Wrigley Field on June 8 after the Mets had finished a doubleheader in New York against the Pirates the prior evening. Johnson, disgruntled with having to wait for Strawberry to get to the ballpark, nonetheless put him in the starting lineup at the last minute, as the sleepy slugger responded with an 0-4 effort on four meekly hit ground ball outs, further enraging the manager. "Chicago got to him," Hernandez said cryptically of the young outfielder, noting there was no escape from the dreaded afternoon starting times at Wrigley and the need to make it to the stadium in the morning. "I've done my share of 4:30 a.m. arrivals at the hotel there. Chicago is just one of those towns [where] you have to suck it up and get to the park the next day." Johnson fined and benched Strawberry once again, letting him appear as a pinch hitter in the middle contest against the Cubs (as he struck out looking in the ninth inning with two out and the tying run on first base) before sitting him out altogether in the finale. But afterward, Johnson considered the matter closed and looked forward to moving on. "I'll shake his hand when he hits a home run," the Mets' manager told the press. "We don't have to talk about it. It's not important to love each other and as far as I'm concerned, everything's over."[34]

Hernandez, meanwhile, had taken drastic measures to shake another recent slump. On June 10 he had shaved off his signature mustache and responded with 2 home runs that day against the Cubs.

In the midst of their perpetual turbulence, the Mets readied themselves to face the Cardinals in Flushing Meadows with another important series between the two clubs on the line. A half-hour before the opener on June 29, Tudor—still over a month away from being ready to pitch—shook hands with Lyons in front of the Mets' dugout, showing that there were no hard feelings.

With New York holding a 7–3 lead going into the top of the seventh, Herzog's men rallied with four runs and ultimately triumphed in eleven innings by an 8–7 score in a battle lasting beyond four hours, as Coleman led off the final frame with a walk, took second for his 50th steal, and scored on a Smith single. Dayley finished things off for his first save, which kept the Mets, Expos, and Cubs all tied for second place at seven-and-a-half games out— the Cardinals biggest lead in a divisional or league race since 1968. "Am I uncomfortable being seven and a half out?" Johnson was asked in the home locker room. "Anything 'out' is uncomfortable. We need to win the next two." Howard Johnson was more pointed with his comments: "If we don't win the next two, we'll be in serious trouble."[35]

Picking themselves off the mat, the Mets were indeed victorious in the final two games of the series, which included Gooden going the distance in the middle contest for a 3–2 win and his fifth-straight victory against St. Louis. The deciding tally was an RBI single down the left-field line in the bottom of the ninth by Johnson, who claimed that Danny Cox had been intentionally throwing at him the previous night when Cox hit him in the ribs in the first inning. "The next time he comes in on me, that's it," HoJo publicly warned the St. Louis pitcher with whom Johnson had feuded in the past. As for Cox, the hitter's statement was nothing he had not heard before from Johnson and many other opponents. "I wake up every morning and I hear the birds chirping," the pitcher dismissed. "He is just opening his mouth before he thinks. He'll get his wish to come true if he wants."[36]

Strawberry was at his antics once again, refusing to play in either of the two Mets' victories, citing a stomach virus, and he was once again criticized by his teammates. "I feel, and the rest of my teammates feel, that we lost respect for the man," said veteran Lee Mazzilli, who took Strawberry's spot in right field for both wins. "This was a very important game to us, and we feel he should be out there playing. Even at 70 percent, he's a lot better than most players at 100 percent, including me. I'm saying this as a caring friend, however he takes it. We all like Darryl, but he has an obligation to us. He let us down."[37]

Despite dropping two of three in New York, the Cardinals maintained the best record in baseball entering July, and while Tudor was still absent from the pitching staff, the offensive side appeared to be getting healthier. Having convalesced from his back and hamstring injuries, Lindeman played in a doubleheader in Louisville on July 3 and went 4-6 with a double, triple, and a home run to raise his average to .288 in his seventeen-game rehab stint with the Triple-A team. After the long day he caught a 9:00 flight the following morning to Atlanta, where Lindeman was slated to be in Herzog's starting lineup that night against the Braves. The Cardinals' manager asserted to the press that, due to their physical setbacks, the baseball world had yet to see the "real" Tony Peña or "real" Jim Lindeman in 1987.

The recall of Lindeman also meant the release of Tito Landrum, who in turn refused an assignment to Louisville and thus closed his remarkable eight-year run as a valuable backup outfielder in St. Louis. Landrum decided to instead test his worth on the market, where the veteran would be picked up by the Dodgers six days later. Signing with the Cardinals as an undrafted free agent in 1972, Landrum spent eight seasons in the Minors before finally making the big leagues in 1980. After being sent to Baltimore in August 1983, he was a hero for the Orioles two months later in the American League Championship Series with an extra-inning, pennant-clinching home run. Rejoining the Cardinals the following spring, Landrum once again rose to postseason excellence in the 1985 World Series.

Landrum, in trying to overcome a variety of injuries since the start of spring training, had been among a host of players who could not seize the regular right-field job in St. Louis after the departure of Van Slyke to Pittsburgh in early April. In just the first seventy-five games of the year, Herzog had already used seven different starters at the position. Upon Lindeman's return and insertion into the spot, Jim would go 0-3 against Atlanta left-hander Zane Smith on Independence Day (part of what would become a new 2-18 slump for the rookie) and was picked off second by catcher Ozzie Virgil in his lone visit to the basepaths after reaching on a force out. The Cardinals were nonetheless able to sweep the Braves in three straight, thanks to dominating performances on the mound from starters Forsch, Cox, and Mathews, as the staff allowed a mere 2 runs in the three games.

At the halfway point of the Cardinals' road games for the season, they were now 28-13 away from St. Louis, which included an 18-7 mark on grass surfaces—in spite of being labeled as a turf-only team. Sitting twenty games over the .500 mark for the first time on the season (49–29) while leading the Expos by seven-and-a-half games and the Mets by eight, the Cardinals had proven they could surmount grass fields, Astroturf fields, injuries, young starting pitchers, a closer still looking to find his form, and a nightly mix-and-match starting lineup, among other obstacles. In the next couple of days, they would prove they had physical and mental fortitude as well.

When the Cards returned to Busch Stadium on July 6 to open a series against the Dodgers, a wave of thunderstorms began pounding the St. Louis area. A violent round of hail followed, which hit the ballpark during the series opener and forced the cancelation of a 3–2 Cardinals lead in the fourth inning—as well as an unusual individual feat that, along with the game that day, would be forever wiped from the record books.

In the Cardinals' second inning, Ozzie Smith found himself picked off and caught in a rundown between first and second. Watching the proceedings while cautiously taking a few steps off the third base bag was Magrane, the starting pitcher in the would-be opener. In the pregame meeting in the locker room, the Cardinals had been instructed by Herzog to sprint for home anytime the Los Angeles second baseman Sax was holding the ball, due to his difficulty with throwing.

While Sax was running Smith back to first, Magrane saw the infielder freeze momentarily. The pitcher instinctively bolted for the plate and, without a play being made on him, stole home—the first Cardinals' pitcher to do so since Slim Sallee in 1913 and the first time any pitcher had achieved it against the Dodgers since 1930. The confused Sax never let go of the ball as Smith returned safely to first as well. "I bobbled the ball before I threw it, and that's why I didn't throw it," Sax tried to explain. "I don't know if I would have gotten [Magrane]. It would have been close."[38]

Shortly thereafter, the teams dashed to their clubhouses as the hail began pelting them relentlessly. Down the street at Forest Park, a performance of *Cats* at the Muny Theatre had simultaneously been halted. Sitting in the press box in front of an empty stadium with little else to do, Hummel recognized that Magrane's accomplishment, soon to be vanished from the archives for eternity, would have given him as many steals of home as Coleman and one more than Lou Brock ever had. "Anytime a pitcher steals home, you know the rains are coming because that's not supposed to happen," Magrane said in the clubhouse in mourning the erasure of his feat.[39] But nearly four decades later, he appreciated the free

POWERING THROUGH

rein of improvisation that Herzog afforded nearly everyone on the team. "That was the great thing about the Cardinals organization," Magrane added in 2024. "They didn't teach hitters this and pitchers that; they taught *all* of us *baseball*."[40]

What Mother Nature had thus left behind for the Cardinals and Dodgers were two back-to-back doubleheaders on July 7 and 8, forcing both managers to further juggle their pitching staffs, as Horton made his first start of the season. Preparing for austerity measures with a shortage of arms, Herzog even approached the left-handed John Morris about the possibility of the outfielder taking the mound over the next couple of days. Morris, always willing to perform any role that would help the team, responded in the affirmative while reminding Whitey he had pitched in high school as well as at Seton Hall University. "I don't care if you can throw the ball over the plate," Herzog waved his hand dismissively as Morris was trying to lay out his credentials. "But can you get out of the way of a line drive?"[41]

Entering in the seventh inning in relief of Dayley after Horton had worked into the sixth, Worrell polished off a 5–4 victory in the first of the four contests. Intermittent rain was in the forecast indefinitely, with multiple downpours still to impact the entire night. With the trip being the final one to St. Louis for the Dodgers and with no common off days between the two teams for the remainder of the season, the players were forced to wait out recurring delays that stretched far past midnight, as Tunnell was summoned to start the nightcap—or "morningcap."

With the Cards trailing 4–2 in the bottom of the ninth, Steve Lake, getting a rare start with Peña having caught the opener, came to bat with one out and Pendleton on first. As Lake stared out at the Dodgers' pitcher Matt Young, far off in the distance he could see the Stadium clock on the scoreboard, standing among the empty seats behind the outfield wall and reading 2:33 a.m.

Lake found a pitch on the outer half of the plate and was able to pull the ball off the façade of the left-field stands for a home run, only his second of the season, which tied the game. Young turned his back and went behind the mound, folding his arms in disbelief.

After Dayley held the Dodgers scoreless in the top of the tenth, the battle was pushing three in the morning by the time the Cardinals came up again in the bottom half. Lawless—who had appeared in only seven games to date and was hitless in as many at bats—attempted a sacrifice bunt but forced Ford at second base. Lawless atoned for the misplay by promptly stealing second himself and then scored the early-morning game-winner on a Clark single with Dayley victorious by the same 5–4 count as the opener. Only a handful of the original forty thousand were on hand to witness it. "They were either under the influence of alcohol or they didn't have watches," Herzog figured.[42]

To the few scribes who had stuck around to ask questions in the Cardinals' clubhouse, Lake called it "The greatest thrill of my career.

"The homer—not staying up until 3:00 a.m.," he clarified.

Bill Dawley replied from across the locker room, "I can testify Lake's been up until three before."

The catcher responded, "They call me a 'Three o'Clock Hitter,' and I guess I am. They never said if it was a.m. or p.m."

Dayley, the winning pitcher in game two after having worked in the first contest as well, then went into a narrative about his own past twenty-four hours. "Today was my little girl's birthday. We had a birthday thing scheduled at noon, so I was up and awake with that. Me and ten little rug rats."[43]

The two teams went right back at it for two more games starting the following afternoon, as they yearned for the All-Star break that was a mere five days away. Another pair of victories followed for St. Louis, as Clark tied a National League record by walking six times in a doubleheader. The Cards needed another extra-inning effort to prevail in the last matchup, as Pendleton singled home Oquendo with the bases loaded for an 8–7 victory against Orel Hershiser, whose contributions were required from the bullpen with Lasorda having no one else to whom he could turn. It was only Hershiser's second relief appearance of the year, the first having come at Busch Stadium back on May 2 when he earned a save, his first since his rookie season of 1984.

Pendleton, who had played in every inning of all four games, slumped back into his locker afterward and nearly fell asleep in his uniform. "I like baseball an awful lot, but not that much," he told Tom Wheatley, as Hummel had abandoned his typewriter and headed for home hours earlier.[44] Pendleton would later say of the following morning that "I woke up and had never been so sore. I never woke up that sore playing football."[45]

There was no rest for the weary. Immediately arriving in town was manager Roger Craig and his San Francisco Giants on Thursday, July 9, for a four-game set in advance of the All-Star break. But before the treasured off days would arrive, another blow was struck to the Cardinals' starting pitching staff.

After Chris Speier walked to lead off the top of the seventh for San Francisco with the Giants leading 2–1 in the series opener, Mike Aldrete drove a liner off the right foot of Cox as the pitcher was completing his follow-through. Although Cox was able to retrieve the ball and throw Aldrete out at first, the impact had broken his fifth metatarsal bone, which leads from the little toe to the ankle. Cox was able to continue on as the injury numbed up, pitching through the eighth. The bullpen then took over, as the Redbirds were able to again post an extra-inning victory by a 7–6 score, overcoming 3 runs by San Francisco in the top of the tenth with 4 of their own in the bottom half. Herzog's men had won eight in a row.

Just like the Easter Sunday victory against the Mets back in April, the long-term cost of the win was a concern. It was expected that Cox would be shelved for a month, while Tudor was still not due back for another three weeks. In consideration of the depleted staff, an old name thus began circulating around the Cardinals' offices who might be able to help: Joaquín Andújar.

Andujar had spent the majority of the first half of the season on the disabled list with a bad hamstring and had made only nine starts for Oakland by the All-Star break, posting an ERA near 5.00. Nonetheless, some of the Cardinals appeared to be in favor of his return. "We need pitching," said Ozzie Smith. "We know his arm is fine. I'd like to have him back."

When asked about the rumors while with the A's in Boston, Andujar responded in his unique and noncommittal way. "I cannot say anything in the newspapers. You know that."

For his part, Herzog doubted there would be a reunion but did not dismiss the idea as a bad one. "I don't think it's likely. He could probably help us. He's sure as hell not tired." Maxvill, however, put any further speculation to rest. "There have been no conversations with the A's, and I don't anticipate we'll be having any."[46]

The St. Louis starting rotation—as remotely as it resembled one—thus stood pat, with Forsch as the stabilizer, while Mathews, Horton, and Tunnell continued to log important innings in the midst of Magrane finding consistency. Instead of depth for the mound, extra help was imported for the outfield—which was supplied by one new face and an old familiar one.

Speedy youngster Lance Johnson was recalled from Louisville, where he had been hitting .330 with 29 stolen bases and 9 triples. During his collegiate career at the University of South Alabama, Johnson set the NCAA single-season stolen-base record with 84 in 1984 and, in 1986, had led the Texas League with 49 steals at the Cardinals' Double-A affiliate at Little Rock. (The Cardinals had another left-handed speedster at Little Rock in 1987, Alex Cole, who, by the end of the summer, would pace the Texas League himself with 68.) Despite the crowded nature of the St. Louis outfield with both established veterans and young players like himself, Johnson hoped to remain part of the organization for the long term. "Deep down, I really want to be a Cardinal. I'd love to be part of a winning ballclub, and I think I'm suited for Whitey's game."[47] His initial taste of the big leagues would last only a week, as Johnson was returned to Louisville on July 17. But Herzog was impressed. "I like him. He's got great speed. He's going to be a pretty good player."[48]

A day after Johnson arrived, David Green was signed to a Minor League contract and took Johnson's place in Louisville. After being the property of the Giants and Brewers and having spent most of 1986 in Japan, the one-time Cardinal and 1982 World Series participant was looking for a place to play. Green had even approached the local amateur Mon-Clair League on the Illinois side of the river across from St. Louis but declined to join when he was told that the men's league did not pay its players.

The indefatigable Redbirds took home another victory in thirteen innings on the day of Johnson's activation on Friday, July 10—the St. Louis winning streak stretched to nine. It was snapped the following day, but the momentum returned in the finale on Sunday with seven strong innings from the starter Horton, although it was initially feared he had become another casualty on the mound.

In a frightening scene, the left-hander was forced to leave the game after a line drive from Joel Youngblood nailed his pitching forearm. Horton's effort, as well as that from Perry, Worrell, and Dayley who followed him, allowed the Cardinals to beat Craig's team again, 3–2, as Horton continued to sport a perfect record at 5-0 with 7 saves. The Giants' manager had been upset with Jack Clark, thinking the Cardinals' first baseman had unnecessarily bowled over San Francisco catcher Bob Melvin in the twelfth inning of Friday's contest—an inning before Clark would end things with his 26th homer, which now gave him a circuit clout against every club in 1987.

An angry Craig, who was a pitcher on the Cardinals world championship team of 1964 and had coached or played on four World Series winners in his career, warned St. Louis that payback was coming. "We're going to beat them in the playoffs," he stated in predicting a conquest against Herzog's troops in the National League postseason. "Ain't no question about it. They're just on a good streak."[49]

5

All Hands on Deck

It's a wholesome scene now. It's quiet on the bus. It's quiet on the airplane. It's quiet when you travel with them. It's a great bunch now, enjoyable to be around.

—Jack Buck on the Cardinals, July 1987

HAVING WON TEN OF THEIR LAST ELEVEN HEADING INTO THE All-Star break, the Cardinals had a nine-game lead atop the Eastern Division with the best record in baseball at 56-30. The team was averaging just under 6 runs a game—a far cry from the dry spells of 1986, with Ford (.323), Oquendo (.321), Pendleton (.315), Clark (.311), McGee (.302), and Smith (.301) all over the .300 mark and Coleman (.288) not far behind, while Morris (6-13) led the sharp squad of pinch hitters who continued to come through in clutch situations.

The individual achievements were wide and varied and not limited solely to batting averages. Clark had totaled 86 RBIs and 83 walks (the latter putting him on pace to threaten the existing National League record of 148), and his 26 home runs were already the most in one season by a Cardinal since Ted Simmons hit the same number in 1979 in a full year; Ozzie Smith, the top All-Star vote-getter in either league, had struck out a mere 15 times and displayed his typical superlative defense; Coleman, despite missing the last four games before the break to undergo a painful dental surgery, was easily outdistancing the Reds' Davis for the NL lead in stolen bases (52 to 33); McGee, although having stolen just 6 bases himself in uncharacteristic fashion, was embracing his role as a run-producing number-five hitter; and Pendleton's 105 hits was second in the NL only to Gwynn's 117.

Trailing right behind Pendleton with 102 hits was Jeffrey Leonard of the Giants, who was fresh off of his first All-Star selection and, after failing to hit a single home run in 411 at bats as a rookie with Houston, had developed into a long-ball threat with San Francisco. With his newfound power stroke, the flashy Leonard circled the bases with one arm tucked closely at his side on each homer he drove out of the park, which he called his "one flap down" ritual—his announcement to the world that the pitch he hit had nothing on it.

As had been the case in 1985, the performance of the Cardinals' relief corps had been a true team effort in the first half of 1987. With Herzog annually setting a goal of getting 45 to 50 saves from the bullpen, the Cardinals had already earned 30—led by 18 from Worrell and Horton's 7, but also with contributions from Dayley, Dawley, and Perry. "If it wasn't for Horton and Pat Perry early in the season," Herzog granted over the break, "I don't know where we'd be."[1]

While Clark and Smith had been voted in as starters for the All-Star Game by the fans, McGee was the only Cardinal selected by National League manager Davey Johnson as a reserve for midsummer classic, which would take place in Oakland on July 14 near McGee's home in the Bay Area. The St. Louis trio went a combined 0-9 but were not alone in struggling at the plate in perhaps the greatest pitching duel the All-Star Game had ever seen—ironically nested in the middle of what would become one of the most heavy-hitting regular seasons in recent memory. The National League held on for a 2–0 win over the American League in extra innings, with Tim Raines tripling home the game's only runs in the top of the thirteenth.

At the conclusion of the midseason intermission, the rest of the Cardinals met up with Clark, McGee, and Smith in California as the second half of the schedule commenced with an eleven-game West Coast trip starting in San Diego. While the team was away from St. Louis, it learned of important news from back home: after throwing a couple batting-practice sessions, Tudor was cleared to take the mound for Triple-A action in Louisville, where he was expected to pitch in three games before returning to the Major League roster.

With Tudor's extended absence along with that of Cox, Mathews had stepped into a leadership role alongside Forsch on the starting staff, posting a 5-3 record and a 2.68 ERA in the ten starts he had made since returning from the Minors. On July 17 he took a shutout of the Padres into the ninth inning at San Diego before Worrell entered to help with his 19th save. "I wanted [the shutout]," Mathews said afterward. "I wanted to step forward and show I'm capable of picking up the slack as well as our other starters. I want to go into the ninth inning and not have anyone warming up in the bullpen."[2] Peña, who saw his average reach a high of .276 at the end of June before falling back to .253, delivered his first game-winning RBI of the season. "Let's hope it doesn't take another 88 games or whatever," Herzog joked in prodding the catcher for another one soon.[3]

Lindeman, the other right-handed bat looking for rhythm, had struck out 22 times in 46 at bats since getting injured back in April, and 32 times in his 92 at bats for the season, as the team left San Diego and split the four-game series. "He's got big league-itis," Herzog said. "He's just overmatched right now, [and] I don't know how to get him out of it."[4] Did the rookie still have confidence in himself? "I don't know where it is, or if it's still around or what," Lindeman admitted. "It seems like I've been struggling the whole season."[5]

Clark was thus once again left as the lone power source, coming out of a brief 1-13 slump by nailing 2 home runs against the Padres on July 19. The second shot pushed the Cards to a win in ten innings and gave him 28 for the year as he reclaimed the league lead from Eric Davis. Davis was recently passed by the Cubs' Dawson for the most RBIs in the National League, while Dawson was creeping up behind Clark in the home run chase as well.

Herzog's team next took aim at Lasorda's men, with the Cardinals storming into Chavez Ravine to sweep three straight from the Dodgers. Forsch, batting .405 for the season, outdueled Valenzuela in a complete game in the opener, and Dayley picked up two relief wins in the second and third contests. The finale saw Los Angeles shortstop Mariano Duncan commit 3 errors; he blamed the mishaps on a migraine headache. "You can have your headaches at Albuquerque," Lasorda told the player in sending him to Triple-A the following day.[6] The Redbirds were now 9-3 against Los Angeles for 1987, ensuring a winning record in a season against the Dodgers for the first time in nine years. They were also twenty-nine games over .500 (61-32), pushing the gulf in the Eastern Division between them and the nearest competition to nine-and-a-half games over the Expos, ten and a half over the Mets, and twelve over the fading Cubs.

Everything kept falling into place. Down at Louisville, Tudor hurled three innings in a Triple-A game and reported no pain in his healing leg.

But as baseball can so quickly humble an individual player or an entire team, a cold spell was about to strike the Cardinals at a most inopportune moment. Perhaps looking ahead on the schedule to a crucial series with the Mets at Busch Stadium upon returning home, the Redbirds failed to complete the entirety of their road business before leaving California.

At the last stop on the trip in San Francisco, they dropped four straight games—something they had not done all season—that were decided by a total of eight runs. In Roger Craig's mind, the sweep exacted a measure of revenge after the series in St. Louis two weeks prior and gave more credence to his prophesy of an upcoming San Francisco victory for the National League pennant. With the blink of an eye, the Cardinals' lead over the Expos had shrunk from nine games to six.

Not around to witness the team's sudden freefall in the Bay Area was Jack Buck. On the last day of the road trip on Sunday, July 26, the famed announcer was on the other side of the country, being enshrined into the National Baseball Hall of Fame with his receipt of the Ford Frick Award. "The biggest kick I get," Buck told the crowd in his acceptance speech, "is to communicate with those who are exiled from the game—in hospitals, homes, prisons, those who have seldom seen a game, some who cannot travel to the game, those who are blind.

"And after all these years, I realize that my energy comes from the people at the other end."[7]

In an interview with Hummel earlier that week, Buck—who had had broadcasted Cardinals games since 1954—credited Whitey Herzog directly for prolonging his career behind the microphone, as both men lamented the apparent passing of the game they had once known. "For a few years there, I was embarrassed to be around them," Buck said of what he saw of the Cardinals during the pre-Whitey days before 1980. "The players would be getting on the airplane wearing sandals, and earrings, and jeans with holes in the butt. That ain't me, man. It was like junior high. You'd hear all the loud music all the time. I said, 'What the hell am I doing here?' I'm 55 years old.'" But it all changed when Herzog took over. "It's a wholesome scene now. It's quiet on the bus. It's quiet on the airplane. It's quiet when you travel with them. It's a great bunch now, enjoyable to be around."[8]

Buck's triumphant return from Cooperstown to Busch Stadium only heightened the local emotion for the showdown with the Mets, which began on the night of Tuesday, July 28, when Buck took his seat alongside his longtime partner and former Cardinals player Mike Shannon in the KMOX broadcast booth. The New York team had just finished an eleven-game homestand at Shea Stadium, of which they had won six. The Mets players had pledged to no longer turn around and peek at the scoreboard to see what the Cardinals were doing. "If it was up to me," Gooden joked, "I'd say keep the Cardinals off our scoreboard."[9]

Word quickly spread amid the flock of media representatives covering the games that Tudor was ready to go, and though not likely to face New York, he would probably be scheduled by Herzog to pitch in the following series against the Pirates on August 1. In addition to the larger contingent of writers that crammed into the press box, other new faces were hanging around the batting cage before the game—such as a man who was wearing a St. Louis jersey with No. 72 and *Lee* on the back. The man was Kwang Lee, the manager of a Korean baseball team who had been a guest of the Cardinals since spring training while observing the club's practices and operations.

The fireworks began right away. Magrane, winless in his last five starts, reacted angrily when he walked Tim Teufel in the first inning on a borderline pitch that was called a ball by home plate umpire Randy Marsh. Next was Keith Hernandez, who also walked on another pitch that Magrane thought was a strike—as did Peña, evidenced by the catcher firing the ball down to second base in thinking that Teufel was trying to steal. The ball went into center field for a throwing error as Teufel scooted to third.

Then came the slugger Strawberry, who bounded a chopper to Herr at second base as Hernandez bowled into his former infield mate at the bag. Herzog, already irritated by Marsh's early interpretation of the strike zone, stormed onto the field and made a beeline for second base umpire Joe West, claiming that Hernandez interfered with Herr's attempt at a double play. West quickly sent Herzog to an early shower, while Mets coach Bill Robinson would also be ejected later when arguing a close play with first base ump Paul Runge. In the end, errors in the outfield by Coleman and McGee led to the Mets rallying to overcome a 4–2 deficit, winning 6–4. A frustrating evening for St. Louis had gradually gotten worse, as in the eighth inning Ozzie Smith sprained an ankle in running out a ground ball and was replaced at shortstop in the ninth by Oquendo.

Despite the Cardinals tying the game in the ninth inning the following night, the Mets nonetheless prevailed in the tenth by a 6–4 score once again—this time on a home run by the blossoming star Howard Johnson, his 24th of the season, which gave him one more than Strawberry, who himself had left the yard in the second inning.

The Mets had made a strong statement with the two tough wins, and the tightening of the divisional race was now palpable. "As far as I'm concerned, we're back in it," Davey Johnson said.

Herzog's opinion was not changed one bit in hearing the comment. "As far as I'm concerned, he was never out of it."[10]

The angst in the St. Louis clubhouse was somewhat assuaged when Smith showed he was able to shake off the ankle injury and, despite not starting, entered the second game of the series in the seventh inning. But in the course of events, another key player in Herzog's lineup had gone down.

Taking a lesson from the Giants, Davey Johnson decided that

to be successful against the Cardinals, his pitchers had to take the bat out of Jack Clark's hands. In their series sweep of the Redbirds in San Francisco, the Giants had walked the slugger nine times, and St. Louis hit into ten double plays—including three by McGee, who was still batting fifth in the order behind Clark. In the second game of the Mets-Cardinals tilt, Clark had already been walked twice intentionally in his first two trips to the plate. After taking his position at first base in the top of the fourth, he was involved in a collision with New York speedster Mookie Wilson, who hit a slow bouncer on the third base side of the mound to Horton. In his haste to get the out, Horton grabbed the ball and turned quickly, firing an errant throw to Clark, who had to go up the line to meet it. The subsequent impact with Wilson caused bruises on Clark's arm, shoulder, and elbow, as he was lost for the remainder of the middle contest and the third game as well.

With Clark temporarily out of the picture, Johnson's club was now in an even a stronger position to sweep the visit to St. Louis—and even more so since he had shuffled his rotation at the beginning of the week to ensure that Gooden would throw in the critical series. "If we were closer, I probably wouldn't do it,"[11] Johnson revealed of the decision to hold Gooden in reserve to face the Cardinals in consideration of their eight-and-a-half-game distance from the first-place Cards when they arrived in town. The Mets' manager also possessed a relief corps that matched the quality of Herzog's. "I remember Keith [Hernandez] saying that if we got into another team's bullpen, we were in good shape," Roger McDowell said. "And with the Cardinals, it was more equal with our bullpen to theirs, because they had tandem closers like us in Dayley and Worrell. Being a co-closer with Jesse [Orosco], a system which started in the middle of '85, we knew the teams we would be pitching against during the back end of games."[12]

Powered by McReynolds's first triple of the year that plated two runs off Mathews in the first inning, Gooden beat the Cardinals for his sixth straight time by a 5–3 count, as the Mets took all three games. The last run crossed the plate in the eighth inning, when Howard Johnson homered off Dawley. Johnson, never having batted over .245 in the past four seasons, was now hitting .395 against St. Louis for the year. "The ball I hit against Perry [the previous night of July 24 to win the game] was an absolute missile, maybe as good a ball I ever hit right-handed in my life," the player recalled in 2023. "I was hitting the ball well. I had changed a lot about my swing and my approach to being an everyday player."[13]

Now, after hitting his 25th round-tripper in the series finale, Johnson was thought by the Cardinals to be staring at Dawley as he passed Smith at shortstop on his trot around the bases, and then at Cox in the home dugout as he came down the third base line. At that point, the Cardinals could not contain their suspicion of Johnson's sudden 1987 success any longer.

With Herzog already on his way out to home plate, Peña bent over and grabbed Johnson's bat. Johnson attempted to take it back from him, but the St. Louis catcher refused to hand it over and instead gave it to West, the home plate umpire for the game.

The Cardinals claimed that Johnson's bat had been hollowed out and filled with cork, an illegal move designed to lighten the wood but still maintain its strength and composition to let the batter get the bat head through the strike zone more quickly. Herzog and the Cardinals demanded that the bat be x-rayed. "He looks like Babe Ruth up there, and I know he ain't that good," Herzog told reporters. "I know the bat is corked. I'll take a hatchet to it. I tried to get it last night, but the bat boy got it before it hit the ground. What gets me about him [Johnson] is the way he shoots off his mouth all the time and then showboats it around the bases."

After a cursory examination, the umpiring crew found no abnormalities with the bat, and West stated later that his crew would have given the bat back to Johnson if the player had been scheduled to come to the plate again later in the game. "The bat is not corked," Johnson retorted in the Mets' locker room after it had been delivered to the New York clubhouse by Runge and a police escort, with several newspaper writers scurrying close behind. Johnson held the bat up for the reporters to see while running his fingers over it. "It is perfectly normal. You can see the grain is perfect. There isn't even any paint on it."

Johnson's explanation and the umpires' decision did not satisfy Herzog, who doubled-down and claimed that other Mets were guilty of the same practice, such as Johnson's fellow infielders Teufel, Wally Backman, and Rafael Santana. "He's not the only one on that club who is doing it. And they aren't the only club in the league doing it."[14]

Whatever the cause, eyes had been opened to the increased number of home runs across the Major Leagues in 1987, which some attributed to a supposed lively ball being secretly introduced. The idea of local cheating elicited laughs around the Cardinals' locker room, as no one suspected any impropriety from Punch and Judy Club members such as Vince Coleman or Ozzie Smith—who were still homerless going back to 1985 over a combined total over 2,000 at bats. "Ozzie might hit one," Herzog predicted, "But I don't think Vince will. Not with that bat he uses. They won't be checking him for cork."

He scratched his chin and then corrected himself. "It might be *all* cork. And no wood. Or balsa wood."[15]

Joking aside, Herzog remained serious in his pursuit of justice against Johnson and joined other managers Lanier, Craig, and Buck Rodgers of the Expos in wanting the bat sent to the National League office for a full investigation. Whitey was convinced, however, that a complete inquiry would never occur. "That's the last we'll hear about it," he was resigned to say. In addition to his soaring batting average, Johnson had already doubled his career high for homers in a single season, a fact also noted by Herzog. "That'd be like Jack Clark hitting 50 this season when he had only hit ten before."[16]

Despite Herzog's doubts of anything coming of it, the Cardinals eventually filed an official grievance with the National League and requested that a specific procedure be put in place for umpires to follow when an illegal bat was suspected. "The umpires didn't know what to do here," Herzog added about the confusion that transpired when Johnson crossed home plate after his 25th blast. "I know you can't go out there and challenge every bat. The game would never be over."[17] Ultimately, Ueberroth's office decided that managers would be granted one challenge of an opponent's bat per game, but enforcing that protocol would be problematic as well, according to Herzog. "What if a manager chooses to use it in the second inning? After that, the other team can say, 'OK, boys, go get your corked bats. They can't ask us anymore.'"[18]

Regardless of the pending inquiries, the fact remained that the Mets' sweep extended the Cardinals' season-worst losing streak to seven, with no more games scheduled between the two clubs until September 11 in New York. In a troublesome reminder of 1986, the floundering St. Louis offense had scored a total of 23 runs during the weeklong skid, as the lead over the Expos was now four games and five and a half over Davey Johnson's team. A week earlier, it had been nine and a half and ten and a half, respectively. "If they lose two out of three to the Pirates," an unnamed Met said to the New York newspapers about the Cardinals' next series, "they could fold. It would be a two-team race with us and Montreal."[19] The Cardinals, fighting for their third pennant in six years, had gotten their wake-up call, and the Mets were on the other end of the line.

HEADING INTO AUGUST, ONE LEFT-HANDED PITCHER WHO had been instrumental in the Redbirds' World Series championship run in 1982 was dismissed to make room for one who was key to the title chase in 1985. When Dave LaPoint struggled again in the Cards' second loss in San Francisco on July 25, it would be his last appearance in a St. Louis uniform. On July 30, the man who had been part of the trade with the Giants for Clark in 1985 was sent to the Chicago White Sox for Minor League pitcher Bryce Hulstrom. The deal was specifically constructed to create space on the Major League roster for Tudor, still slated to pitch against the Pirates on Saturday, August 1. With the Cardinals' lead in the division dwindling, the team was desperate for Cox to return as soon as possible. But Dr. Stan London declared that the hurler needed another week, or perhaps two, to allow his broken foot to completely heal.

The Cardinals had to overcome a 3–1 deficit in the eighth inning in the first game against Pittsburgh in Busch Stadium to keep the losing streak from reaching eight. Able to salvage a 4–3 win, three of the unsung heroes of the pitching staff—Forsch, Perry, and Dayley—had combined to keep the contest within striking distance at the end.

The victory primed the team and city for the return of Tudor as scheduled on the following night of August 1, with Herzog hoping for at least 75 pitches out of him. On the hill against Tudor for the Pirates was thirty-eight-year-old veteran Rick Reuschel, a longtime battler for mediocre Cubs teams in the 1970s and early '80s. Reuschel had found a career resurgence in Pittsburgh, crafting an 8–5 record and a 2.36 ERA in 1987, as the highly impressed Pirates' pitching coach Ray Miller—recently dismissed as the manager of the Minnesota Twins—said Reuschel was "the greatest sinkerballer of this generation."[20]

Tudor lasted four innings in his return, permitting the Pirates to build a 5–2 lead that later stood at 6–4 by the bottom of the ninth. But another furious comeback pulled a 7–6 St. Louis win out of the fire, followed by a clean sweep of the three games with a 9–1 Sunday victory for Magrane (his first since June 21) that took place with a sweltering downtown heat index of 111 degrees and 130 on the Astroturf, with hundreds of spectators forced to visit the first-aid rooms at Busch Stadium. "I've never seen that many fans have to leave the ballpark by the third inning," Herzog observed of the conditions. "I'd say 65 percent were gone by the seventh inning."[21] Nonetheless, the hurler welcomed the environment. "I always liked pitching in day games or earlier games," Magrane noted in 2024, "because you get the butterflies when you pitch once every five days, and your competitive instincts make you ready to go do your thing. I didn't want to wait around all day."[22]

Still nursing his bruised body from the collision with Mookie Wilson, Clark was absent from the lineup in the first two games against the Pirates, which allowed Lindeman to get a couple of starts at first base. And while the St. Louis slugger was out of commission, the Cubs' hot-hitting Dawson took hold of the league lead in both home runs (34) and RBIs (95) in the first week of August. When Clark returned for the last game of the series, Lindeman was moved to right field and finally hit his 4th home run of the year and his first since April 13. He would homer again the following night when the team went on the road to play the Expos, and he was now 7 for his last 21. Giving a vote of confidence was his former winter league manager Nick Leyva: "He can play here. I really believe that. I've seen him. A lot of times [slumps] happen when you get platooned. You say to yourself, 'I might not get to play for three or four days, so I have to do it in this at-bat.'"[23] Peña, the other right-handed bat who was seeking consistency, was 8 for his last 18 and homered in the opening game against Montreal as well. "I'm on my way back," the catcher declared. "I'm really working hard and trying to be patient."[24]

When the Cardinals had arrived in Montreal, they entered the visitors' clubhouse to find a bat hanging from a locker with little pieces of cork taped onto it. With the Mets having just been in town, it had been left specifically for Herzog's men as a joke by Johnson, who hit a grand slam during the series. The Cardinals were not amused—especially Dawley, who had given up the last home run Johnson had hit in Busch Stadium. "He just might have to get drilled," the reliever said, getting in line behind Cox on the list of Cardinals pitchers who wanted to deliver a message to the New York third baseman.[25] A couple days later, Johnson hit his 27th home run against the Cubs in New York, with Strawberry also notching his 26th and 27th in the game. Dawson hit two as well for the Cubs, bringing his league-high total to 34. When Strawberry had stolen a base against the Phillies on August 4, he and Johnson became the first teammates with 20 home runs and 20 steals in the same season since Frank Robinson and Vada Pinson of the Reds in 1963.

After the Mets' offensive outburst against the Cubs, Chicago manager Gene Michael joined his fellow skippers and demanded that Johnson's bat once again be sent to the National League offices for another examination. In spite of no evidence of tampering found yet again, Herzog refused to relent in his fight. "I say, if they challenge the bat and it is corked, then suspend the player for life," he uttered in upping the ante. "That might stop some of that stuff."

"Was that not a bit harsh?" he was asked.

"That's cheating. If you want to stop it, you have to put some teeth into the rule. Talk is cheap. I'm waiting for some pitcher to be killed because some guy uses a corked bat."[26]

The Cubs' Sutcliffe, who pitched the night after the New York aerial bombardment and surrendered 2 more homers to Santana and Carter, agreed. "I hope it doesn't come to the point where someone gets hurt seriously and cork is found in the bat. I would hate to sleep with that on my conscience."[27]

Johnson, still providing evidence of his innocence, was fed up with the accusations. "I don't care what he [Herzog] says anymore.

He can say what he wants. He's convinced that I'm doing something illegal, and I don't know what it's going to take to change his mind."[28]

Cox finally returned to the team in Philadelphia, and it was just in time. The Cardinals had gone 12-13 in their twenty-five games without him, with Mathews having been victorious only once in his last eight starts and blowing leads of 5–0 and 5–1 in his last two. With Cox ready to pitch the following night, Magrane had been able to record only four outs (and Tunnell only five after him) on August 7, as the Phillies built a 12–1 lead. When the Philadelphia advantage had worsened to 15–5, Herzog was forced to summon Oquendo to the mound; when asked by Herzog if he wanted to first throw a few in the bullpen, Oquendo told him he did not need any warmup tosses.

With the game out of hand and no position players left on the bench, Ricky Horton played an inning in right field, where he watched helplessly as the Phillies' Glenn Wilson rocketed a double over his head. "But at least I hit the cutoff man," he proudly told Jim Palmer for an upcoming ABC television broadcast.[29] Even Tudor was mustered for extra duty, as he was sent in to pinch-hit for Dawley in the eighth—and he horrified Cardinals observers by stumbling over the first base bag when trying to beat out a double play. Tudor's knee remained intact on the play, but the loss meant the lead over the Mets was now down to three-and-a-half games.

With Cox back on the active roster, the Cardinals, for the first time in 1987, had all twenty-four players whom they originally expected to have when they broke spring training back in early April. Limited to 70 throws, Cox was removed from the game on August 8 with nobody out in the top of the fifth after issuing 68 pitches, deferring to the bullpen, as the Cards' offense slugged out a 9–5 win.

Having Cox and Tudor back in the rotation allowed Horton (6-1) to return to the bullpen to aid Worrell, who had blown his 9th save in 31 opportunities in Montreal, while other pitchers, such as Conroy at Louisville, were dealing with minor aches and pains that hindered their ability to assist the big league club. "I'm back with my buddies," Horton said happily. "Whatever they want me to do. I'll even pinch-hit."[30]

Before leaving Philly, the team's stamina was tested once again in what would become the Cardinals' twelfth extra-inning game since the middle of July. On Sunday, August 9, Ford and Morris were both injured after being pressed into service by Herzog as two of the twenty-one players the manager used, leaving only the healing starting pitchers Cox, Tudor, and Magrane as the lone men in uniform not to appear in the game. Ford, having fractured his right hand two months earlier, suffered a full break while striking out in the ninth and could no longer hold onto a bat. Morris, meanwhile, had crashed into the outfield wall and bruised his hip on the last play of the game in trying in vain for a Steve Jeltz triple, which won the game for the Phillies in the fourteenth inning, 8–7. (Despite losing, the Cardinals had surpassed their 1986 total run output of 601, now having posted 604 for 1987.) While Morris was expected to only miss a few days, Ford headed back to St. Louis to have surgery to repair the bone and was projected to be out at least six weeks.

Like an army filling gaps on the battlefield with companies in reserve, other troops arrived as able replacements. After a four-game split in Philadelphia, the team traveled on to Pittsburgh the following night, where Forsch became the Cardinals' first 10-game winner and garnered the 153rd victory of his career—tying him for third all-time in franchise history with Bill Sherdel and trailing only Jesse Haines and Bob Gibson—with a 6–0 shutout. In his last five starts, the red-hot Forsch had woven a dazzling ERA of 1.40. "I can't think of anybody throwing better," Ozzie Smith said of the wily veteran who still owned an important place on the club among all the talented young throwers around him. "He knows how to pitch when you get a lead. Maybe everybody else learned from that tonight."[31] The franchise record of 251 wins was still a way off, however. "I won't catch Gibson," Forsch said with a laugh.

Also during the evening, Clark broke the National League record by walking in sixteen consecutive games, bringing his season total to 113, which was only 3 shy of the team record for a season held by Miller Huggins. Clark was also closing in on the Major League record for combined walks and strikeouts in a season of 290, set by the Astros' Jimmy Wynn in 1969. Coleman stole two bases against the former Cardinals' catcher LaValliere, to give him 76 on the year, and Smith contributed 2 hits, including a double. Continuing a year of unprecedented offensive production for the shortstop, Ozzie had more RBIs (57) through the first week of August than five players in baseball with 20 or more home runs—Bo Jackson, Brook Jacoby, Ozzie Virgil, Rob Deer, and Tom Brunansky.

Only the young starting pitchers, who had contributed so effectively earlier, seemed to be waning. Magrane lost again on August 12, as the Cardinals were shut out for the first time of the year by an 11–0 score in Pittsburgh. The only offensive highlight was Lawless getting his first hit of the season in the ninth inning, beating out a high bounder to short. The achievement, he joked, doubled the fan mail he discovered in his locker when he and the Cardinals got back to Busch Stadium—from the three or four notes he typically found there to almost ten. "Half of them are bills anyway," he said.[32]

As the Phillies came to St. Louis, the story of the series was the venerable Schmidt, who drove his 23rd home run out of Busch Stadium to break his longest dry spell of the season with his first since July 26, a span of 78 homerless at bats. Schmidt would go deep twice more the following night and almost hit a third, doubling high off the wall in the ninth inning. The pair of blasts came off Forsch, who had served up 11 to Schmidt in the fourteen years they had been facing each other, his most against any pitcher. Yet amazingly, Schmidt, for the first time since 1974, would not hit any home runs in Chicago's Wrigley Field during the season after having hit 47 in the Cubs' home park in his career to that time.

The bombs by Schmidt provided the victory for Phillies' pitcher Kevin Gross, who had been winless in all of his starts since June 30. Gross was supposed to be serving a suspension for ten days for altering a baseball with sandpaper, as accusations of cheating around the game had now creeped from the batter's box up to the pitching mound. Only a week earlier, Joe Niekro of the Minnesota Twins had also been caught with sandpaper in the pocket of his game pants in addition to an emery board. The latter, though receiving the most attention in the media as Niekro attempted to surreptitiously throw it out of the umpires' sight, was legal to possess—as one typically did not file one's nails with sandpaper. Niekro wound up with a ten-day suspension himself after umpire Tim Tschida presented the proof to the American League office.

"Niekro already was a known ball scuffer, of course, and rather than tossing balls out of play, I was putting them in my extra pouch in case we needed evidence," the umpire revealed. "Those balls didn't have the normal nick. They had gouges the size of a half-dollar."[33]

Gross's penalty was under appeal, and thus he was available to play against the Cardinals. "I don't think he should have pitched," Herzog said in objection. "But there's not a hell of a lot we can do about it. I'm sure the Cubs didn't think he should be pitching when he beat them in the 13th inning the other day."[34] The Cubs did concur, as their general manager Dallas Green was of the opinion that if a pitcher was caught scuffing up a baseball, that particular game should be replayed. "He was pitching so badly, we didn't say anything," added Gene Michael, who followed Tschida's lead and gathered twelve scuffed baseballs from the game Gross had pitched against his club. "For the youth of America, set a good example and play by the rules."[35]

The Cardinals' pitchers made it clear they did not want any part of such activities. "I don't operate on that level," said Worrell. "For me to cheat, it would take away the challenge of the game. What satisfaction is there if you go up on the mound cheating? You're not beating somebody if you're cheating." Added Horton, "It's opening up the game to scandal if you allow it to continue. I would like to see stricter, more uniform measures in regard to cheating. . . . For the people who don't cheat in baseball, it's not fair."[36]

With 100-degree heat once again bearing down on Busch Stadium on Sunday, August 16, the Phillies took three of four from the Cardinals despite two homers from Clark, as Tom Herr had to be rushed to the hospital with sudden abdominal pains. The Mets themselves had avoided a four-game sweep at Wrigley Field in setting a team record for runs scored with a 23–10 romp over the Cubs, as Strawberry drove in five runs, scored five, and posted a double, a triple, and a three-run homer.

The lead for the Cards was at four games, and given their history in Houston, it was destined to get smaller in their final visit to the Astrodome the following three days. Having batted .208 in the "Eighth Wonder of the World" in 1987—more than forty points lower than their performance in any other National League ballpark for the season—Herzog's men scored a total of 5 runs in dropping all three games. After a high-water mark for the season of 61-32 on July 23, the Cardinals had gone 9-18 since.

Despite Magrane pitching well in Houston while losing 2–1, Herzog's confidence in the young left-handed starters was weakening. "I hope they get going. It's tough to make a pitching schedule with Magrane and Mathews in it."[37] Run support for all the hurlers had noticeably slipped. Since the All-Star break, Herr and the previously struggling Lindeman were the only ones who had seen a rise in their batting average, as Herr—who in the past week had tied Pepper Martin for tenth on the all-time Cardinals' stolen-base list with 146—improved from .270 to .306, and Lindeman went from .191 to .244, while key figures such as Clark (from .311 down to .296), McGee (.302 to .261), and Pendleton (.315 to .269) had endured significant drops.

Watching their descent with glee from afar were the Mets, ready to pounce. "St. Louis is doing some finger-pointing," noticed Keith Hernandez. "They lose some games and somebody blames the bullpen or somebody says the pitching had done its job but the hitting has let them down. I was enjoying every comment."[38]

Needing a boost at the plate, the team recalled Pagnozzi and Lance Johnson from Louisville on August 21. In the three months Pagnozzi had spent at Triple-A after his brief major league stint in April, the catcher had hit .318 with 14 home runs and drove in 70, while Johnson was batting at a .333 clip with 11 triples and would be named the American Association MVP for the season, with Pagnozzi also named to the league's All-Star team. "They called up the snail and the rabbit," joked the slow-footed Pagnozzi.[39]

On his first night back up in the Majors, Johnson was given the starting assignment in right field in his hometown of Cincinnati, where his father, mother, brother, and three sisters were in attendance. Having grown up rooting for the Reds, Johnson played against the Reds' talented new shortstop Barry Larkin in high school when Johnson was at Princeton and Larkin was at Moeller. "We beat up on each other," Johnson recalled of those days. "They beat us in football and we beat them in baseball."[40]

While Maxvill had authorized the promotions to hopefully provide some punch in the lineup, the West-leading Giants— already having acquired pitchers Craig Lefferts, Dave Dravecky, and Don Robinson in the preceding weeks—bolstered their pitching depth even further by picking up Reuschel from the Pirates. In speaking of the work done by his general manager Al Rosen, Roger Craig said, "I told Al, he's done his job. Now it's up to me."[41] News of the move irked the former Giant Jack Clark, who thought that Maxvill should have been on the phone looking for veteran pitching help such as Reuschel.

With the Mets creeping to within two-and-a-half games of the Cardinals and the Expos right behind them at three back, Herzog attempted to jolt the pitching staff by temporarily moving Forsch to the bullpen to supply it with more right-handed help. As Magrane still held only one victory since the third week of June, the manager was seeking a bona fide stopper from the starting staff, and Tudor, also struggling since his return from the broken leg, finally showed his 1985 form on August 21.

With Lindeman hitting his 7th homer off his fellow Bradley University product Guy Hoffman, Tudor (despite leaving the game early because of slight arm stiffness) headed off the Cardinals' five-game losing streak in besting the Reds in a tight 2–1 score in Cincinnati, assisted by nearly three innings of scoreless help from Worrell. In the four seasons he had played in the Senior Circuit, Tudor had now beaten every team in the National League.

Keeping the momentum going, the Cards would rally from a 7–1 deficit the following night to beat the Reds again, 9–7 and subsequently sweep all three games—the first time they had done so in Riverfront Stadium in fourteen years. The three losses dropped the Reds to two games behind the Giants in the Western Division, as Cincinnati owner Marge Schott, nervous in reading about the bevy of trade deals other teams were cutting across baseball, mandated that General Manager Bill Bergesch get moving on some proposals. A week later, they would acquire Pat Perry from the Cardinals for fellow pitcher Scott Terry.

The arrival of Lanier's Astros to Busch Stadium on August 24 began a stretch in which twenty-six of the Cardinals' final thirty-nine games would be played at home, while the Mets had only sixteen of their last thirty-eight at Shea Stadium and the Expos a mere thirteen of thirty-eight in Montreal. Clark notched his 100th RBI in beating the Astros on the 25th, while on the 26th, Coleman achieved the first outside-the-park home run of his career off Jim Deshaies of the Astros after 1,914 plate appearances.

When Oquendo's suicide squeeze scored Clark in the ninth for a 4–3 win on August 30, it was the Cards' 44th come-from-behind victory of the season. August was capped by their sixth win in a row the following night, as Tudor and Worrell excelled together once again in combining for a 4–0 shutout of the Reds. With Labor Day looming, the winning streak had provided some extra breathing room between the Cardinals and the Mets, as the latter was five-and-a-half games off the pace. But an on-going storm of challenges would make the September chase for the pennant unlike any other.

Fig. 1. Todd Worrell.
Courtesy of the National Baseball Hall of Fame and Museum.

Fig. 2. Whitey Herzog.
Courtesy of the National Baseball Hall of Fame and Museum.

Fig. 3. Tom Herr.
Courtesy of the National Baseball Hall of Fame and Museum.

Fig. 4. Vince Coleman.
Courtesy of the National Baseball Hall of Fame and Museum.

Fig. 5. Terry Pendleton.
Courtesy of the National Baseball Hall of Fame and Museum.

Fig. 6. Jim Lindeman.
Courtesy of the National Baseball Hall of Fame and Museum.

Fig. 7. Willie McGee.
Courtesy of the National Baseball Hall of Fame and Museum.

Fig. 8. Tony Peña.
Courtesy of the National Baseball Hall of Fame and Museum.

Fig. 9. John Morris.
Courtesy of the National Baseball Hall of Fame and Museum.

Fig. 10. Jack Clark.
Courtesy of the National Baseball Hall of Fame and Museum.

Fig. 11. Ozzie Smith.
Courtesy of the National Baseball Hall of Fame and Museum.

Batboys - Tony Simokaitis and Jeff Brinegar.
First Row (Seated) - Vince Coleman, Dave Ricketts, Johnny Lewis, Rich Hacker, Whitey Herzog, Mike Roarke, Nick Leyva, Red Shoendienst, Terry Pendleton.
Second Row (Standing) - Clubhouse Men Rip Rowan and Kurt Schlogl, Traveling Secretary C.J. Cherre, Jose Oquendo, Tito Landrum, Tom Herr, Bob Forsch, Bill Dawley, Todd Worrell, Mike Laga, Danny Cox, Jack Clark, Dave LaPoint, Willie McGee, Tom Lawless, Clubhouse Manager Frank Coppenbarger, Trainer Gene Gieselmann, Equipment Manager Buddy Bates.
Third Row (Standing) - Ozzie Smith, Curt Ford, Greg Mathews, Pat Perry, John Tudor, Rick Horton, Steve Lake, Jim Lindeman, Tom Pagnozzi, Ray Soff, Tony Pena.

Fig. 12. The 1987 St. Louis Cardinals. Courtesy of the author.

Fig. 13. A twenty-year reunion in 2007 of a portion of the Cardinals' pitching staff from 1987 (*left-to-right*): John Tudor, Danny Cox, Greg Mathews, Joe Magrane, Ricky Horton, and Bob Forsch. Courtesy of Alamy.

6

Down Goes Jack, and Out Goes Terry

*When I went to spring training, I thought we had the best staff we
ever had. But it didn't work out that way until later in the year.*

—Whitey Herzog, 1987

THE CARDINALS' RUNNING GAME FOUND ITS FIFTH GEAR IN
August, posting a season-high 53 stolen bases during the month
while being caught only 9 times. On August 29 they had grabbed
4 against Charlie Puleo and Ozzie Virgil of Atlanta to give them an
even 200 for the year, making the Cardinals the first team since 1915
to steal at least 200 for three straight years. Their sweep of three
games against the Braves in Busch Stadium to close the month
had been emblematic of the overall National League interdivisional
play for 1987, as entering September the Eastern Division was fifty-
three games over .500 (224-171) against its Western counterpart.

With the Mets keeping pace in the first week of September at
three and a half back, the Cardinals kept finding new ways to
win. On the morning of Friday, September 4, the thirty-year-old
Peña took a page from Keith Hernandez's book and shaved off
his mustache for the first time since he was seventeen, seeking
anything that would shake a slump in which he was batting .181
for the past two months. That night in St. Louis, with two out in
the eighth inning and Pendleton on first, the clean-faced catcher
slugged a two-run homer for the difference in a victory for Worrell
over the Padres, 4–2.

Not having as much luck that weekend was Herzog, who on the following Sunday morning awoke with an advanced ear infection but made it to the ballpark anyway. "It scared the hell out of me," he described the experience a few days later. "I was having breakfast and, when I got through reading the paper, I was looking at the wall, and it was moving. I broke out in a cold sweat."[1] The only way Herzog could relieve the pain was to lie flat on a training table in the clubhouse, as he watched the game from a TV monitor while turning over the managerial reins to Red Schoendienst. The two Southern Illinoisans communicated through walkie-talkies, as the Cardinals won, 6–4, keeping the Mets and Expos at bay.

After showering and leaving the locker room that day, Coleman, McGee, and Pendleton found a woman with a flat tire in a parking garage near Busch Stadium and helped her with the repair. "I'm forever grateful," said the woman, who was in the midst of especially difficult times with her husband battling cancer. Pendleton spoke for the trio of heroes in being happy to do it. "It was no big deal, really. I would hope that anybody would help out somebody like that."[2]

The Cardinals were glad to receive all the karma they could get. On the Labor Day holiday of Monday, September 7, the team started a series in Montreal—the city that Herzog had dreaded visiting the most in the earlier part of the decade, calling it "the easiest baseball town to score in—and I ain't talkin' runs" when problems with recreational drugs were ravaging the Cardinals and the rest of the sport.[3] Behind their emerging young first baseman Andrés Galarraga, who batted an astounding .481 (26-54) against St. Louis for the season, the Expos proceeded to take three straight to make them 10-4 against Herzog's club for the year, keeping the Cardinals under .500 for their last 52 games, at 25-27.

But a blow to the Cardinals' pennant chances far beyond the loss of a single game hit them in the final contest of the Montreal series on September 9. Trying to ignite the Redbirds from a 7–2 deficit as he led off the sixth inning, Jack Clark sprinted down the first base line after hitting a slow roller to Expos' third baseman Tim Wallach. In a situation similar to when Ryne Sandberg injured himself earlier in the summer with Clark on defense at first base, Clark saw Galarraga leave the bag to pursue an errant throw and changed his stride to avoid a tag attempt he knew would be coming. Clark caught his cleats in the same treacherous rug that had gradually ruined Andre Dawson's knees over ten years. But instead of the decade's worth of damage Dawson had sustained, Clark rolled his ankle on the turf in one split second and had to leave the game. The Expos surged on to an 8–3 victory, leaving the Mets only a game and a half out of first and the Expos two. The Cardinals had been in the top spot in the National League East for 113 consecutive days but were now down to their smallest lead in the division since leading the Cubs by a single game on June 3.

An examination revealed no broken bone, but Clark was expected to be lost for at least a week. It was feared that the slugger's absence would once again destroy the makeup of the team as it had in 1986 and had nearly done in 1985.

Taking his place was Dan Driessen, the man who had been sitting at home in June when Lee Thomas signed him to a Triple-A contract as a long-shot insurance policy—which the Cardinals now looked to cash in. Having batted .244 with 7 home runs in fifty-eight games at Louisville, Driessen had performed a similar role twelve months earlier for Lanier's Astros during Houston's playoff run in September 1986, as had former Astro César Cedeño in subbing for Clark in St. Louis in late 1985. Also helping out at first base would be Mike Laga—recently brought up from the Minors as well—while Lindeman was still being used against left-handers. But with Lindeman experiencing back problems once again, Herzog sought an extra right-handed-hitting outfielder and first baseman. It prompted the return of David Green to a Cardinal uniform after redeeming himself in Triple-A ball, where he batted a sizzling .356 with 21 doubles at Louisville. Green was given jersey No. 18, formerly belonging to Andy Van Slyke.

With the Cardinals heading to New York without their biggest bat, the Mets felt the timing was perfect for an attack. "The last time we played St. Louis, I didn't see that much," the unimpressed New York shortstop Santana said. "I didn't think they had that much. I don't think any club starts out strong and ends strong. Everybody has a time to drift. This may be their time. All we've got on our minds is seeing St. Louis sink."[4] Howard Johnson was even more confident than before. "We're definitely going to win this thing," he announced.[5] He and the other Mets had been preparing the whole season for this ultimate encounter. "We've waited a long time for this," Hernandez said. "I guarantee we'll take two out of three."[6] Even Davey Johnson hinted that the Cards seemed to him to be folding. "They haven't really played well since the All-Star break. And I thought they played over their head in the first half."[7]

The Mets, winners of eight of their last ten, had seized the momentum. In front of a raucous sellout crowd of 51,795 in Shea Stadium for the opener on Friday night, September 11, Strawberry immediately turned Tudor around for a two-run homer in the bottom of the first inning after Ozzie Smith had shot a line drive back at the Mets' Ron Darling in the top half, which bruised the pitcher's left wrist. With the Cardinals obviously missing Clark (and his .470 career average against Darling), they would manage only 1 hit through the first eight innings, a bunt single by Coleman in the sixth. "We played awful until the ninth [inning]," Herzog would say afterward.[8]

On Coleman's bunt, Darling suffered his second injury of the evening, and a more serious one. In diving for the ball, he damaged ligaments in the thumb of his throwing hand. He gave way to relievers Randy Myers and McDowell, as New York had upped the lead to 4–1 heading into the ninth inning. Along the way, Howard Johnson stole second base in the bottom of the fourth to become the eighth player in MLB history with at least 30 home runs and 30 steals in a season, and the second man to do so in 1987 after the Reds' Davis had accomplished the feat on August 2.

McDowell permitted a lead-off walk to Smith but then retired Herr and Driessen, putting the Mets one out away from being a half game out of first place. With Smith on second, McGee laced a single to center that cut the Mets' lead to 4–2 and kept the Cards alive for Terry Pendleton, who had been hitless in his last 12 at bats since the start of the series in Montreal. "But with the crowd standing and howling for the kill with two down in the ninth," wrote Durso in the New York Times, "the Cards nailed McDowell in a stunning sequence."

Swinging at a devastating McDowell sinker on the first pitch, Pendleton feebly dribbled the ball foul as it skittered through the batter's box. McDowell went with his best pitch again, and

Pendleton was ready for it. "Until I get to two strikes, I've got to try to hit it out of the ballpark," the Cardinal said of his strategy in the situation. "He threw me two good sinkers. I pounded the first one into the dirt.

"Then I moved up front in the box and got the next one early, and I was able to catch up with it."[9] This time, he hit it on the screws.

In one of the most iconic Cardinal at bats of all time, he sent a long fly ball toward straightaway center field. Out there for the Mets was Mookie Wilson, who tracked it to the 410-foot sign but ran out of room. "I knew he hit it well, but the wind was blowing in," the seasoned outfielder judged. "It just kept going, so evidently the wind didn't hurt it."[10] The ball went over the wall, tying the game at 4 as Pendleton pumped his first while circling the bases.

The game moved to the tenth, when Herr—like Pendleton, without a hit to that point on the road trip—snapped a 1-25 skid with an RBI single off Orosco (the same pitcher he victimized for the grand slam back in April), which was followed by another run when Driessen hit into a force out with Mets trying for a double play. In his second inning of work, Dayley blew through Strawberry, McReynolds, and Carter to seal the dramatic 6–4 triumph. For Dayley it was his ninth win, as the bullpen had accounted for 34 of the Cards' 82 victories so far on the year. Moreover, often lost amidst the memory of the Pendleton home run was the middle-relief performance on the night of Scott Terry (the newcomer from the Reds) and Steve Peters (a left-hander up from Louisville only for the past month), which kept the Cards in the game.

In a dejected Mets' clubhouse, Hernandez gave an honest appraisal. "Give him [Pendleton] credit. He is not a home run hitter, but that's what it called for, and he got it. He probably got the biggest hit of the year for them. If they win it, that'll be the hit that did it."[11]

Earlier that afternoon, Peña—himself in the midst of yet another tough stretch at the plate, this one 5-44—decided he would bypass a chance at free agency in the off-season and signed a two-year contract extension with the Cardinals, taking him through 1989 at the same 1987 salary rate of his $1.15 million. The conscientious Peña was taking lots of extra batting practice in an effort to work his way out of the slump. "Sometimes I can't sleep at night. It's really tough. I've never been through a slump like this in my life—not the whole year." Herzog was worried he might overwork himself and thereby detract from his catching abilities, which remained superior. "I wish he wouldn't take extra hitting every day. If batting practice made Hall of Famers, I'd be in."[12]

The avalanche of Cardinal red cascading upon Queens continued into Saturday. The flu-ridden Gooden was shelled, giving up 5 runs in the first inning of an 8–1 loss to Mathews and his complete game, while Coleman stole his 100th base in the seventh. After permitting a sixth Cardinal score in the second inning, Johnson removed his ace right-hander in what was Gooden's earliest departure in his 120 starts to date in the big leagues.

To make matters worse for the Mets' leader, it was announced that Darling was lost for the season, and he would undergo surgery a few days later and be in a cast for four weeks. Until this time, Darling had been the lone starter on the New York staff not yet felled by some form of injury or off-field matter, and the only pitcher to start more than twenty-seven games. Ojeda was finally back on the mound but only in a limited relief role, having not pitched since May 9 before appearing in two innings in relief on September 8 against the Phillies; Davey Johnson felt he was not yet strong enough to make a start. The fourth member of the talented rotation and another southpaw, Sid Fernandez, missed three weeks in August with a knee injury and had won only twice since returning. "I don't know exactly what we'll do the rest of the season," the dejected New York skipper said.[13]

The Mets gained some soggy consolation in the final game, winning a rain-soaked 4–2 decision that was delayed two separate times for nearly two hours during each storm. After being bombed in Montreal, Cox was ineffective again, as he had posted only one victory in the eight starts he made since returning from his broken foot.

As the Cardinals were getting ready to leave town, Howard Johnson bumped into Herzog outside the clubhouse and offered an olive branch to the Cardinals' manager:

Whitey was coming through the tunnel. I was usually one of the last guys out of the locker room, and on this night, he was as well.

We ran into each other, and it was the first time we really had a chance to talk about everything that had been going on. I said, "I just wanted you to know that you guys are tough, and it's always fun playing against you." And he said, "You know I'm only messing with you with the corked bat stuff. Maybe we should get your forearms checked next time."

A typical Whitey saying! It made me respect him even more. It was a fun rivalry, and we just didn't like the Cardinals. I liked hitting in their ballpark, but it was difficult to play them because of their style. Coming off 1985 when we almost got there, and 1986 when we did get there, we knew that the Cardinals were regrouping and were going to be tough—and they were every bit as tough as we thought they would be.[14]

With three weeks remaining and everything still up for grabs, both teams kept an eye on the final three games of the schedule starting on October 2, which looked to be a winner-take-all series between the Mets and the Cardinals in St. Louis. Desperate for starting pitching, the Mets on September 15 traded for John Candelaria, the grinning veteran left-hander of thirteen Major League seasons and four postseason appearances, the most recent of which came the previous autumn in the American League Championship Series for the California Angels. Despite being hit hard in his three starts for New York, Candelaria would win two of them.

The next stop for the resilient Redbirds was a pair of games each in Philadelphia and Pittsburgh, starting in Veterans Stadium on September 14, where the man who had been a five-tool prospect with the Cardinals five years earlier made his first start in right field and batted cleanup. "So far, so good," Herzog said of David Green's return. "His reactions and quickness have been very good, both at first base and in right field. His bat speed has also been very good. We were really due a [pleasant] surprise." The manager hinted that Green, pending his continued progress, even had a shot at the regular right-field job in 1988 if the position was still unclaimed by then. "This is my last chance," Green acknowledged, "And I'm trying to take advantage of it."[15]

After a split of the games in Philly, the St. Louis lead over the Mets remained at a game and a half. On their first night in Pittsburgh on Wednesday, September 16, the Cardinals recorded an 8–5 win over the Pirates, with McGee driving in his 100th run and fellow outfielder John Morris scoring 2 runs himself.

Later, in the early hours of the morning of Thursday the 17th, Morris was awakened in his hotel room by a knock on the door. When Morris looked through the peephole, he saw that it was Herzog and Gieselmann with grim looks on their faces. They had been unable to reach Morris by phone, as the player had taken the receiver off the hook because of prank calls he had been getting. They had come to tell Morris that his father had passed away back in New York. Morris's mother and father had both been diagnosed with cancer earlier in the year.

After absorbing the shock, the player sat on the edge of the bed with his head down, seeking advice from his manager. "What should I do?" he asked Herzog.

"Just go home, take care of your family," Whitey responded.

"When should I come back?"

"Just come back when you're ready. Don't worry, we've got this."

Morris immediately headed for home. "I had the wake for my father on Friday, the burial on Saturday, and decided I was going to catch the first flight out Sunday morning back to St. Louis for our one o'clock game against the Cubs," he recalled of the whirlwind of events. "My first flight out of LaGuardia was canceled. I got on the next flight, which was about nine o'clock in the morning and I arrived in St. Louis at eleven. I hopped in a cab and got down to Busch Stadium at noon."

A lot had happened while he was away. Another key game was interrupted on the 17th by multiple rain delays (four of them that totaled nearly three hours) before a 1–0 win was claimed for the Pirates by former Cardinals prospect Mike Dunne, who was part of the Peña trade, had reached the Majors in June, and quite possibly had been the best rookie pitcher in the National League for the year. Morris had also missed Cox losing to the Cubs, as the team returned home to St. Louis on Friday night, and Magrane helping the team bounce back with a win on Saturday, in which the pitcher homered at the plate and Herr registered his 1,000th career hit to keep the Mets at one and a half back.

When Morris got to the Cardinals' clubhouse on Sunday, he

was stopped by Clark while walking to his locker. "Hey, Whitey's looking for you. He wants to see you."

Just before entering Herzog's office, Morris noticed that the lineup was not posted on the bulletin board in the hallway like it normally was. "I walk in all blurry eyed. I can't think straight. I haven't touched a ball or a bat in four days," Morris continued in his recollection of the emotion-filled time. He sat down in front of the manager.

"Hey kid, great to have you back," Herzog greeted him. "I'm really sorry about your dad. What do you want to do?"

"What do you mean?" Morris responded, confused with the question.

Herzog reached into a drawer. He pulled out two lineup cards and held them up side by side. He repeated his question. "What do you want to do? I've got your name on this one," he said in lifting his left hand. "But if you're not ready to play, I'll see you in the seventh inning and you don't have to start, and I'll use this other one. But, *what do you want to do?*"

Knowing that he was being challenged, Morris accepted the task. "I want to play."

Morris started in right field and batted seventh in the order against the struggling Cubs' rookie Maddux, who had not won since July 24 and possessed an ERA near 6.00.

In 2023 the outfielder could still vividly remember the fifty thousand people in the stands and the warm, sunny Sunday afternoon at Busch Stadium—in addition to a supernatural force that was guiding and driving him:

> My first at bat, I hit a line drive just over Shawon Dunston's glove at shortstop that drove in 2 runs. Next at bat, there was a man on third with one out, and the infield was back. I hit a ground ball to Dunston to get the guy in for another RBI. Next at bat, I get another single and another RBI. I get to first base, and I got a standing ovation from the crowd. [Cubs first baseman] Leon Durham says to me, "Man, that is really cool." I realized that everyone in the stadium knew what I was going through and were saying, "Welcome back." It was the only game in my career that I had 4 RBIS.

Despite the single being Morris's last hit of the day in the 10–2 Cardinal romp, he was not finished at the plate. "In my last at bat, I hit another line drive to left field—and my dad would always say, 'Take two and go to left.'"

It taught Morris something about himself which he has never forgotten. "Whitey had many other options that day—he could have put Curt Ford out there, or Lance Johnson, Jim Lindeman, or Jose Oquendo. But he chose to challenge me, knowing that sometimes in adversity, young men rise to the occasion. I am forever grateful for that moment and that Whitey chose to put me in there that day."[16]

The crowd that had inspired and supported Morris had also set the St. Louis attendance record for baseball. With the Cardinals' Sunday victory over the Cubs, a total of 2,650,452 had watched them at home on the year, surpassing the 1985 record of 2,637,563. To reach three million—something which no team outside of Los Angeles had ever done—the team would need to average just under thirty-two thousand a game in their eleven remaining home dates.

While the Redbirds were tangling with the Cubs, the Mets had followed the Cardinals to Pittsburgh—where Howard Johnson was asked about the significance of dropping two of three games to St. Louis in the key series the previous week in Shea Stadium. "We were playing a good team. We were playing the Cardinals. It's not like were playing the Pirates." But Johnson and the Mets proceeded to lose two of three to Pittsburgh as well, with Andy Van Slyke serving the crow at the end. "There isn't a team in the National League that doesn't want to beat the Mets. Every team in the league wants to see them lose. They're a great team, but they don't have to let you know about it all the time."[17]

If the pursuit of another championship did not give the Cardinals exclusivity among the sports attention in St. Louis, the events of the following week certainly consumed whatever ancillary interest remained among the other pastimes. On September 22, the National Football League Players Association ordered their members to walk off the job, marking the second work stoppage in professional football in the past six years. By December the city would bid a permanent goodbye to football Cardinals as owner Bill Bidwell packed the team for Phoenix after considering Jacksonville and Baltimore as well.

In an attempt to inject some much-needed levity into the sports world, the Anheuser-Busch company had one of its "spokesmen" pitch its products at the ballgame in Busch Stadium that night. Throwing out—or actually nosing out—the first ball before the Cardinals' battle against the Phillies was Spuds MacKenzie, the company's canine mascot who promised a party with Gussie's products anywhere he happened to emerge around the world and made his way around the infield before the first pitch. It is unknown if Spuds stuck around to watch the reliever-flipping employed by Herzog at the end of the game, in which Worrell and Dayley took turns in right field and the pitching mound, for after Worrell surrendered a homer to Schmidt, Dayley entered to retire the left-handed-hitting Von Hayes before Worrell came back to the hill to get Rick Schu and Darren Daulton for his 32nd save. In consideration of his work on the evening, Dayley felt slighted by proceedings. "Spuds rides in a limo, and I get relieved by the right fielder," he joked.[18]

To clear his mind from the pennant chase, Herzog had resumed his September routine for game days while the team was in town—it was the same every year, whether the Cardinals were in the pennant race or not. "He's in his bass boat at 6:00 a.m.," Dave Dorr of the *Post-Dispatch* informed his readers, "fishing on abandoned strip mining pits near Freeburg, Illinois. At 9:00 he returns home, showers, and takes a nap."[19]

While the tension continued to build, so did the realization that a division title was drawing near. As the hour came ever closer, the Cardinals could not wait to get to work each day. "Last time I was here, we were 20 games out of first place," Lindeman recalled of his initial big league experience the previous September. "It was fun, but not as much fun as now. Everyone wants to get to the clubhouse early and get something accomplished."[20]

The offense, however, again seemed to be dangling precariously over a pit of complete collapse without the services of Jack Clark. When the Cardinals headed to Chicago for their last road series of the year against the Cubs and dropped a 2–1 opener, they had scored only 10 runs in their last five games despite winning three of them. The newest stretch of ineptitude with the bats was symbolized by the momentary return of Clark that afternoon, who attempted to pinch-hit in the ninth inning. After taking the first pitch from diminutive Chicago left-hander Frank DiPino for a ball, Clark then tumbled to the ground after swinging at the next offering, unable to keep his balance on his sore ankle. Peña had to take his place as the second pinch-hitter in the same at bat.

Despite the Cubs taking two out of three from the Cardinals during the penultimate weekend of the season, the Chicago team remained entrenched in last place in the East after having threatened for the division lead in the early part of the summer. Before the weekend, the Cubs had only won two of their last eleven and would go 9-18 for September, as Green unloaded on the players in the city's press. "I want to apologize to the fans of the Chicago Cubs," the general manager said in frustration of the team's performance. Green had terminated Michael as the field manager two weeks earlier, having turned the reins over to Frank Lucchesi while the search for a permanent leader would commence shortly. "The reason I have to apologize is because we quit. I was slapped in the face and so were the Cub fans. They forgot we had another month to play."

Green quickly corrected himself. "No, they didn't forget. They didn't care. Danny Cox and John Tudor went down and Jeff Lahti was lost for the season, but the Cardinals didn't quit."[21]

In spite of Green's comments, many around baseball had no problem with Dawson being the front-runner for the MVP award while playing for a team at the bottom of the standings. "If you're going to have a Cy Young Award for the most outstanding pitcher, then the best player should get the most outstanding player award," Herzog stated. "That's the purpose of it." For his part, the humble Dawson deferred to his lame-duck rival. "I probably won't win it. It usually goes to someone who's been on a winning team. Jack Clark has been the big weapon in the St. Louis lineup all year."[22] Clark, meanwhile, thought that as many as four or five Cardinals had a chance to take the honor—while Herzog believed there was a case for Oquendo to be the team's MVP.

As the Mets continued their pursuit of the Cardinals, some of their comments about the Pirates in the previous week—and New York's subsequent loss of the three-game series—did nothing to deter Gooden from continuing the team's verbal assault on

Pittsburgh. Entering his start against the Pirates on September 26, the Mets right-hander had been 7-0 against them in his career. Stating there was "no way" he would be defeated by Jim Leyland's club and that "they belonged in the little leagues,"[23] Gooden was ambushed for five runs in the first two innings, including a two-run homer by second-year star Barry Bonds. The game ended up an 8–2 laugher for the players from the Steel City. "Not bad for a bunch of little leaguers," Leyland proudly said of his club.[24]

Coupled with Tudor's win over Sutcliffe and the Cubs—thanks to a homer from a certain substitute first baseman for Clark, which prompted Hummel to proclaim that "Cesar Cedeno is alive and well in Dan Driessen's uniform"[25]—the Mets' setback increased their distance from the top to three-and-a-half games.

The trip to Wrigley ended the road portion of the schedule for the Cardinals, and the club headed home and enjoyed their final off day on Monday, September 28. The team had proven to be a most compelling draw for fans in other cities; in eighty away games on the year (one short of a full slate), the Cardinals had set the National League record for road attendance with 2,321,960. Now, with a week left at Busch Stadium, they would be defending a lead on the Mets that had just been trimmed to two and three over the Expos—both of which they would face in the coming days.

With Herzog having issued a thinly veiled challenge to Mathews and Magrane about their importance to the team's hopes, the young starting pitchers were assigned to the doubleheader that opened the crucial series with Montreal on September 29. They responded like veterans. Before a half-empty stadium as the crowd was slow to fill in for the doubleheader, Magrane pitched the best game of his rookie season, shutting out the Expos in the first contest, 1–0. The key play was made by the hot-fielding Pendleton, who grabbed a smash down the third base line and threw out the Cardinals-killer Galarraga to end the Expos' sixth with Wallach on second; a hit would have given Montreal the first run of the game, and with it, the momentum. Instead, the lone score followed in the bottom half of the inning and came in St. Louis–garden variety. Coleman drew a walk, which was followed by Smith singling him to third and Herr driving him in with a sacrifice fly. Magrane, who had now permitted only 4 earned runs in his last thirty innings, went the distance in allowing a scant 3 hits and 2 walks. "He is being *mobbed* by his teammates on the mound!" Jack Buck declared over KMOX after the final out.[26]

Decades later, the day still stands out in Magrane's mind:

I went out there, and the defense was amazing. They were catching everything that wasn't nailed down.

The thing I remember most was coming back into the clubhouse after the game. Greg [Mathews] was going out to get warmed up for the second game. As I was sliding carefully across the locker room concrete with my spikes on, I said, 'Match that, mother—!' He certainly did. He responded, and that's a day we revisit with each other from time to time.[27]

In a one-day showcase reminiscent of the near double no-hitter performed by Paul and Dizzy Dean in Brooklyn in September 1934, Mathews followed up by being just as good in the nightcap.

After visiting an eye doctor, the desperate Peña—batting only .174 since the beginning of July—had started wearing glasses and had also grown his mustache back. He provided the first Redbirds' hit in game two in the sixth inning, a bloop double to right field that broke up a no-hitter for Montreal's Bryn Smith and led to three Cardinals runs. It was all the support needed for Mathews (six innings) and Worrell (the final three), who blanked the Expos for the second time on the day, 3–0—the first back-to-back shutouts by Cardinals' pitchers since Andújar and Cox performed the feat in May 1985. The brilliant performance from the young left-handers had pushed New York back to three and a half behind, as the Mets had been shut out themselves in Philadelphia by a 3–0 score. "That's what we've been waiting for all year from Magrane and Mathews," Smith said plainly. "This is what we saw in spring training from these guys, hoping they would be able to do it all year. I guess they couldn't have picked a better time to really come to the forefront."[28]

Clark, yearning to return and make his own contribution to the championship charge, tried to get back in shape by taking extra batting practice. Unfortunately, his session in the late afternoon of September 30 was cut short. With the recent NFL strike, replacement players had been hired by the teams to keep the 1987 schedule going. When Clark strutted out of the dugout to take some swings, he was stunned to see the substitute football Cardinals on the Busch Stadium turf holding practice. "That's the worst I've ever seen," Clark moaned about the intrusion. "Here we're trying to win a pennant. We've got four days left and the —ing scabs are on the field taking up our time. Unbelievable."[29] Clark vowed to be out there again at the same time the following evening whether football practice was occurring or not. "If they're there, I'm going to hit line drives at their butts," he warned. But when the next day had come, the slugger had cooled off and allowed the strike-breaking version of the Big Red to go through their drills before commencing an eighteen-minute round of extra hitting.

By the end of the night, the Redbirds had secured a tie for the division title; despite the Cardinals losing in St. Louis that evening, the Mets dropped a ten-inning game in Philadelphia on a home run by Phillies reserve Luis Aguayo.

The Eastern Division crown became solely theirs at 10:15 the following night, October 1. With temperatures in the midthirties at Busch, Cox finished a complete game by fielding a tapper off the bat of Montreal's Tom Foley and throwing on to Driessen at first. Driessen, who also had 2 hits and 3 RBIs in the game, had earlier made a diving stop of a Raines grounder down the line as Cox raced over to beat the lightning-fast speedster to the bag. And in the eighth, the first baseman dug a Smith throw out of the dirt to complete a double play on Raines, thereby stopping another rally.

The Cardinals thus cemented themselves permanently where they had been since May 20—first place in the East and on their way to the National League Championship Series. As the celebration got underway, the normally reserved Herr ripped off his jersey and waved it over his head in front of the Cardinals' dugout, while some nearby fans replied in kind by taking off their own shirts and launching them onto the field. In the locker room, Coleman was conducting an interview when a gallon of milk was suddenly dumped on his head from behind—but as on the basepaths, he never broke stride in his comments to the reporter.

The clinching against the Expos rendered irrelevant what had been eagerly anticipated for most of the summer—the season-ending series with the Mets on the final weekend. After Tudor won his 10th game, aided by four innings of scoreless relief from Horton and Peters in a 3–2 win over New York on Friday, a tribute reserved especially for the St. Louis fans was in store for the following afternoon.

On Saturday, October 3, Brenda Slover of Orchardville, Illinois, became the three millionth fan to pass through the Busch Stadium turnstiles in 1987, making the Cardinals only the third team ever to achieve the feat after the Dodgers had done so once again in 1987 (for the sixth time) and the Mets had also joined the elite list earlier in the week. New York reached the figure while drawing from a metropolitan area of nearly 19 million people, while the St. Louis region totaled just 2.5 million. "We stopped at Centralia [Illinois] and bought us a lottery ticket," Ms. Slover said while being interviewed at the game. "And I said, 'This is my lucky day—I'm either going to win the lottery or I'll be the three millionth fan.'"[30] She and the rest of the crowd watched a lineup of reserves lose to New York 7–1, as Barry Lyons deposited a three-run double to the wall off Dawley in the ninth.

The regular season closed the following day with another loss, 11–6, with many of the starters back in the batting order. The end of the NFL strike had, in part, accounted for a less-than-sellout figure of 41,890 for the finale, bringing the Cardinals' total attendance for the year to 3,072,122—the highest in the Majors for 1987 and the seventh-largest total in Major League history behind the Dodgers' top six years. When the day was concluded, the Cardinals stood in front of the first base dugout and tossed their batting gloves, wristbands, and other personal articles to the grateful fans.

The conclusion of the regular-season schedule, however, merely meant unfinished business for the St. Louis faithful—the Cardinals' front office was in the process of receiving over a million postcard entries for their playoff ticket lottery.

There was no such problem for those handling the mail at the headquarters of the Minnesota Twins, which while getting ready for their appearance in the American League Championship Series against the Detroit Tigers, still had fifteen thousand unsold postseason tickets as the regular season was ending.

THE 1987 CAMPAIGN HAD BEEN A TRUE TEAM EFFORT FOR the Cardinals, as repeated hardship had hit the team again. After the Cardinals peaked at twenty-nine games over .500 just after the All-Star break, they struggled through a sub-.500 mark of 34–35 the rest of the way. With every starting pitcher on the Cardinals' staff having to rebound from injury, inexperience, or some other hurdle, the team was the first division champion to have no starter with at least 14 wins. Topping the Cardinals' list was a modest 11, achieved by Cox, Forsch, and Mathews, while Tudor added 10, Magrane and Dayley 9, and Worrell and Horton 8. In going 10-2, Tudor's record in his three seasons with the Cardinals stood at 44-17—which overtook Mort Cooper for the best winning percentage in team history for a pitcher with at least 50 decisions.

New York writers such as Durso bemoaned the injury bug hitting the Mets' revered starting rotation, which some predicted at the start of the season would get 20 wins each from Gooden, Ojeda, Darling, and Fernandez. By season's end, their front-liners, in addition to most of the supporting cast, had been put out of action. "In relentless order, Fernandez suffered from a buckling knee and a sore shoulder, Rick Aguilera quit warming up on May 26 when his elbow hurt, David Cone fractured a finger the next day, Terry Leach won ten straight games and then tore the cartilage in his knee in August and Ron Darling tore the ligaments in his thumb in September."[31] Davey Johnson's plans for the off-season, along with his review of 1987, sounded much like Herzog's summary of 1986. "Going fishing," Johnson said. "Do some fishing, work on my golf game, develop some property. This is a year I'll never forget. Everything that could go wrong in every possible way did."[32]

Unlike the Mets, the Cardinals—with their own myriad injuries—found ways to overcome. The Cardinals were 77-7 in 1987 when leading after seven innings and 75-2 when ahead after eight, illustrating the growth of Worrell and the strong return of Dayley, the latter of whom retired 200 out of the 253 batters he had faced during the year. "The most surprising development of the entire season," Herzog said of Dayley's complete recovery amid a season full of surprises. For his part, Dayley never doubted he would resume an effective role on the mound. "From day one, I told myself that I was going to pitch again somewhere. I didn't know if I was going to be the same type of pitcher, the power pitcher that I've always been. But I told myself that, and I told my wife that I was going to be back somewhere, sometime. The way that it happened was miraculous, and I thank the Lord for the opportunity." As Herzog saw it, the southpaw was an irreplaceable component. "I doubt very much that we could have finished in the top three in the division if Ken Dayley hadn't come back."[33] His partner in the pen, Worrell, finished with 33 saves to become the first Redbird with back-to-back 30-save seasons.

By the end of the year, the preseason potential that Herzog had foreseen for the pitching staff had matured. "When I went to spring training, I thought we had the best staff we ever had. But it didn't work out that way until later in the year."[34] After the bats had carried the team in the first half of the season, the Cardinals' pitchers had their best ERA month in September while atoning for the team's simultaneous .226 team batting mark. The Cardinals were dead even for September (14-14) and October (2-2)—the only two months in which they were not above .500.

Nonetheless, the Cardinals finished with a .264 average at home and .263 on the road, which brought them back to their exact 1985 overall figure after their 1986 downturn. After a rough beginning in April, Ozzie Smith's .303 final average would be the only time he would hit .300 in his nineteen-year Major League career, which was even more impressive because he had batted second in the order behind Coleman all year. Smith also committed his fewest errors in a season on defense with 10, posted his most stolen bases to date as a Cardinal (43), and drove in 75 runs without the benefit of hitting a single home run—which fell just one short of the team record of Milt Stock in 1920.

Despite his season essentially having ended back on September 9, Clark had nonetheless set a Cardinals' record with 136 walks during the year. Herzog had once again been prophetic about Clark being an irreplaceable power source; his 35 home runs were 23 more than the second-place man Pendleton, who finished with 96 RBIS to trail Clark (106) and McGee (105, the most ever for a Cardinals center fielder), which nearly gave the Cardinals three men with 100 for the first time ever. Yet McGee, after grounding into 8 double plays the previous season and only 3 in his MVP year of 1985, followed Peña from 1986 in leading the National League by hitting into 24, perhaps a lingering effect of recovering from his off-season knee problems. "It's hard to believe," Herzog reflected. "You'd think he wouldn't have 25 in his career."[35] Nonetheless, McGee had also posted 37 doubles and 11 triples, which suggests that the knee was not a factor in sprints of longer distances.

The newfound patience of Coleman at the plate had paid off. Only seven times all year had he swung at a 2-0 pitch, leading to impressive numbers of 70 walks and a .289 average to go along with his league-leading 109 stolen bases, including 22-27 in stealing third. His patience naturally resulted in a commensurate rise in his strikeout total (126, from 74 in 1986), but Coleman no doubt had discovered a rebirth in the batter's box. In only 14 of his 151 games did he fail to reach base by a walk or a hit, which included 14 hits via the bunt.

Even the subs had their individual achievements—such as the ultra-versatile Oquendo, who became the first player to start at seven different positions since former Cardinal Jack Rothrock had done so with the Red Sox in 1928.

TO GET TO THE WORLD SERIES, THE CARDINALS WOULD HAVE to conquer a team from the West that harbored a lingering animosity toward Herzog's men. In the homer-happy baseball season of 1987, the Cards were the only Major League club to hit fewer than 100, with their forthcoming opponent in the National League Championship Series, the San Francisco Giants, pacing the National League with 205.

7

A Giant Fight

I don't like Jeff Leonard. It's not a secret to him or anyone else.

—John Tudor, October 1987

LIKE THE TWO TOUGHEST KIDS IN SCHOOL FINALLY COLLID-ing on the playground, the showdown in the 1987 National League playoffs was the culmination of a heated undercurrent that had lingered for more than a year between the St. Louis Cardinals and the San Francisco Giants. The resentment could be traced to the middle of the Cardinals' frustrating 1986 season when the teams clashed on July 22 at Busch Stadium.

With the Cardinals already having built a 10–2 lead in the bottom of the fifth inning, Coleman walked and proceeded to steal second and third, giving him 60 stolen bases on the year. When he came to bat again in the seventh inning, he was hit in the leg with a pitch by San Francisco reliever Frank Williams as the benches emptied. After the players from both sides displayed their typical harmless jockeying with no physical damage, calm momentarily returned. But when Herzog and Roger Craig encountered each other at home plate near the end of the melee, the managers entered into a shouting match and, within seconds, had to be restrained from one another. Ignoring Craig's unrelenting overtures as the San Francisco skipper trailed behind him, Herzog then stormed down the third base line and went after Joel Youngblood, who was wrestling with Ricky Horton—the pitcher whom Youngblood would strike in the arm with a line drive twelve months later. But unbeknownst to Whitey, the two were just playfully mocking the rest of the scene before Herzog threw them both to the turf. Young-blood, however, would later be serious in voicing his displeasure with Coleman. "It seems like the only time he hustles is when it's going to benefit himself."[1]

After peace had been restored another time and the players appeared to be returning to their dugouts, the situation turned ugly again when Giants third baseman Chris Brown went after Coleman and tackled him. Brown joined Craig and Williams in being ejected and, before departing, appeared intent on going into the stands behind the San Francisco dugout to confront a fan who had thrown an object in his direction. "This is the kind of thing that is remembered for a long time," warned Cardinals' television announcer Ken Wilson over the airwaves.[2]

The trouble between the two teams continued into 1987. On the evening of May 4, Giants outfielder Candy Maldonado drove a home run off Cox out of Busch Stadium in the seventh inning and taunted the St. Louis pitcher with a slow jog around the bases. Brown, who happened to be next in the batting order, was forced to pay when he was struck in the face with a fastball that broke the batter's jaw. Cox later admitted to throwing inside on Brown because of Maldonado's actions but denied trying to hit him. San Francisco would get its revenge served cold, as Aldrete's line drive off Cox would break the pitcher's foot the next time the pitcher faced the Giants two months later on July 9.

And now, with a trip to baseball's ultimate prize on the line, Cox—the only Cardinal pitcher to start at least twenty-five games in each of the past four seasons—was Herzog's choice to open the National League Championship Series, with Tudor slotted for the second game and Magrane and Mathews for Games 3 and 4.

Grabbing a copy of the *Post-Dispatch* on the afternoon of the series opener on October 6, the relaxing Mathews had played eigh-teen holes of golf the previous morning while looking forward to another few days of relaxation presumably ahead of him. While enjoying the paper, Mathews suddenly sprang to his feet. An article in the sports page announced that Cox had been injured and that Greg Mathews was taking his place to start Game One.

A GIANT FIGHT

Due to a sudden neck strain, Cox found he could not complete his pitching motion without pain. In the presence of the newspaper writers at Busch Stadium several hours before the opening game, he was seen wincing while attempting to do some practice windups in the Cardinals' locker room. Herzog had been on the golf links himself when he got the news. "I had just hit a drive 280 yards right down the middle. When I heard Dal [Maxvill] called, I thought Lindeman's back had gone out or that somebody had been in a wreck."[3]

Cox told Herzog he was not able to throw. At 4:00 p.m. Mathews, on one day rest after his two innings of relief in the regular-season finale, was officially inserted to start in Cox's place against the Giants' Rick Reuschel.

With temperatures dropping to the upper forties by nightfall, 55,331 patrons filled Busch Stadium for Game One—the largest crowd for any event in the history of the building, as playoff baseball returned to St. Louis after a one-year absence. As part of T-shirt promotion occurring downtown during the day, many of the fans were holding small white towels, which they waved furiously as the Cardinals took the field. "I did not sleep last night," the veteran Peña shared about his first career postseason appearance. "It is like my first year in rookie ball. I could not wait to put my uniform on and get to the field."[4]

Like the Giants, the Cardinals had operated with twenty-four players for nearly the entire year and would continue to do so in the playoffs. When probed by the media about not employing an extra eligible man, Maxvill responded, "Who cares? You're not going to use 25 anyhow."[5] When thinking of the sudden and strange misfortune of Cox, Herzog added, "I hope Tudor doesn't get pneumonia sitting in the dugout tonight."[6]

Mathews, answering the most unexpected summons, went right after Craig's men. He was able to get leadoff hitter Robby Thompson to tap a slow one-hopper to Driessen at first, who having been activated on August 31 (ten days before Clark's injury) made him eligible for the postseason. But Driessen bobbled the ball, leading to the first run of the series scoring in an unearned variety.

After Reuschel retired the first seven St. Louis batters, the Cardinals evened the score in the third, as Peña singled to center, was bunted to second by Mathews, and scored on a Coleman hit—his first RBI against the Giants in 36 at bats on the year, as he was barely able to push a groundball past shortstop José Uribe. But in the first stolen-base attempt against Reuschel in the nine starts he had made for the Giants since arriving from Pittsburgh, Coleman was gunned down by catcher Bob Brenly on a pitchout. Experts had decided that the Cardinals would have to assert their running game to be successful in the series, as their 14-24 performance in stolen bases against the Giants was their worst rate (58 percent) against any team for 1987, with Coleman being 3-8, although he had missed four of the games between the two clubs.

Leading off the top of the fourth for San Francisco was the outspoken Jeffrey Leonard, wearing the No. 00 on the back of his jersey and making only his seventh start since the third week of August because of a lingering wrist injury. In what would essentially be Mathews' only mistake through seven innings, Leonard clubbed a long home run deep over the center-field wall. After making contact, he immediately pointed to the stands in that direction with his right index finger, and, while rounding the bases, Leonard brazenly taunted the St. Louis crowd with his one-flap-down gesture.

The Cardinals answered Leonard immediately. Smith, entering the game batting .435 in nine LCS games in his career, tripled. A Driessen pop fly to left failed to drive him in and elicited boos from the crowd—from a combination of his failure in the key moment, his error in the first inning, and the fans' general yearning for Clark. McGee, whose availability for the series was in doubt due to a sprained wrist and thumb he had suffered when going for a Hubie Brooks fly ball on September 30, singled Smith home on a ball that mimicked Coleman's earlier RBI, sneaking it through the left side of the infield for a 2–2 tie.

The score remained knotted until the bottom of the sixth when the Cardinals snatched a 3–2 lead and loaded the bases with two out as Mathews came to the plate. Despite the pitcher having hit .191 during the 1987 regular season (although a marked improvement from his .047 rate of his rookie year), Herzog felt compelled to let Mathews swing the bat, given the shortage of arms on his staff and after processing all the conceivable alternative scenarios in his head.

On a hanging slider over the outer half of the plate from Reuschel, Mathews reached out and poked a single to center field. It drove in two runs, nearly matching his season RBI total of 3 and increasing the Cardinal advantage to 5–2. Mathews tried switch-hitting the previous year but had returned to right-handed only in 1987, exposing his pitching arm to injury and deciding it was worth the risk. "The reason why I started hitting left-handed was because I was hit in the left elbow in a game against the Giants last season [on July 21, the day before the brawl]," he explained. "I thought I had to protect myself."

After walking Thompson with one out in the eighth, Mathews was met at the mound by Herzog and given a standing ovation by the sellout crowd at Busch upon being lifted, to which he tipped his cap before descending down the dugout steps. He was replaced by Worrell, who grunted audibly with every fastball. Dayley helped in the eighth and finished the ninth as well, posting the save in a 5–3 victory, which ended on a Smith-to-Herr-to-Driessen double play and a final throw that the veteran first baseman dug out of the dirt. "He was the difference," Roger Craig said of the starter Mathews. "He kept us off balance with his great changeup. And he had just good enough of a fastball to keep us honest."[7]

With a more powerful windchill factor making the following afternoon feel even colder, the same record total of 55,331 crammed the ballpark the next day, as the teams quickly returned to play at 2:00 St. Louis time on Wednesday, October 7. While Tudor was making his first appearance of the year against the Giants, a southpaw was also on the hill for the Giants in Dave Dravecky. Herzog was thus counting on Lindeman to take Driessen's place in the lineup at first base, as Clark would miss his twenty-eighth consecutive game since his ankle injury. But despite his sore back finally feeling better, Lindeman showed up in the locker room now stricken with the flu. "It's been quite a year," the frustrated rookie granted.[8]

Lindeman would fight through the sickness and play, but his fatigue would permeate the rest of the healthy lineup in Game Two. "Despite a stadium full of red coats and sweaters," reported the

Post-Dispatch, "the lethargic performance kept most fans huddled in their seats."[9]

After the Cardinals were retired in the bottom of the first (when they requested to home plate umpire Ed Montague that Dravecky remove his white undershirt and wear a dark one instead), Craig's men went on the attack. In his first career at bat against Tudor, the Giants' second-year sensation Will Clark, the sweet-swinging first baseman from Mississippi State University, nailed a two-run homer over the right-field wall in the second inning. Clark, whose 35 round-trippers in the regular season were the most by a San Francisco player in fourteen years, almost passed the runner on first, Maldonado, who had stopped to watch the flyball and even retreated back toward first as Clark nearly ran into him.

When Leonard struck in the fourth inning with a solo blast once again to straightaway center to make it 3–0, he slowed his trot to nearly a walk when he went around the bases as another tidal wave of anger crashed upon the San Francisco outfielder from the spectators. "But St. Louis fans rank no higher than 'fourth or fifth in the league' for obnoxious behavior to visiting teams," Dave Luecking quoted from the Giants' outfielder. "'There's Philadelphia, New York, Chicago ahead of them,'" the Philly-native Leonard claimed.[10]

The sunny day gradually gave way to an overcast sky, as the shadows disappeared from the field along with the St. Louis bats. With the uncertain status of Cox, Herzog again was hesitant to go deep into his bullpen and had Tudor labor through eight innings. The southpaw, still regaining his strength from his interrupted regular season, issued 10 hits over the course of a 5–0 San Francisco win. It was a masterful two-hit performance from Dravecky, who after the Pirates' Brian Fisher was the only pitcher to shut out the Cardinals at home all year. It was also the Redbirds' first-ever loss of a League Championship Series game in Busch Stadium. Dravecky had pitched three other shutouts for the Giants since arriving in a trade from San Diego on July 5 and had broken at least five St. Louis bats on the day by consistently running his fastball on the inside corner. Furthermore, with his sleight-of-hand mechanics toward first base, Dravecky had also shut down the St. Louis running game with the only steal attempt coming from Peña, who was thrown out on another successful pitchout called by Craig. In Coleman's lone time on base, Dravecky threw over to Will Clark eight times. The Cardinals never got a runner to third all day. The performance meant the left-hander had now run his string of scoreless innings in the playoffs to nineteen and two-thirds, trailing back to his 1984 work with the Padres—with whom Dravecky had beaten the Giants to clinch the Western Division title that season. "I'm not going to stand here and say I was ever any better," he said in the visitor's clubhouse. "This is by far the best game I've ever pitched."[11]

As the series shifted to the West Coast with the teams even at one win apiece, the Giants' renewed confidence perhaps caused them to pour gasoline on the rhetorical fire. Some of the San Francisco players claimed that an error by Ozzie Smith in the eighth inning of Game Two (which allowed two extra runs to score) was a result of Smith "hot dogging it" and that the St. Louis club was nothing without their speed. For their part, the Cardinals absorbed the barbs with little mind. "Even before the playoffs started, their manager said he was supposed to be playing the Mets," Jack Clark scoffed, pointing to his team's 95 wins during the season, which were 5 more than San Francisco had accomplished. "We feel privileged to be standing on their sacred soil. They've already won the World Series."[12] A bit more diplomatically, Herr reminded that "Los Angeles shut down our running game early in the 1985 series, too. I think it's a little premature to say they [the Giants] have shut down our running game." Pundits were pointing to the four-straight games the Cardinals lost at Candlestick back in July, when they grounded into eight double plays in just two of the games and Craig ordered his staff to pitch around Clark. Before the Cardinals arrived in town for that set, the Giants had dropped twenty-one of their previous thirty-one games at home.

There was also the idea—one which had been perpetually regurgitated from the newspapers for the entire decade—that Herzog's club could not play on grass. It was a refrain of which the manager had grown weary. "You guys really make a big deal out of that," the manager shot back at the writers. "How many times did we beat the Mets at Shea? Four times. How many times did the Mets beat the Giants? Nine out of twelve. Don't you think the Giants are glad they're not playing the Mets?"[13]

Even so, Herzog made certain his team was as prepared as possible for the unpredictable ecosystem of Candlestick Park, where virtually no one enjoyed playing—let alone during the cold winds of fall, and where former Giants center fielder Bobby Murcer was known to take his bats into the sauna in between innings. "That's what we like to hear," Roger Craig said of the disdain visiting clubs had for the stadium. "People come to our park and say, 'We just want to play three and get the hell out of town.'"[14] Added Maldonado, "When it's cold and windy, we like it. When it's foggy, we *really* like it."[15]

After the Cardinals arrived in California early on the off day of October 8, Herzog scheduled a workout for 5:30 p.m. to coincide with the time of the first pitch for Game Three the following evening, the part of the day when distracting shadows started to creep over the grandstand. During the practice session, Herzog took a page from one of his first mentors, Casey Stengel (to whom many compared Whitey because of Stengel's baseball acumen), by mostly hitting pop flies and few ground balls during infield practice. Stengel had stunned onlookers in doing so during pregame warmups with his newly formed Mets in the early 1960s, but he reasoned that balls up in the Bay's unpredictable winds would give his defenders the most trouble.

During the workout, another discouraging injury blow struck the Cardinals, and it occurred on one of the limited ground balls taken by the infielders. Pendleton, wearing turf shoes instead of cleats for the practice on the natural surface of Candlestick, slipped on the damp grass while fielding a grounder and twisted his ankle, putting his status for the following night in doubt.

As in St. Louis, a record crowd in San Francisco had greeted the teams for Game Three. On a mild, clear evening of 63 degrees but with near-drought conditions persisting in northern California since March, a total of 57,913 filled the seats for the ballpark's first postseason game in sixteen years. Herzog anointed the rookie Magrane with the pitching assignment, while the home team would send another left-hander to the mound in Atlee Hammaker, who had missed all of 1986 with rotator-cuff surgery after having been a Herzog selection for the 1983 National League All-Star squad.

Having made every effort up through the Cardinals' batting

practice session before the game to loosen his ankle, Pendleton finally informed Herzog he was unavailable—thus forcing the manager to juggle things once again. Standing in left field and shagging flies during pregame was Tom Lawless, who had logged only 25 at bats all season. Red Schoendienst picked up his fungo bat and got Lawless's attention with a line drive near the player's feet, as Lawless was waved toward the dugout and informed he was starting at third base for the first time on the year. The absence of Clark and Pendleton from the lineup meant that Lindeman would be batting in the cleanup spot for only the second time all season and the first time since April. "It was terrible for us that Jack and Terry got hurt," Lindeman said in 2023, "but that gave myself and Dan Driessen the opportunity to play first base—and I was much more comfortable there than in the outfield. Unlike now with the playoffs, where a wild card team can get hot and win, back then it was the two best teams. So, the intensity of the League Championship Series against the Giants was great."[16]

That intensity carried over from the field to the seating area. Similar to before Game One in St. Louis, the reserve and starting players from both sides were introduced to the crowd in San Francisco. Sitting along the third base line behind the dugout were the Cardinals' wives and other family members, who had lugged along large bunches of red and white balloons that they planned to release when the players were announced. But many of the balloons were popped by nearby Giants fans with lit cigarettes, while Nick Leyva's three-year-old son had a souvenir ball ripped out his hands. "Pushing, shoving, and some other discourtesies were reported," read the news story of the scene.[17] After ushers intervened, the family members were invited to watch the rest of the game in the Giants executives' area of the luxury boxes. Herzog, while sympathetic to the alleged assault (especially when getting reports that his wife Mary Lou was shaking her clenched fist at some folks and was ready to fight), offered that "if you're going to bring balloons, they're going to be popped."[18]

The Giants did not waste any time in getting their bats popping. After a flurry of hits and a Magrane wild pitch had quickly made the score 3–0, Leonard added a fourth tally with his third home run in as many days, touring the bases once again with one flap down as he waltzed through his most time-consuming stroll to date. "Leonard's gait became slower and slower, until, finally, he walked the last few steps down the third base line," noticed Mike Smith in the *Post-Dispatch*. "A rowdy reception in the on-deck circle and a curtain call for Leonard followed."[19] With the television camera squarely upon his face in the dugout and the crowd beckoning him, Leonard could be seen uttering, "Let 'em wait!" as he delayed his reappearance.

A more dramatic display, however, was sure to follow—and was even promised by Leonard himself. "He's got one [home run trot] that takes 45 seconds," Maldonado warned with a laugh. "Wait until he hits one he knows is gone." Leonard confirmed that he had grandiose plans. "I've got four or five of them," he revealed of his celebratory home run jaunts—the best of which, he claimed, had already gone on display a couple of years ago against the Cardinals. "[St. Louis pitcher] John Stuper knocked me down. Next time up, I hit one out. I walked all the way from third."[20]

Desperate for his own clout, Herzog ordered the hobbling Jack Clark to the plate as a pinch hitter in the fifth. When Hammaker ran the count to 0-2 on the former Giant, the crowd rose to a standing ovation. Clark went down looking on strikes as he was serenaded back to the dugout by an acoustic version of the song "Aloha 'Oe" over the speakers, which was customary when an opponent struck out at Candlestick.

All watching inside the stadium and across the country on television were convinced the punchless Cardinals were dead for the game, and perhaps, the series. But while one veteran was unable to turn the momentum, another soon would.

Taking over the pitching duties for Herzog in the bottom of the fifth was Bob Forsch, who promptly hit Leonard on the right shoulder the next time he came to the plate. Forsch then short-circuited a Giants' assault with one out and the bases loaded, which otherwise could have blown the game wide open. "Ex-Cardinals from the 1987 team still talk about Forsch hitting Jeffrey Leonard," Horton would say in 2023. "He was great player and had a great series. He owned most of us on the pitching staff, me in particular. But he had put the one-flap-down one too many times, and when the emotional tide was turning in favor of the Giants, the ship was righted when Forsch basically said, 'We're not going to take that anymore.'"[21]

Lindeman, who like Clark had watched a third strike from Hammaker go past him in the fourth inning, got things going on the offensive side in the sixth by driving a two-run homer to the opposite field in right, just out of the reach of at outstretched Maldonado at the fence to plate the Cardinals' first runs in sixteen innings. In the top of the seventh, five straight soft hits followed along with a Lindeman sacrifice fly for a sudden 6–4 St. Louis lead.

The Giants fought back when pinch hitter Harry Spilman, who had one homer all year, took Worrell deep for the first run ever given up by the Cardinals' pitching staff in the ninth inning of a League Championship Series game, closing the gap to 6–5. But there it would remain, as the Cardinals grabbed the pivotal game in the series thanks in large part to Lindeman's resurgent bat. "Jimmy's going to be the man for us," Ozzie had correctly predicted to his wife before the game that night, to which Mrs. Smith agreed.[22] In a microcosm of the 1987 season, key contributions were witnessed during the evening from not only unexpected starters Lawless and Lindeman but also Oquendo, Ford, Driessen, and Lance Johnson off the bench.

THE CANDLESTICK BASEBALL ATTENDANCE RECORD LASTED only one day, as a new mark of 57,997 jammed inside for Game Four on October 10. Temperatures were again pleasant for autumn in the region, settling in the lower sixties, although the winds had picked up from the west at sixteen miles per hour and, as was typical at Candlestick, occasionally gusted and swirled with even greater ferocity. After being plunked by Forsch, Leonard was expected by the Cardinals to come back swinging—with words, if nothing else. "There hasn't been anything that has stopped him from popping off or saying anything to the press," Worrell said before the fourth game. "I was sure he was going to have some retort."[23]

It was finally Cox's turn to take the mound, wearing no undershirt and ignoring his recent neck stiffness. Opposing him was Mike Krukow, winner of only 5 games during a rough 1987 campaign after notching 20 the season prior. Krukow, who had sustained bruised ribs in the July 1986 brawl in St. Louis which landed him on the disabled list, denied there was any remaining individual resentment toward the Cardinals. "It adds spice to all of this, and it puts people in the seats, and it sells newspapers," he told the press of the previous scraps. "But this really isn't personal. There are no real ill-feelings here. I have a lot of respect for their organization and their manager. Mike Roarke used to be my pitching coach [with the Cubs], so you know I respect him."[24]

San Francisco's main target, Coleman, however, again drew the ire of the Giants early in the contest by sliding outside the baseline near second base and knocking over the shortstop Uribe. (Having been the property of the Cardinals for four years until being part of the trade with the Giants for Clark, Uribe had previously gone under the surname of Gonzalez—which according to Vin Scully, broadcasting the series for NBC, truly made him "the player to be named later.")[25]

After jumping out to an early 2–0 lead, the Cardinals were soon overwhelmed with the Giants' power. A home run by Thompson got Craig's men on the scoreboard, as the tally stood at 2–1 as Leonard strode to the plate in the fifth inning with the crowd whipped into an anticipatory frenzy.

Leonard swung and lofted what seemed to be a routine fly to left, under which Coleman got camped. While tracking the ball, the outfielder suddenly began taking a few walking steps backward that quickly turned into a gallop. The baseball had gotten caught in a sudden Candlestick zephyr and kept carrying and floating along, finally coming back to earth just over the chain-link fence that lined the warning track. Young fans dropped down from the bleachers that stood several feet back from the field and scrambled after the souvenir as Leonard, who after July 31 hit only 3 home runs in the regular season, had knocked his 4th of the series—which already tied a League Championship Series record shared by Bob Robertson of the Pirates and Steve Garvey of the Dodgers.

Bob Brenly followed with a solo shot in the eighth, while Krukow—like Reuschel, a veteran who had found greater success later in his career after beginning his playing days with the Cubs—continued dumping his slow curve into the strike zone. He and Cox both went the distance as the Giants prevailed 4–2, with all of the San Francisco tallies coming on the 3 home runs, while the

Cardinals posted 9 hits that were all singles. For the first time in League Championship Series history, both teams used only nine players, as each manager sought to preserve his roster for the protracted battle that lay ahead. Brenly, who shared the Giants' catching duties with Bob Melvin, was among the many who were already physically and mentally spent from the long season. "By the end of the year," he said of the men who worked behind the plate like himself, "you feel like a used car."

The brash, rampaging Leonard was now batting .538 over the first four games and did not care if he was insulting anyone with his words or actions. "I'm the kind of guy if you invite me over for dinner," he described himself, "and your wife or mother bakes a cake and it's terrible, I'm gonna tell her it's terrible."[26]

FOR THE THIRD STRAIGHT DAY ON OCTOBER 11, A RECORD crowd to watch a baseball game had squeezed into Candlestick, with the figure rising measurably for Game Five to 59,363—made possible by the selling of tickets in a pavilion normally used only for 49ers football games, offering those willing to purchase them an obstructed view of the action. The San Francisco weather for the Sunday afternoon continued to warm further, reaching an unseasonable seventy degrees for the 1:30 p.m. start time. But the locale's infamous wind would become a factor as the day wore on.

In a rematch of Game One, Mathews and Reuschel were again pitted against one another, and Morris received his first start in right field in the place of Curt Ford, with Herzog looking for someone who could drive the ball and with Ford struggling to come back from his hand injury. Through Game Four, the pitchers had ironically led the way for the weak Cardinal offense in posting a total of 3 RBIs, while the big bats of Clark (still out of the lineup), McGee (1 RBI in the series), Pendleton (1), and Herr (0) were largely silent. In the first inning, Herr was finally able to break through by producing a sacrifice fly to give St. Louis an early lead, but the Giants answered in the bottom half with a run of their own.

Not only had the Cardinals been unable to convert hits into runs, but they also continued their inability to steal bases against the San Francisco pitchers and catchers. The relentless Giants, meanwhile, were taking control of the series with the weapons they had relied upon all season—hitting home runs and turning double plays on defense, two categories in which they would match or exceed LCS records in the third and fourth innings.

San Francisco thwarted a Cards attack in the third by notching another twin-killing, their 10th double play of the series, which set a new LCS mark after having led all of baseball during the season with 183. "They've got the best young infield in the league," Herzog claimed. "They're a lot like we were in '82."[27] It was followed in the bottom half with a homer by Kevin Mitchell, the former Mets' prospect and part of New York's trade for McReynolds with the Padres before coming to San Francisco on July 5, along with Dravecky. Mitchell's blast was the Giants' 9th home run of the series, tying the Cubs' LCS record from 1984. Ultimately, Mathews was forced from the game with a strained right quadricep. Furthering the sense of an impending collapse by St. Louis, McGee became the third Cardinal runner in the series to be caught stealing on a pitchout and hit-and-run during the Redbirds' fourth, despite Pendleton trying to protect him by throwing his bat at the Reuschel offering and missing.

Amid a shadow of doom surrounding Herzog's squad, a troubling atmospheric event was enveloping the field as well. A fierce wind had picked up by the middle of the game, measured only at twelve miles an hour while the teams had been taking batting practice but had increased up to twenty-five by the fourth inning. Spontaneous cyclones were legendary at Candlestick Park, where the infield was given extra water before games to keep the topsoil from blowing into patrons' eyes in the lower stands. Once, the infamous wind had knocked the cap off the head of Mets pitcher Ed Lynch during his delivery and was propelled all the way to the center-field fence before it could be retrieved.

"A beach ball blew onto the field," noticed Horrigan from the press box, as home plate umpire Jim Quick was forced to stop play to retrieve it. "Balloons blew onto the field. Hot dog wrappers blew from the first-base line to the left-field fence. The wall line looked like a New Orleans gutter during Mardi Gras. Things were getting uglier by the second."[28] Another beach ball surprised Driessen as it rolled up from behind and struck him in the back of the legs near first base. It was a humorous sight to behold when Eric Gregg, the girthy umpire working the right-field line for Game Five, tried to run down a roll of toilet paper that was twisting through the outfield grass like a jungle snake.

Unlike the previous day, Forsch could not stem the San Francisco offensive tide. Bombarded in the fourth in relief of Mathews, he allowed 3 hits and a walk while retiring no one, as the Giants' lead increased to 6–3. There the final score would remain, as Reuschel was rescued in a tremendous relief effort by mountainous left-hander Joe Price, who after seven years in the Majors was making his initial playoff appearance. Price permitted a lone hit and a walk over the final five innings, as Craig's men were now up three games to two, putting them only one victory away from his July prophesy of topping Herzog for the National League flag. With McGee's lone stolen base attempt, the Cardinals were now unsuccessful in that department in four of the first five series games, keeping them at a 77-28 record in 1987 in games in which they had stolen at least one base but 20-28 in games in which they had not. Ironically, Leonard was the only Giants' starter not to reach base in the game, as Will Clark passed him for the series lead in hits with eight.

As the series went back to the Midwest with Cardinals' fans knowing their team's back was against the wall, Leonard was asked if he were concerned about the reception he would receive for the second round in Busch Stadium. Channeling Dizzy Dean, he answered ambiguously. "I may run my mouth too much, but I'm like that. I'm outspoken. When I started off my career, I was like that. I got no respect. I was just a big guy with a big mouth. When you say things, you have to back them up."[29] Besides, Leonard added, he was too concerned with individual vendettas to worry about any abuse from the crowd. "I've got a personal thing that I still haven't taken care of," he said in speaking of Forsch, whom Leonard said he would have charged at the mound in Game Three had it not been a playoff game.[30]

Herzog was hopeful that one more twenty-four-hour stretch of rest for Jack Clark on the travel day of October 12 would have him ready to play in Game Six. By the afternoon of the 13th, however, he was still unable to go. Devising alternate possibilities with Dravecky once again on the mound, the manager toyed with the idea of putting Peña at first base and Lake at catcher, with the latter having batted .308 against left-handers on the year. But despite Peña being seen with a first baseman's glove during pregame warmups, Herzog decided to keep Lindeman at the position. When word reached the television booth that Clark remained unavailable, it was humorously suggested by Scully that Clark's absence was so meaningful that he should be named the series MVP if the Cardinals lost.

As for the actual front-runner for the award wearing the Giants' uniform, the starting pitcher for the Cardinals in Game Five pulled no punches. "I don't like Jeff Leonard," John Tudor said unconditionally. "It's not a secret to him or anyone else."[31]

Those making their way to the seats at Busch Stadium demonstrated their agreement with Tudor with equal clarity. From the moment Leonard emerged from the dugout for batting practice, the St. Louis fans relentlessly tormented him everywhere he ventured on the field during the night—through several pitches into his first at bat, when he stood on base, as he jogged out to his position, as he ran back to the visitors' bench, and anywhere else he dared to show his face at the corner of Broadway and Clark. In a scene reminiscent of the 1934 World Series in Detroit with Dean's Cardinals teammate Joe Medwick, debris was even fired at Leonard's direction from the left-field bleachers, including a cowbell in the bottom of the second inning (which was perhaps the fault of his fellow San Francisco outfielder Chili Davis, who earlier had referred to St. Louis as a "cow town"), an assortment of coins in the third, and, in the sixth inning, another cowbell while Leonard was pursuing a fly ball in the left-field corner—where he was also showered with two beers.

As the umpires and police officers gathered, members of the Giants' bullpen seated down the foul line stood and pointed to the individual in the stands responsible for the beer dumping, and the culprit was ejected. But an unsatisfied Craig continued his protest to home plate umpire Bob Engel while storming back to the dugout and threatened to pull his players off the field for their safety if the behavior continued. Engel got on the phone to stadium public address announcer John Ulett, who reminded the fans that the throwing of objects onto the playing field was a violation of St. Louis city ordinances. The TV cameras, now following Leonard's every move, showed him on the Giants' bench during the next half inning, where he winked and tipped his cap to the audience.

Whether stoked by the spectators' hatred for Leonard or not, a fighting spirit of pitching and defense reminiscent of 1982 and 1985 returned to Busch. Tudor sailed along inning after inning, effectively dangling his superlative changeup on the outside corner and disposing of the San Francisco bats in regular order. After having complained about the lack of inspiring music on the PA system in between innings—claiming "it's not quite like the theme from *Rocky* coming through the speakers"—a small smile could be seen on the face of the stoic pitcher as he left the mound in the third inning with the theme song from the popular boxing movie playing.[32] He was bolstered by McGee, who showed a flash of his defensive days of old, grabbing a line drive in the left-center gap with his left wrist still heavily taped, which saved 2 runs—and ultimately the game and, for the time being, the team's pennant hopes.

The contest's lone run came on a carbon-copy of a play from earlier in the series. Peña, leading off the second inning, drove a sinking liner toward Maldonado, which the right fielder lost in the lights, just as he had done on a similar batted ball in San Francisco. In a sliding attempt to stop it, Maldonado let the ball skip past him to the wall as the Cardinal catcher motored into third with a triple. The Giants' outfielder had a chance at redemption in the next at bat when Oquendo lofted a fly ball down the line, but Peña beat the throw home for the sacrifice fly and a 1–0 lead. The St. Louis crowd frantically waved their small white towels once again, covering the ballpark in an October snowstorm.

After striking out Thompson with two out in the seventh inning and the tying run on second, Tudor—with no baserunners having attempted a stolen base on him and Peña in the fifty-one innings they had worked together on the season—carried the shutout into the eighth when Herzog summoned his two-headed closer of Worrell and Dayley from the bullpen. The game ended with Herr, himself seeming to revert to his '85 form as well, making a great play to rob Uribe. Worrell was seen rushing in to back him up on the play from right field and seal the 1–0 win, as Herzog once again pulled his unique switch in sending Dayley (who now had not allowed a run in sixteen innings in his postseason career) to the mound. The move made Worrell the first player since Babe Ruth in 1918 to pitch and play another position in a postseason game. Dravecky, working on five days' rest since his shutout in the same ballpark, excelled again in allowing only 5 hits, a walk, and 1 run through six innings. The decision for a National League champion for 1987 would thus come down to a single battle.

FOR THE FOURTH STRAIGHT TIME, THE OFFICIAL BUSCH Stadium figure through the turnstiles was 55,331 on October 14, as all seven games in the series had set or equaled new baseball attendance records in both stadiums. Stunned by the paralyzing effect Tudor had on his batters, Roger Craig scribbled out his 123rd different lineup of the season for Game Seven in trying to create the best matchup against Cox, Herzog's choice for the ultimate clash. Craig decided to place the versatile Mike Aldrete in the leadoff spot, with the Giants having gone a perfect 7-0 with him batting first during the season—and thus making him the first hitter Cox would face in the wake of Aldrete having broken the pitcher's right foot with his live drive back in July. Also new in Craig's lineup was veteran infielder Chris Speier, who was on base when Aldrete's liner struck Cox and who sixteen years earlier as a rookie in 1971 had batted .357 for the Giants in their NLCS loss to the Pirates before appearing in the 1981 NLCS for Montreal as well. Speier, in relieving the struggling second baseman Thompson and his .105 average in the series, would be thinking of his father during the game, who was in the hospital back in California after suffering a heart attack.

But the core of Craig's batting order remained the same, including Missouri's Most Wanted villain. Playfully donning Jeffrey Leonard's jacket and heading out to left field during the Giants' batting practice session was Kevin Mitchell, who was immediately assailed with insults from bleacher fans who thought it was Leonard himself.

While Cox was making third start in 1987 when having three days' rest (and being victorious the previous two times, including the Eastern Division clincher against Montreal), Hammaker had posted a 1-8 record on the road in 1987. Leonard struck the initial blow, singling in the first inning for his 10th hit of the series, which tied him with Ozzie Smith's performance in 1985 for the most hits in a single LCS. Leonard, however, was left stranded as the game remained scoreless heading into the bottom of the second.

After opening the Cardinals' turn with a single, the third baseman Pendleton strained his abdomen while bolting from first to third on another hit by Peña. Pendleton was replaced on defense in the next half inning by Lawless, but in the meantime, he was able to jog home leisurely as McGee singled him in for a 1–0 lead. A passed ball by Brenly followed, putting two more men in scoring position for Jose Oquendo, who was making his fourth start of the series in right field. It was the third birthday for Oquendo's daughter Adianez, and her father promised her a present which she would not forget.

Herzog's "secret weapon" waved his bat menacingly at Hammaker while possessing only 2 home runs in his Major League career to date—one in his rookie year with the Mets in 1983 and one for the Cardinals on July 25, 1987, both of which had occurred against the Giants in Candlestick Park.

Oquendo took advantage of a poor curve ball from Hammaker, which floated harmlessly toward him at the letters. He drove it far over the left-field wall for a lightning-quick 4–0 St. Louis lead and only the second Cardinals homer of the series after Lindeman's in Game Three. As Oquendo crossed home plate, one of the first teammates to greet him was the Cardinals' usual power source, a capless Jack Clark, who lifted Jose up in the air as if it were Adianez and her father reenacting a scene at the Oquendo home.

Continuing their defensive brilliance reminiscent of earlier years in the decade, the Cardinals short-circuited a Giants' counterattack in the third on a 3–6–1 double play that was started gracefully by Lindeman with men on first and second and nobody out. Turning the tables on San Francisco and beating them at their own game, Herzog's men doused the Giants' assault with another double play in the fourth on a ball back to Cox, who spun and fired to Smith who leapt high into the air and threw on target to first over a hard-charging Leonard, who attacked the shortstop with a flying elbow as the two players exchanged heated words after the play.

After a decade in the Majors, Ozzie was still picking everything with his glove but continued to make more throws on the run to take the stress off his shoulder. Earlier in the series, Scully respectfully compared the slow-moving baseball coming from the shortstop to "a ping pong ball in a wind storm" as it fluttered over to first.[33] But now, over the national airwaves on NBC-TV, the broadcaster could not hide his admiration. "I've been watching Ozzie Smith for ten years, and each time I think I have seen him do it all, he adds yet another paragraph."[34]

The shortstop was not finished with producing defensive highlights for the evening. Serendipity, karma, and skill would implode together in the top of the sixth as Smith impacted the game with his glove once again.

Cox, still holding the 4–0 lead, quickly retired the first two San Francisco hitters, with Leonard next. He hacked at a low fastball and drove a liner destined for left-center, and with it, the all-time record of 11 hits to overtake Ozzie's mark. But Smith executed a miraculous catch, leaping and initially tipping the ball up in the air before grabbing it on the way back down. In his final at bat in the ninth, Leonard was denied the record once again as he grounded into a force out, keeping his series hit total at 10.

The acrobatic play by Smith lit the flame for one last offensive thrust by the Cardinals and the long-awaited return of Whiteyball in the bottom half of the sixth. With Oquendo on third, Coleman drew a walk, promptly swiped his first stolen base of the series, and then sprinted home behind Oquendo on a line drive single to center by Tom Herr off Craig's ace out of the bullpen, Scott Garrelts, who had fanned 12 Cardinals in just over six innings of work against St. Louis during the regular season. It was a crowning jewel most fitting for the Cardinals' return to the National League's throne, as Coleman's tally proved to be the last run of the night in a 6–0 whitewashing, with Cox going the distance while issuing no walks.

When Chili Davis golfed a fly ball to Coleman for the last out in left field at 10:20 p.m. St. Louis time, Scully told the national audience that Herzog's men were "Minnesota-bound!" to face the Twins in the World Series.

Cox sprinted in the direction of his left fielder with his arms spread wide open and then ran back toward the reserve players charging out of the dugout to meet him at the mound. Leading the cheers in the front row of the stands was Stan Musial, watching St.

Louis win the seventh game of a postseason series for the eighth time in its history—the most by any franchise. The revelry resulted in Smith having his jersey stripped off to reveal his three-quarters undershirt, as he copied Herr's seat-cushion celebration from April and grabbed a spare white towel that had made its way onto the field. Ozzie waved it vigorously above his head, mimicking the sea of those being spun in ecstasy by the delirious fans.

By the time he was corralled by reporter Jay Randolph in the home locker room for an interview, Smith was no longer gripping the towel, but rather a bottle of champagne. In front of the NBC camera, his demeanor had settled down from excitement to one of raw satisfaction when he was asked about the Giants, and in particular, Leonard's flying elbow at him near second base. "Some of the greatest teams in baseball history have been beaten. These guys [the Giants] came in here like they were the greatest thing since Corn Flakes. They had no respect for us at all. I hope those guys learn that you respect every club you play, because you can be beaten on any given day. They came to talk, and we came to play."[35]

Mathews, across the way, was grasping his own container of bubbly. "Send a bottle over to Leonard," he suggested.[36]

In holding the powerful Giants scoreless in the final twenty-two innings of the series and logging two consecutive shutouts, the Cardinals had set another pair of LCS records. As in the regular season, the capture of the National League pennant had been a true team effort, with everyone contributing something, which was Herzog's precise plan every time he left spring training. "I think that's the way it's been all year," Lindeman said in summation. "We had to replace Jack. We can't replace Jack, but we ended up coming through in the end."[37]

As evidenced by the evenly matched battle, Leonard, with his .417 average and 4 homers, was named the MVP of the series despite being on the losing side—the last person so honored as of 2024. As part of a stipulation in his contract that he had signed three years earlier, Leonard would be paid a $50,000 bonus by the Giants for the achievement.

As the Cardinals players continued their partying in the clubhouse and gradually made their way to the showers, Herzog stuck around the to perform the requisite interviews, celebrated quietly with a Budweiser in his office, and then brought home a souvenir to Mary Lou—a congratulatory telegram from Yankees owner George Steinbrenner, which had become something of a tradition between the southern Illinois native and the shipbuilding mogul. "Every time I win something, he's the first person to send me a wire. I've got five of them framed at home."[38]

FOR THE REDBIRDS, IT WAS NOW OFF TO THE TWIN CITIES for the start of the World Series—and to a ballpark dreaded by opponents as much as Candlestick.

8

Battle on the Mississippi

About the only good thing about the Metrodome was that it was super loud. That was cool. I don't think people can understand, unless you were there, how loud it was. You could sit next to each other on the bench and not be able to have a conversation during those games.
—Jim Lindeman, 2023

FOR ONLY THE SECOND TIME IN BASEBALL HISTORY, TWO teams that had posted losing records in the previous season would meet in the World Series. With Las Vegas having set them at 150:1 odds to win the championship at the beginning of the year, the Minnesota Twins had even outdone the Cardinals in surprising the baseball world in 1987. Donning new uniforms, they claimed their first pennant in twenty-two years by winning the American League West with only 85 wins and downed the favored Tigers in the ALCS, making Minnesota the seventh different team to represent the Junior Circuit in the World Series in as many years. They were led by their young manager Tom Kelly, himself born in Minnesota but raised in New Jersey before playing one year in the Majors with the Twins in 1975 as a backup first baseman. He was an organization man through and through, launching a coaching career in the Twins' Minor League system after being released as a player in 1978. Guiding Double-A Orlando to the Southern League title in 1981, Kelly joined the Major League staff two years later before taking the managerial reins for the final twenty-three games of 1986 in replacing Ray Miller. Kelly went 12-11 and was thus able to keep the 59-80 team he inherited out of last place. Despite the successful trial, it would be the end of November before Kelly was named the permanent manager.

Appearing slightly older than his thirty-seven years, with grayed temples and thick-rimmed glasses, the tall, quiet, polite Kelly was the youngest manager in the World Series since Sparky Anderson of the Reds in 1970. He took little credit for the team's success and instead wanted the spotlight shone on the players—such as when he remained in the dugout after the American League pennant clincher at Tiger Stadium while letting his team celebrate by itself on the field.

Kelly's affability had endeared him to those in the Land of Ten Thousand Lakes and beyond. In the days following Minnesota's victory in the playoffs, a man made his way through security and into Kelly's office, where he told the Twins' manager that God had instructed him to pitch in the World Series. Kelly smiled politely, telling the man apologetically that the prospect needed to be on the roster before September to be eligible in the postseason, an explanation that the man accepted before he turned and walked out.

A couple days later, the annual flock of writers converged for World Series Media Day in Minneapolis in advance of Game One. As the proceedings got underway, two local sixth graders had escaped their classroom, made their way into the press conference, and tried to conduct an interview with the manager—which Kelly granted.

In having come through the ranks of the Twins' system as a coach, Kelly had personally developed many of the players he was now managing in the World Series. Despite struggling for the following five years, a bountiful 1982 Minnesota rookie crop that included catcher Tim Laudner, third baseman Gary Gaetti, first baseman Kent Hrbek, outfielders Tom Brunansky and Randy Bush, and pitcher Frank Viola had set a successful foundation. In 1984 they were joined by a stocky center fielder named Kirby Puckett, who in 1987 was the only Twin named to the All-Star Game during the first of three-straight seasons in which he would lead the American League in hits.

They had all grown up inside their intriguing home stadium, the

Metrodome, which debuted the same season as the Twins' grand rookie harvest of 1982 and sat closer to the Mississippi River than did Busch Stadium. Serving the Twins, the NFL's Vikings, and teams of the University of Minnesota, the multipurpose facility had functioned without air conditioning for its first year, causing a stillness that contributed to more home runs being hit early in the stadium's existence before an updated ventilation system was installed. The Metrodome featured an air-supported fiberglass roof that, due to another lack of foresight, had been painted white and thus made every fly ball an adventure for visiting players, and for the Twins themselves on occasion. The majority of the outfield "wall" was also unique, comprised of a soft pliable canvas that stood only seven feet tall in center field but rose to twenty-three feet in right field, where it concealed a stack of compressed football seats. It disparagingly became known as the "Hefty Bag," as balls hit against the material would deaden and fall straight to the ground like a stricken bird. Brunansky, having become the Twins' starting right fielder as a rookie a month after the building opened, had mastered the phenomenon by 1987; he would allow a ball hit off the canvas to take a bounce on the warning track before grabbing it barehanded and, in one motion, setting his body and firing to second base to prevent a double.

In addition to its internal oddities, some found the exterior of the Metrodome to be equally unappealing—such as Ed Sherman of the *Chicago Tribune*, who was quoted by World Series broadcaster Tim McCarver, describing it as "your grandma's old Jell-O mold."[1] Even so, it was the cozy, familiar sanctuary of the Minnesota fans and their beloved Twins, who despite having the worst road record in the Major Leagues in 1987 at 29-52 had won an MLB-best 56 games at home, where their backers waved their Homer Hankies that were similar to the white towels the Cardinals' followers had twirled during the NLCS at Busch Stadium. "The gimmick has become so popular," reported Bill Smith of the *Post-Dispatch* about the Hankies from enemy territory before the start of the World Series, "that more than 200,000 already have been distributed. They sell for $1 each, or 50 cents with a coupon."[2]

The aspect of the Metrodome that visiting clubs found most disturbing, however, was the unparalleled noise generated by

Twins' fans inside the structure, which could easily equal or surpass 102 decibels—the figure registered by a full-sized passenger jet at takeoff. Some opponents, however, embraced the feverish atmosphere. "About the only good thing about the Metrodome was that it was super loud," Lindeman would recall in 2023. "That was cool. I don't think people can understand, unless you were there, how loud it was. You could sit next to each other on the bench and not be able to have a conversation during those games."[3] A handful of the Cardinals (Herr, Peña, Clark, McGee, and Smith) had played in the 1985 All-Star Game held at the site, providing them at least one experience with the sensory challenges of the building.

But with the environment being completely foreign to the majority of the St. Louis roster, Herzog got the team to Minneapolis two days before the start of the Series to get them an extra workout in the strange surroundings. As with the winds of Candlestick, Herzog directed his coaches to concentrate on hitting pop flies to the fielders to let them become familiar with the bright roof, in addition to giving the outfielders some line drives against the Hefty Bag, where pinball-like hops had been known to occur and which only Brunansky's wizardry had been able to conquer.

No doubt, the Metrodome was a laboratory that the Twins had employed to their advantage. Minnesota's team ERA of 4.63 in 1987 was near the bottom of the American League, but it included a staggering 5.46 mark on the road, as the Twins were the first team in history to enter the World Series after having been outscored during the regular season (786 to 806). But as with the Cardinals, the glovework of Kelly's men sparkled, leading all of baseball with only 98 errors, while the Cards had tied the Astros and Braves for the fewest in the National League with 116. Although Minnesota's vaunted power had yielded a total of 196 home runs, it was good for only a fifth-place tie with the Yankees on the year, trailing the A's (199), Orioles (211), Blue Jays (215), and the heavily favored team the Twins had dispatched in the American League Championship Series, the Tigers (225). The Twins were led by the corner men of Hrbek (34 homers) and Gaetti (31), in addition to Brunansky (32), the latter now having posted six straight seasons of 20 or more. Puckett, while finishing fourth in the league batting race at .332, chipped in with 28 home runs and set a Major League record with

21 of them coming indoors. While both the Cardinals and the Twins had gotten the least offensive production in their respective leagues from their catchers, Laudner—though batting only .191 during the year—added 16 homers and showed promise for more, as he had once hit 42 in a Minor League season.

For the Cardinals, therefore, it was yet another test of their speed game against an elite power outfit, which they had first passed in the 1982 NLCS against the Atlanta Braves and in the World Series that same year against the Milwaukee Brewers.

In spite of being separated between the American and National Leagues, several of the Cardinals and Twins had crossed paths in their baseball lifetimes. Gaetti, the MVP of the ALCS with a .300 average and 2 home runs against Detroit, had grown up dreaming of playing in the World Series in Busch Stadium—albeit in a Cardinal uniform, as he was raised in the southern Illinois town of Centralia, an hour from St. Louis and the same distance from the city as Herzog's home southwest of Centralia in New Athens, Illinois. Puckett and Lindeman had been teammates as freshmen at Bradley University in Peoria, Illinois, in 1981, as the Chicago-native Puckett left the school after one year to enroll at Triton Junior College near the city, from which he would be the third overall pick in the 1982 draft by the Twins.

Further back in 1978, John Morris and Frank Viola had faced each other in the Nassau County (New York) High School Championship Game—although the roles were reversed, as the junior Morris was a pitcher for Mepham High and the senior Viola was a slugging first baseman for East Meadow. While growing up on Long Island, Morris had also been a childhood friend of Twins reserve player Gene Larkin, who grew up two blocks down from the Morris residence and, after high school, proceeded to break many of Lou Gehrig's records at Columbia University. Viola made his way to St. John's University, where he would pitch against Morris at Seton Hall and, in what some have called the greatest game in college baseball history, against Ron Darling and Yale on May 21, 1981. In the NCAA Northeast Regional contest, Viola posted eleven shutout innings against the Bulldogs, but was more than matched by Darling and his no-hitter, which he carried into the twelfth—at which time St. John's managed to push across a run for a 1–0 victory at dusk over a darkened field, with a standing ovation for both young men coming from the crowd that was virtually unseen to the players due to the nightfall.

By 1987 Viola had become the ace of the Twins' pitching staff and was the winningest left-hander in baseball over the previous four years with 69 victories, making him Kelly's selection to start Game One. Kelly had also considered veteran Bert Blyleven for the opener but opted for Viola and his superior ability to hold runners on and thus get off to a good start against Herzog's fleet assortment of baserunners. Despite their lack of stolen bases against the Giants, the Cardinals' speed was expected to run roughshod over the Twins, as they had permitted 168 stolen bases on the season while throwing out only 46. Minnesota would rely heavily upon Laudner, as backup Sal Butera did not throw well, and Tom Nieto (a member of the Cardinals 1985 pennant-winner and a better defensive catcher than either man) was not eligible for the postseason after missing most of the regular season with a broken bone in his hand. Blyleven, scheduled to start Game Two, suggested a new strategy against St. Louis in his usual good humor. "We might let their pitchers get on just to clog up the bases."[4]

In the midst of heading to the mound for Game One, Viola was saddled with a personal conflict, as he was supposed to be the best man at his brother's wedding back on Long Island that day. But with John Viola and his fiancée Donna having set the date a year and a half earlier, there were no hard feelings in light of Frank's unforeseen and sudden new work assignment. "He's so upset he can't come," John told the guests. "I said, 'No problem—I'm getting a lot of publicity from this.'"[5] Upon returning from a Caribbean cruise for their honeymoon, John and Donna would be flown by Frank to Minneapolis to attend a later game in the Series.

The Twins were rested and healthy, enjoying nearly a week off in between their five-game ALCS victory over Detroit and the start of the World Series. The World Series did not pause to sympathize for the casualty-laden Cardinals, on the other hand, who continued to be shorthanded with a variety of problems, the likes of which Herzog had been dealing with for two years in trying to piece together an effective batting order. Pendleton's abdominal injury in Game Seven of the NLCS limited his services to left-handed batting only, while Clark, still unable to swing a bat after giving it one more try in the team's first round of batting practice in the Metrodome, was taken off the active roster and replaced by Lee Tunnell to give the team an extra pitcher. (Clark's ankle trouble was actually more serious than had been revealed in the preceding weeks by the Cardinals, so as to give the Giants the notion that he might play.) As in the NLCS, Clark would be in uniform for the World Series but withheld to the bench. "The fact that Jack is not on field doesn't mean we lose all of his leadership qualities," Herr pointed out. "He's still in the clubhouse and he's still in the dugout. He has a patience about him that others can feed off of."[6] But with Pendleton and Clark and their 202 RBIs out of the lineup, the press was beginning to call Herzog's limping collection the "Out-of-Gas House Gang." Herr admitted that the downside was more obvious. "We're going to have to play perfect baseball to win this series since we'll be playing without two of our most important players. Everyone is going to have to concentrate a little bit harder."[7]

In addition to Pendleton being replaced at third base by the little-used Lawless—who was only the fourth nonpitcher in eighty-four years to start a World Series game with 2 or fewer hits during the regular season, and the first since 1925—the Cardinals had three rookies in the lineup for Game One. Lindeman was at first base, Pagnozzi was the designated hitter, and, at the pitcher's spot, Herzog gave the ball to Magrane, who had once thrown a few years earlier in the Metrodome as a collegian.

WITH AMERICA HOLDING ITS COLLECTIVE BREATH OVER THE miraculous rescue of eighteen-month-old Jessica McClure from an abandoned well in Midland, Texas, on television on October 16, the nation looked for relaxation, as the first World Series game ever to be played indoors received the national attention the following night. In addition to the Cardinals having lost their last eight games in domed stadiums (five in Montreal, which now had an enclosed roof, and three in Houston), Viola had not lost at the Metrodome since the third week of May.

Viola started strongly, hopping off the mound to successfully field a bunt from Coleman, who was appearing in his first World Series action after missing the 1985 battle with the Royals, to open the game. The left-hander followed by striking out Smith, Ozzie's first whiff in 55 World Series plate appearances. But in the second inning the Cardinals were able to draw first blood as Lindeman blooped a double in front of Puckett, moved to third on a fly ball to the center fielder, and then scored on a ground ball to Minnesota shortstop Greg Gagne.

The young Magrane initially rose to meet the tense occasion but was ultimately engulfed by the fury inside the dome. "He was great for three innings," Herzog would say of the first-year south-paw.[8] The Twins' fourth time at the plate saw Gaetti, Don Baylor, Brunansky, and Hrbek register hits to start the inning, which was followed by a walk to second baseman Steve Lombardozzi before an out was recorded. The inside noise grew stronger with each baserunner that reached, with the Twins' wives being among the most boisterous in leading the way by blowing whistles in between their screams. "The hardest working crowd in baseball," McCa-rver had called the animated Metrodome faithful. "They resem-ble 55,000 Scandinavian James Browns."[9] Looking back in 2024, Magrane agreed. "That's the loudest stadium I've ever been in, either as a player or a broadcaster. Even going up there later to see Packers-Vikings games, I've still never heard it as loud as it was in the 1987 World Series."[10]

After Magrane loaded the bases without retiring a batter, Forsch entered the scene and allowed a hit to Laudner to make the score 4–1 in favor of Minnesota, with the bags remaining full.

Next to fire away was Dan Gladden, the fireplug Twins' left fielder who had arrived from the Giants at the start of the season. With Gladden on first base in the third inning, Magrane had thrown over nine times before Gladden ultimately stole second, adding to the 25 steals he logged during the regular season, the most by a Twin since Rod Carew in 1978. Now, Forsch notched two strikes on Gladden. At that point, a beach ball entered the outfield and began rolling around on the Astroturf, as if having found its way across the country from San Francisco and into town. It wound up being an evil omen, as Forsch served up a beach ball of his own on the next pitch. Gladden drove a hanging breaking ball out of the yard to left, the first grand slam in World Series play since Baltimore pitcher Dave McNally hit one in 1970.

Desperately needing innings, Herzog left the venerable Forsch in the game to weather the storm for three innings. Horton mopped up afterward in what ended as a 10–1 rout, as an anemic St. Louis offense saw Coleman, Smith, and Herr go a composite 0-12 for the first time all season. Viola cruised easily through eight, permitting no walks and 5 hits in giving way to Keith Atherton for an inning, with the core of the Minnesota bullpen of left-hander Dan Schatzeder, swing man Juan Berenguer, and elite closer Jeff Reardon able to extend their rest. Like Gladden, Berenguer had also came from the Giants and quickly became the workhorse in relief, exemplified by the Twins' June 2 game against the Red Sox in Boston when he threw 114 pitches in three-and-two-thirds innings. Reardon, also new to the Twins in 1987 after a dominating six-year run in Montreal, was the only pitcher in baseball with at least 20 saves in each of the past six seasons and joined Worrell as the only pitchers in 1987 to get saves in four consecutive games played by their teams. The southpaw Schatzeder was yet another pitcher new to the Twins after coming to Minnesota from Philadelphia in June and offered Kelly an option against lefty hitters.

Wishing to save Tudor for Busch Stadium, Herzog once again brought Cox back on three days' rest for Game Two. The manager received a bit of good news before game time from Pendleton, who reported that running was not as painful for him as it had been and that he would be able to start as the designated hitter against the right-hander Blyleven—although Pendleton was still unable to field, throw, or bat from the right side. Taking Lindeman's place at first base was the left-handed-hitting Driessen, who eleven years earlier had been the first National League designated hitter in World Series play for the Reds in 1976.

Blyleven, who as a teenage rookie in 1970 had pitched for the Twins in their last ALCS appearance, retained one of the most devastating curve balls in the game and was the owner of 244 wins and over 3,000 strikeouts. He also tended to surrender the longball; in 1987, he had given up more homers during the regular season (46) than the Herzog's patchwork starting lineup for Game Two had hit altogether during the year (38). "If it doesn't bother him, it doesn't bother me," Kelly said of Blyleven's home run figure.[11]

Before moving to Morehead, Kentucky, Magrane had spent part

of his childhood in the Twin Cities while his father was on the faculty at the University of Minnesota conducting research on adrenal gland cancer. Joe recalled a story of seeing one of his first heroes in person—about which he and the hero would laugh for years to come:

This went the way of the hula hoop, but at Metropolitan Stadium in Minnesota, they used to have the pitcher warm up right next to the on-deck circle. I loved Bert Blyleven; I was a kid, and I wanted to see his curve ball up close. I was just six feet away from him, and I could literally hear the ball ripping off the seams from his curve. I said, "Hey Bert—throw another curve ball!"

And I heard Bert say, "Hey, kid—get f—'n lost."

I went back to my dad, who sitting was on the other side of the stadium by the Oakland A's dugout because Blyeven was throwing against Catfish Hunter that day. My dad said, "It looked like you and Bert had a conversation. What did he say?"

"He said he is busy and can't talk right now."[12]

As in the opening game, a quiet 1–0 contest after three-and-a-half innings—this time in the Twins' favor, due to a Gaetti home run—belied an overwhelming attack that was soon to follow. After totaling only 28 pitches in the first three frames, Cox labored through 34 in a disastrous fourth, mirroring the experience of Magrane and Forsch twenty-four hours earlier. Cox allowed 6 earned runs in the inning to give him 7 for the game, both figures tying World Series records established nearly eighty years earlier. It had gotten so loud in the Metrodome during the Twins' offensive onslaught that home plate umpire Lee Weyer had been forced to yell when wanting to say something to the catcher Peña.

For the second straight evening, Minnesota combined its hitting with a fine pitching effort, as Blyleven worked through seven Cardinal turns, inducing groundballs with his outstanding curve that he kept low in the strike zone. He allowed just 2 runs en route to an 8–4 win and a quick 2–0 lead for the Twins in the series. Blyleven, in his eighteenth Major League season, was now 5–0 in the postseason for his career, and Kelly's lineup was hitting .358

with runners in scoring position for the 1987 playoffs. Despite Coleman finally achieving a stolen base against Berenguer in the eighth, the Cardinals' running game had once again been stymied, due to the large early deficit and despite the protests of Herzog, who after the Cardinals batted in the second and fourth innings complained to Weyer about what he believed to be Blyleven's illegal actions on the mound. Herzog claimed that Blyleven, who had not been called for a balk over the past two seasons in covering 73 starts (in the traditionally balk-barren American League), was not coming set with his hands before proceeding in his motion toward home plate. After the game, Herzog insisted to the writers that he had counted eleven balks that were not called.

It was indeed a tough night all around for the Cardinals, as Rod Booker's wife Kathryn—a cousin of Jackie Robinson—had been struck in the head with a foul ball while sitting next to their seven-year-old son (and expecting their second child) and was taken to a local hospital with a concussion. And while the Redbirds had been falling in Game Two in Minneapolis, the soon-to-be dispatched football Cardinals were out on the dreaded sod of Candlestick Park in San Francisco, losing to Joe Montana and the 49ers by a 34–28 score.

The two early victories were exactly what Kelly needed, as the Twins had managed only a 40-49 record during the regular season in games without Viola or Blyleven. Although they possessed only the two quality starters, Herzog believed Minnesota was at a great advantage, with two off-days scheduled during the series instead of the usual single one. "I'm not knocking Les Straker," Herzog said of the rookie in the number-three spot in the Twins' rotation slated to take the mound at Busch Stadium in Game Three, "but during the season, two guys could pitch five out of eleven games. Now it's five out of *seven*."[13] With his team conquering the ALCS in five, Kelly did not need Viola or Blyleven to make an extra appearance late in the series against the Tigers. Plugging holes in a starting staff that was thin all season long, the Twins had even added Steve Carlton to the roster in a trade with the Indians in July, as the legendary left-hander contributed seven starts.

As the series shifted to St. Louis, the Cardinals had now dropped ten-straight games indoors and five World Series contests in a row, having been outscored 37–7 in those five losses. With the team's charter flight not arriving in town until 2:30 in the morning of Monday, October 19, Herzog decided to not schedule a practice at Busch Stadium for the open date. While the Twins worked out, Herzog was the lone Cardinals' employee present at the ballpark; he decided to conduct a brief press conference before telling the writers he would continue his comments down the street at the Missouri Bar & Grille downtown on North Tucker Boulevard for anyone interested. There, he held court with scribes from all over the country while sipping a Bud Light at the bar. "We've got an off day, so we're having a victory party," the Redbirds skipper raised his bottle and toasted in self-deprecation.[14]

In between their discussion of the Series, the group occasionally glanced up at the television inside the tavern where the midday news was covering the plunge of the stock market. The end of the afternoon would see the Dow Jones Industrial Average lose 508 points—which was over a fifth of its value after having topped the 2,500 mark back on July 17.

The freefall of the economy did not seem to bother the low-key Kelly, who after the Twins' practice considered heading to the horse track at Fairmount Park across the river in Illinois. Instead, he opted for a sandwich at a deli near the team hotel, returned to his room, and watched television. There was apparently little to do in the vicinity of the Twins' lodging, as the Cardinals had booked them at a place some thirteen miles outside downtown in the suburb of Frontenac, Missouri, rather than at the Marriott across the street from Busch Stadium where opposing teams normally stayed. Hrbek was particularly disappointed to miss out on the action happening in the center of the city. "It's dead out there," he said of the team's quarters. "People sit in the lobby. Then they get up and sit in the restaurant. This is more like spring training than the World Series."[15]

When corralling some of the Cardinals later that evening, the writers asked Herr if he had lost money in the stock market crash. "I haven't checked," the second baseman responded with his mind on other things. "But they said the ratio of losers to winners was 49 to 1, and I'm sure I'm not the 1." Reports were circulating around town of Gussie Busch losing as much as $150 million on paper from the events of October 19. "I bet he really misses it," laughed Herzog.[16]

Ignoring what was perhaps the coldest night of the season, another new record crowd of 55,347 gathered in Busch Stadium for Game Three and the 7:00 p.m. local-time start. Herzog, conducting one more session of interviews with the media in his office a few hours before game time, resumed his vigorous protest about Blyleven's motions on the mound. He held up the rule book for all to see, pointing to the section that stated the pitcher had to come to a complete stop in the stretch position. A short time later as the Cardinals were beginning batting practice, the manager angrily confronted umpire Ken Kaiser on the field (who was dressed in a suit, having yet to change into his umpire's uniform) to raise the issue once again. Herzog contended that Kaiser, the third base umpire in Game Two, had the clearest view of Blyleven's hands and yet failed to properly enforce the balk rule.

To counter Minnesota's Homer Hankies, St. Louis fans took to their frosty seats with the same small white towels they had whipped during the NLCS. Even Gussie Busch himself waved one above his head as his team of Clydesdales rode onto the field upon the left-field wagon gate flying open. Shortly thereafter, Ozzie Smith made his own unique contribution to the rising pregame crescendo by doing his patented backflip for the roaring crowd when going out to his position at shortstop. It would take more than acrobatics, however, for him and the Redbirds to turn things around; Smith entered the night batting .145 in World Series play in his career, while his partner at second base Herr sat at .136— the third and fourth worst marks all-time in World Series action for players with more than 40 plate appearances.

Relaxing in the box seats and watching his two former infield teammates take their warmup ground balls was Keith Hernandez, enjoying his thirty-fourth birthday on what was also the fifth anniversary of the Cardinals' Game Seven win over the Brewers in 1982 in which Hernandez played a hero's role. He was sitting alongside another former St. Louis infielder, Ted Sizemore, who was Hernandez's initial second baseman when he came up with the Cardinals in 1974.

Tudor, who did not experience the 1982 title like Hernandez, Smith, Herr, McGee, and Forsch, took the mound. Looking to focus solely upon his fastball and changeup, the left-hander openly declared he would throw his curve ball only to Hrbek. The Cards' hitters, meanwhile, figured to pile up some runs in their home park against the first-year pitcher Straker, who had been born in Venezuela and paid his dues by spending ten years in the Minors in nine different cities, and among three different organizations.

Herzog's men were unable to capitalize on a balk called on the rookie in the second inning by Kaiser, who had rotated to second base for Game Three. Straker instead confounded the Cardinals and the millions watching on television by staying stride-for-stride with the veteran Tudor, with each man posting a shutout through five innings.

A two-out hit by Brunansky plated the game's first score in the top of the sixth, the first run permitted in the last thirteen postseason innings by Tudor, who had thrown 45 of 60 pitches for strikes.

Straker continued to silence the St. Louis bats, clinging to the 1–0 lead heading into the bottom of the seventh. Not wanting to push his luck with the rookie who had only 1 complete game among his 26 starts over the season, Kelly decided to lift Straker and go to his bullpen, playing into his preferred pattern of giving the set-up man Berenguer two innings and the closer Reardon one.

After an Oquendo hit opened the Cardinals' seventh, Peña was called upon to bunt by Leyva from the third base coaching box. But with the count advancing to two strikes, the catcher reached back and instead slapped at a curve ball from Berenguer, slicing a single to the outfield as Oquendo raced for second. Inserted to bat for Tudor was the still-ailing Pendleton, pinch-hitting for only the second time all year after tripling in the role back on August 20. A capable bunter, Pendleton successfully moved the runners ahead on a sacrifice to set the table for Coleman, who like Smith and Herr behind him continued to struggle at the plate. But Coleman responded, zooming a double down the left field line on an 0-2 count for a 2–1 lead for the home team. Seizing the energy of the moment, Coleman immediately grabbed third for his second stolen base of the night.

Next for redemption was Smith, who singled him home for a

3–1 St. Louis advantage. Smith had recently stated he was tired of manufactured scores being called "Cardinal-like" runs in the media. "I don't care how you get it. A run is a run."[17]

Worrell entered the game; his only imperfection over the final two innings was a two-out triple for Puckett in the eighth, as he closed the door for Tudor in a 3–1 gem to get the Redbirds back in the hunt.

RELYING AGAIN UPON A MAKESHIFT LINEUP, HERZOG PUT the second-year pitcher Mathews and his sore leg muscle on the mound for Game Four, the switch-hitting Oquendo in right field, and the right-handed Lawless at third base for the rematch with the left-hander Viola with temperatures in downtown St. Louis still mired in the upper thirties.

After Lawless missed a chance by striking out looking in the second inning with two out and runners on first and second, the teams fought to an even battle through the third, when the light-hitting Minnesota shortstop Gagne homered—his first in 129 at bats versus left-handers on the season—before Lindeman, another right-hander whom Herzog wanted in the order against Viola, tied the game with a two-out RBI single in the bottom half.

In the top of the fourth, Mathews, pitching effectively, felt a twinge in his injured left quad and had to be removed for Forsch, who completed the inning with no damage done to the scoreboard.

After Peña and Oquendo opened the Cardinals' bottom half with a walk and a single, Lawless came to the plate once again. Despite his tiny unimposing sum of 2 base hits for the entire year, Herzog could not afford to have Lawless bunt with the pitcher's spot waiting behind him, because the manager wished to have Forsch continue in the game and once again eat some necessary innings, as he had done for Magrane in Game One.

Shrugging off his failure from his first time up, Lawless leapt upon a Viola fastball that stayed up in the strike zone. He drove a deep fly to left, taking a few walking steps out of the batter's box to watch the ball, along with the 55,347 once again in attendance, sail through the frigid night. All eyes were upon Gladden, giving chase. But in the end, the left fielder could only watch as well, as the ball bounced off the front of the bleachers for a home run.

Lawless triumphantly tossed his bat high into the air and went into an elongated jog in circling the bases—a fling and a trot full of warranted pride, which Mike Smith of the *Post-Dispatch* compared to "a cross between Jack Clark's and Jeffrey the Great [Leonard]."[18] The three-run homer was only Lawless's second in the Majors and his first in over three years (the other having come off Ken Dayley in 1984 when Dayley was with the Braves). The 3 RBIS on the one swing of the bat, meanwhile, matched his total number of runs driven in from 1986 and 1987 *combined*.

It lit the fuse for 3 more Cardinals runs to follow in the inning, which included Coleman stealing his 4th base of the series against Schatzeder, who had relieved Viola and against whom Coleman had stolen second and third during the regular season while Schatzeder was with the Phillies.

With Kelly suddenly incurring a depth problem on his own pitching staff, Joe Niekro was summoned to the mound in the fifth inning and a 7–2 deficit for the Twins. In the wake of his ball-scuffing scandal from the summer, Niekro had thus attained a World Series appearance for the first time in his twenty-one-year career, topping Walter Johnson's former Major League record of eighteen. (Niekro's brother Phil would never pitch in a World Series in a twenty-four-year career that had just ended with the close of the 1987 regular season.) He and George Frazier quieted the St. Louis bats for the rest of the way, but Forsch and Dayley did the same to the Twins' offense, leaving the final tally at 7–2 and squaring the series at two games apiece.

Naturally, Lawless and his powerful blast was the center of attention in the home locker room afterward. "When I saw the umpire signal home run, I said, 'Holy cow, the ball went out,'" reflected the man of the hour, who had no intention of showing off when the surreal moment happened. "Then I kind of went blank. I saw the TV replay where I flipped my bat, but I don't remember doing it. I had never been in that position before. You dream about these things as a kid." The homer and the victory capped a huge day for Lawless, who had just moved into a new house in St. Louis that same morning.

Giving the unlikely star the requisite hard time, an unimpressed

Tudor rolled his eyes from across the locker room. "I would have drilled you," he informed Lawless about his bat flip.

Lawless smiled understandingly. "I would have taken it and sat down." Pausing to think further, he added, "I probably wouldn't even have felt it."[19]

WHEN THE SUN ROSE THE NEXT MORNING ON THURSDAY, October 22, Herzog sought to take advantage of his club's momentum for his own personal benefit, feeling it was a good opportunity to go fishing—and by the afternoon, he was able to pull nine bass from a southern Illinois lake before heading to the ballpark. Those fans with the patience to hold tickets for Game Five were rewarded with better weather, as St. Louis temperatures soared into the lower sixties with light winds from the west that had gusted to over twenty miles per hour during the afternoon but had died down by the first pitch. The redundant, maximum figure of 55,347 was counted through the turnstiles, as the crowd settled in for the year's final ballgame at Busch Stadium. Oquendo, though in the starting lineup once again, had become the latest individual on the Cardinals' roster who was riddled with casualties. In Game Four, he dove for a foul fly ball along the right-field line and jammed his shoulder on the rubberized warning track, making his ability to execute throws in Game Five limited.

In a rematch of Game Two, Cox faced Blyleven with both men working on three days' rest. The two right-handers with ample postseason experience served up a classic duel. When Blyleven struck out against Cox to open the top of the third, it would be the last at bat taken by a Twins' pitcher in the series and made American League pitchers 0 for their last 63 at the plate in World Series competition, with Tim Stoddard of the Orioles achieving the last hit in 1979.

The contest remained scoreless heading into the Cardinals' sixth, when Whitey's men were able to break through in their inimitable fashion. A Coleman single started the inning, which was followed by a bunt hit by Smith so perfectly placed down the third base line that Blyleven could only pick up the ball and walk back to the mound. As soon as the veteran hurler toed the rubber against the next batter Ford, Coleman and Smith took off on a double steal. With men quickly placed on second and third, Ford, following Lawless as the obscure hero on this given night, followed with a single to score both men.

When Coleman and Smith each added another stolen base in the seventh inning, it gave Coleman 6 in the series—one shy of Lou Brock's World Series record—while the Cardinals' 5 in the game was the most in a World Series contest since the 1907 Cubs. The Redbird lead had increased to 4–0, as those in the home stands were unaware that an era of Cardinals' baseball was simultaneously going by the wayside.

A moment of dread followed in the bottom of the eighth when Peña singled and quickly grabbed his hamstring in agony at first base, prompting Herzog to send in Lance Johnson as a pinch runner. Peña, however, had only foiled himself and fooled his manager, for he was not actually hurting but instead attempting to decoy the Twins into thinking he was actually injured because he wanted to join the stolen-base parade himself. Despite the intensity of the game situation, it was nonetheless indicative of the playful, enthusiastic color that Peña had added to the team and what his teammates loved about him. "Tony brought energy; that was always the best part of him," Ricky Horton would say in 2023. "He was always energetic and fun to watch play."[20]

As they had done so many times, Dayley and Worrell kept their inherited lead intact, bringing home a 4–2 victory for Cox and the eleventh consecutive loss on the road in World Series play for the Twins and Washington Senators franchise dating back to 1925. In a final gesture to the Cardinals' style of play in the '80s, the home team had won on 10 hits that were all singles. When the fireworks went off after the game and wrapped themselves around the top of the Gateway Arch off in the distance, it was among the very last vestiges of Whiteyball the fans in Busch Stadium would see, as their boys headed back north, just one win away from the title.

THE CARDINALS LANDED AMID THE STARK MINNESOTA weather and held a practice inside the climate-controlled Metrodome on the off day of Friday, October 23. The Minneapolis forecast for the morning of October 24 called for the possibility of flurries; Oquendo, never having seen a snowfall in his life, set the alarm clock in his hotel room to wake up early in the hope of catching a glimpse of it.

In the only afternoon game of the series and the first day game in the World Series in three years, the Cardinals were hoping that the sunlight coming through the roof of the dome at the 2:30 starting time would give them a better—or at least, different—view of balls hit in the air. "There's nothing more I can say about it," muttered a frustrated Willie McGee, who had lost track of multiple fly balls in the first two games in Minnesota. The center fielder, accustomed to instinctively reading balls right off the bat, had instead been forced in the Metrodome to wait and locate them as they made their descent. "You can't take your eye off the ball. You can't hear anyone call for it. You have to get a feel, a sense of where the other guy's going to go. That could be a problem if you're running flat out." Coleman, who was fighting a slight bout with the flu, was blunter. "I can't even see why they play baseball in this place. It's not worth playing in."[21]

Herzog, believing that if the Twins won Game Six they would have momentum that would be nearly insurmountable, decided to slide all his chips in the middle of the table. Instead of saving Tudor for the seventh game and thereby giving him a fourth day of rest, Whitey sent his left-handed ace to the mound in the hope of wrapping things up. The statistics supported the strategy, for although it was the first time in 1987 that Tudor would work on only three days off, he had posted a 9–1 record and a 1.27 ERA to date in his Cardinals career in such circumstances. He would face Straker, having to take another turn for the Twins in what would become a back-and-forth affair.

Herr unloaded for a long home run in the first inning, sending the ball high above the Hefty Bag into the seats in right field. It was his first extra-base hit since the first week of September, his first RBI in World Series play since 1982, and his first left-handed homer in 1987. Tudor was unable to hold the lead, as the Twins responded immediately with 2 runs in the bottom of the first, starting with a Gladden lead-off triple—making him the first Twin to reach base in the first inning during the series. The Cardinals fought back with flurry of hits in the fourth and fifth innings to build a 5–2 advantage. But Tudor imploded again, giving up 4 more runs in an assault capped by a blow from yet another of Kelly's seemingly endless array of sluggers.

Despite 331 home runs in a career that included a 1979 MVP award, the veteran Don Baylor had not yet homered for the Twins in his 63 at bats since being acquired from Boston on September 1, with his last round-tripper having come *against* the Twins on August 23 at Fenway Park against Carlton. But with Puckett and Gaetti aboard to start the inning, Baylor powered a Tudor pitch over the wall in left that tied the game at five. Horton entered with nobody out and was able to finish the inning, but not before another run crossed the plate to put the Twins in front.

An inning later, it was Hrbek's turn. After his first two at bats versus Tudor that afternoon and a third against Horton, the Minnesota-native first baseman was 0-16 in the postseason against lefties. But on the first pitch from the newly entered Dayley— who had replaced Forsch specifically to face the hitter from the left side—Hrbek launched a towering home run to straightaway center field with the bases loaded, making it only the second time in World Series history (since the 1956 Yankees) that one team had hit two grand slams in a single Series. It was also the first longball surrendered by Dayley to a left-handed batter in over two years, since Strawberry had taken him deep at the end of the 1985 regular season.

Pumping his first in the air as he headed for home, Hrbek later said, "I wish I could have run around the bases two times instead of one."[22] The devastating blow lengthened the Twins' lead to 10–5, and the game ended as an 11–5 final, setting up a winner-take-all finale as the Cardinals, for their seventh World Series in a row dating back to 1946, were heading to a seventh game.

In addition to Hrbek, the other Twins' star, Puckett, came out of a slump; he tied a World Series record with 4 runs scored and equaled Goose Goslin's franchise mark of 4 hits in a Series game. In being saddled with the loss, Tudor now stood at 18-14 on the road in his Cardinals' career while maintaining a sparkling 31-7 mark at home.

AS THE CARDS RETREATED TO THEIR HOTEL AND THE TWINS to their homes, the teams were grateful to receive an extra hour rest with the change to Standard Time overnight between Games Six and Seven. When the St. Louis players awoke on the morning of Sunday, October 25, and looked out their hotel windows, they could see a large banner with Latin writing, posted atop a local Catholic church: *Vincente Gemini* ("Win Twins").

With little choice beyond Magrane or Cox, Herzog decided upon the young left-hander to start the all-decisive contest that would begin at 7:00 p.m. in the Minneapolis and St. Louis time zone. Magrane would thus be the first Cardinals rookie to ever start a seventh game of the World Series and the first pitcher in baseball history to start Game One and Game Seven but none in between. His comfort level in working with Steve Lake—the tandem achieving a 5-1 record during the season—prompted Herzog to move Peña to the designated hitter role and give Lake his first start in the series, while Viola, once again on three days' rest, would take the mound for the third time for Kelly.

Lake happened to arrive extra early at the Metrodome that day. He was following the NFL on television in the locker room when Herzog found him and told him he would be playing that night. "One minute I'm watching football, and the next minute I find out I'm starting the seventh game of the World Series," he said. Then, pausing for a moment and considering all the unlikely players who had stepped up for the Cardinals during 1987, he realized it just might be his time to shine. "I could be the hero tonight. Look at all the heroes we've had so far."[23]

As game time approached, three thousand people back in St. Louis had ventured into the 3,500-seat Fox Theatre on Grand Boulevard for $3 a person to watch the game on a twenty-five-foot screen, with beer and hot dogs for sale in the lobby.

Determined to make amends for the Game Seven collapse against the Royals two years earlier, the Cardinals came out fighting. Coleman struck out to lead things off, tying a team World Series record by fanning 9 times. The mark would be equaled by McGee in the third inning—the pair joined Clark, Mike Shannon, and Jim Bottomley for the dubious notoriety. But in the top of the second, hits by Lindeman, McGee, Peña (who after batting .214 in the regular season hit .381 in the NLCS and .409 in the World Series), and the seemingly prophetic Lake sent the Cards out to a 2–0 lead.

Had Magrane been able to navigate through the Minnesota bats early on, Herzog was inclined to give him five innings, perhaps six. But when the Twins came back with a run in the bottom of the second to close the gap to 2–1, Whitey's mind began churning with a dilemma: stay with the rookie or bring Cox back on two days' rest. For the time being, he decided Magrane would remain on the mound.

In the bottom of the third, McGee denied the suddenly hot Puckett from equaling the World Series record of 6 consecutive hits with a leaping catch at the wall to rob his fellow center fielder. Viola settled down, retiring ten Cardinals in a row through the fourth inning with Lindeman, McGee, Peña, and Coleman all striking out by chasing pitches high out of the strike zone, and the latter thus now having the St. Louis World Series record all to himself.

When the Twins came up in the bottom of the fourth, Jorge Orta's Ghost of World Series Past appeared. With Gagne batting, the first baseman Lindeman went to his right to field a ground ball and tossed it to Magrane, a play shockingly similar to the one involving Jack Clark in Kansas City. Magrane, struggling with his footwork around the bag while he received the throw, allowed Gagne to reach with a hit—despite replays showing the pitcher scraping the base with his foot before Gagne reached it.

It was the last batter Magrane faced, as Herzog ordered Cox to the mound for his first relief appearance in three years. "Joe pitched a pretty good game," Herzog said. "I thought he'd get us to the fifth inning, and then Danny could get us to the seventh.

"But Danny couldn't get us there."[24]

On Cox's first offering—one of only 7 of his 21 pitches he would throw for strikes—Puckett lined a game-tying double to the right-center-field gap. Lake saved Cox later in the inning by throwing out Puckett, who attempted to advance to third on a ball in the dirt, and, shortly thereafter, by successfully holding on to the ball when Gaetti bowled him over in trying to score from second, as the Cardinals rushed off the bench out to congratulate the catcher. The two plays would be the only outs recorded by Cox, while not having a hand in either one.

More specters from the 1985 free fall in Royals Stadium began tormenting the visiting team. When Herr got picked off and caught in a rundown between first and second in the Cardinals' sixth, replays showed the umpire Weyer, working first base for Game Seven, missing *two* calls as Herr was clearly safe in a pair of ways upon returning to first. "Hrbek, without the ball, blocked Herr's retreat to first, and Herr should have been called safe because of interference," argued Mike Smith on a first point. "Then, Viola, standing behind the bag, tagged Herr late." The game remained tied.

After walking Brunansky and Hrbek to open the Twins' sixth, Cox was removed by Herzog in favor of Worrell. As the departing pitcher took his time strolling from the mound to the dugout, Cox—àla Andújar the last time the Cardinals were in a seventh game of the World Series—directed his wrath at the home plate umpire, now in the person of St. Louis native and crew chief Dave Phillips. Slowing his exit nearly to a halt by time he reached the foul line, Cox spewed "not one but half a dozen obvious obscenities at Phillips," which the television camera first aired live for viewers and then showed again in slow motion upon returning from a commercial break while Worrell was warming up.[25] The outburst made Cox the last player since Andújar to be ejected in World Series play.

Worrell could not escape the mess bequeathed to him. With two out and the bases loaded, Gaetti delivered a single for a 3–2 Minnesota lead before the Cardinals could get off the field. The dazed catcher Lake, still recovering from the collision with Gaetti an inning earlier, was given smelling salts by Gene Gieselmann upon returning to the dugout.

Gladden, capping a fantastic overall performance in the series, doubled in the eighth inning to plate Laudner with an insurance run for Viola and a 4–2 Minnesota advantage. The Twins' starter then departed the game, giving way to the closer Reardon for the ninth.

After Herr flied out to Puckett in center, Ford, batting for Lindeman, popped to Gaetti in shallow left field. The Centralia native and childhood Cardinals fan then handled the final out as well, firing over to Hrbek on a McGee ground ball, as the Cardinals had been shut out over the final seven innings.

For the Twins, it was the franchise's first world championship since moving from Washington DC in 1961 and its first overall since 1924. With his two victories, Viola was named the MVP of the series, while Tom Kelly, as he had done when the Twins claimed the American League flag, stayed in the dugout as his team formed an exuberant pile in the middle of the Metrodome floor.

It was the first time in World Series history that the home team had won all seven games, and the evidence suggested that no two teams had ever benefitted more from their local support. The Cardinals' pitching staff produced a bloated a 5.64 ERA in the series—but the figure soared to 9.00 in the games in the Metrodome, compared to a miniscule 1.67 for those in St. Louis, with the Twins batting .329 at home but just .184 in Busch Stadium.

What-ifs were lamented by some Cardinals fans, wishing that Busch could have hosted four of the contests instead of three. Some also pointed to the umpire issues in Game Seven as well as rumors of sign-stealing perpetrated by the Twins, the latter an allegation that Herzog and the St. Louis players dismissed. "Stash the excuses," Mike Smith snapped at his readers in the *Post-Dispatch.* "Against an American League upstart, the best baseball team of the '80s had a 3-2 lead in games, and a 5–2 lead in Game Six with their best pitcher of the '80s on the mound, and lost the series."[26]

The Twins' winning share was approximately $88,000 per man— five times Les Straker's top salary for any season in his ten years in the Minors—while the Cardinals received around $68,000 per player. Among those enjoying the victors' booty was Minnesota infielder Roy Smalley Jr., who celebrated his thirty-fifth birthday the night of Game Seven while ending a thirteen-year career in the Majors. The Twins' achievement allowed the Smalley family to join the Niekros in finally getting into a World Series; Roy Smalley Sr. played in eleven big league seasons without appearing in the Fall Classic, while Roy Jr.'s uncle Gene Mauch was in the Majors for seven years, managed for twenty-seven more, and also failed to make baseball's ultimate round.

An exasperated Danny Cox was understandably private in the visitors' locker room after Game Seven. "I don't want to talk," was all he said to reporters, having to repeat his feelings twice over.

Pendleton spoke in the pitcher's stead, as the newspapermen ventured over to his chair. "Every time there is a big game, he's the one who's out there," he said in defense of Cox, pointing at the exhausted hurler. "He and 25 other guys are the reason we made it this far."[27]

THE SPENT COX WAS A MICROCOSM OF THE TEAM THAT LEFT it all out on the field, a group of fighters who departed the Metrodome for their return to St. Louis after having clawed for hardscrabble wins all season long. They may have been the "Ran-out-of-Gas" and "Ran-out-of-Home-Games" Gang, but they never did run out of heart. Nor had their manager, in what was perhaps his finest work.

Epilogue

THE TWINS' .525 WINNING PERCENTAGE DURING THE REGU-
lar season (85-77) remained the lowest ever for a World Series
winner until the Cardinals' next championship season nearly
twenty years later in 2006, when they posted an 83-78 mark (.516).
Six weeks after the completion of the 1987 World Series, Chicago
Bears' coach Mike Ditka incurred the wrath of Minnesotans by
referring to the peculiar Metrodome as the "Rollerdome," prompting cheerleaders for the home team to don roller skates when the
Bears took the field against the Vikings.

The Cardinals' feud with the Giants spilled over into 1988, when
on the Sunday afternoon of July 24 another bench-clearing brawl
erupted two days after the second anniversary of the teams' initial
scuffle in 1986.

With San Francisco ahead 5–0 in the top of the eighth and the
ageless Reuschel, in his sixteenth Major League season, spinning
a shutout, Will Clark—who had put the Giants ahead with a two-
out, three-run homer in the fifth inning—stood on first base with
Maldonado at the plate. The batter squibbed a tailor-made double
play grounder to Smith at shortstop, who scooped the ball and
shoveled it to a waiting Oquendo at the base. Clark began his slide
late, taking him well past the bag and nearly beyond the dirt area
as Oquendo was unable to get his legs untangled from those of the
baserunner. When Clark had finally come to a stop, he found both
Oquendo and Smith lurking over him angrily. Clark got to his feet

and shoved Oquendo, which was followed by a right cross from Smith that missed the head of the Giants' player by a few inches.

Maldonado, having rounded first, entered the fray by sprinting to the scene and knocking Smith over while splitting the St. Louis shortstop's lip in the process. Within seconds the entire rosters of both teams had swarmed the area, as Smith, rarely seen to be so incensed, had to be restrained by McGee from going after both Clark and Maldonado. "I was just trying to get out the way," Oquendo later explained about the play. "I didn't think that was a right slide. He [Clark] slid late." Herzog not only agreed but also accused umpire Randy Marsh of not calling Clark out on a similar play two nights earlier. "Both times, there's no dirt where he slid on the first-base side of the bag," the manager stated. "The rule states you can slide on the first-base side of the bag and your momentum can carry you on that side of the bag. But you cannot break up a double-play and your first mark be on the other side of the bag. They didn't call it, so Clark did it again. I told them if they had called it the other night, this stuff wouldn't have happened."[1]

Clark and Oquendo were ejected by umpire Dutch Rennert, who was working second base on the afternoon and claimed to have not seen Smith's punch. Shortly thereafter, Cardinals pitcher Scott Terry was also tossed by Marsh (now working home plate) as his second offering to the next hitter Aldrete sailed up near the batter's head. Missing the spectacle entirely was Jeffrey Leonard, whom the Giants had traded to the Brewers on June 8 after appearing in only forty-four injury-riddled games for San Francisco.

The frustrations were part of another yearlong plunge by the Cardinals in 1988, as they never fully rebounded from a 3-10 start to the season and, at the time of the slugfest with San Francisco, were ten games below .500 (43-53) and fifteen games behind the first-place Mets. Though maintaining some elements from its core, the Cardinals' greatness from the decade thus began to splinter, as critical departures and a continuance of the injury troubles— through which Herzog had been able to navigate in 1987—sank the team into a period of mediocrity.

Two weeks after the completion of the 1987 World Series against Minnesota, Jack Clark was granted free agency; two months later, he finally won his battle of alleged collusion by the owners and signed a two-year free agent contract with the Yankees. Capable sluggers such as Bob Horner and Pedro Guerrero were acquired by St. Louis to fill the gap over the coming seasons, but the absence of Clark and several others would have a cumulative effect on the chemistry of the team.

After the Mets had beaten the Cardinals 4–0 on the night of April 22, 1988, at Busch Stadium, Tom Herr—twelve months after he had beaten New York in the same ballpark with his iconic grand slam—was traded to the Twins for Brunansky, ending Herr's fourteen-year run with the St. Louis organization after signing as an undrafted free agent in 1974. He retired with the highest all-time career fielding percentage for a National League second baseman (.989) before Ryne Sandberg would overtake the mark a few years later. "I certainly loved my time here as a Cardinal," a dejected Herr told the press in the locker room after playing his final game for the Redbirds, having gone 1-3 with a walk against Darling, who spun a complete-game shutout for New York. "I'm a winner, and the organization provided me a chance to play on a winner. It's really hard to say goodbye. I wanted to play my whole career here, and that dream is out the window."[2] The move had also been difficult one for Maxvill to make. "It's not an easy thing trading a great ballplayer and a fine gentleman. [Tom] helped St. Louis participate in three World Series and has always done everything asked of him by his managers."[3]

Brunansky would naturally step in as the everyday right fielder for the Cardinals, with Lindeman still dragging a sore back that would haunt him the rest of his career. "I was never healthy again in my time with the Cardinals through 1989," Lindeman reflected. "I had two back surgeries, including one after '87. But at some point, they had to make a move for the ballclub." Nonetheless, like most everyone from the 1987 Cardinals, he would retain the glorious memories from the World Series season forever. "Even though we didn't win, it was still a great experience. With it being my first year, I just assumed it would always be like that—that we would always be in contention. Battling injuries in 1987 and beyond was the most frustrating part of my career. But the '87 postseason is something that I'll never forget."[4] By the time he left the organization, Lindeman's Cardinals teammates knew he had given all he could. "I've always felt for Jim," said Ricky Horton, "because he just couldn't do what he wanted to do, and that was no fault of his own."[5]

Brunansky would start eighty-one consecutive games for the Cardinals before sitting out the day of the brawl with the Giants. He stayed with the Cardinals for just over two years while running his 20-plus homers per season string to eight through 1989. But at various points in 1990, McGee, Coleman, Pendleton, Dayley, and others would leave St. Louis, with the breakup of the 1980s Cardinals near completion.

The stabilizing force on the field and in the clubhouse continued to be Ozzie Smith, despite the Cardinals faltering to a fifth-place finish and a 76-86 record in 1988. After finishing second in the 1987 MVP voting to Andre Dawson (and beating out the third-place Jack Clark), Smith would repeat as the top vote-getter for the All-Star Game in 1988, while tying a career high with 57 stolen bases, his highest mark ever in a St. Louis uniform. Remaining a Cardinal through the 1996 season and the age of forty-one, Smith would land an All-Star appearance in every season except one dating back to 1980. To this day, Magrane remains in awe of his former teammate:

Sometimes I would pick up his glove and think, *This is the glove of the best shortstop who ever played the game.* I would put my hand in it—and then I would be cussed out by him. "Put that down!" Ozzie would yell. "I don't need your bad luck on it!"

He was a tremendous example. He wasn't the Wizard of Oz by accident. I liked him very much personally, but professionally he showed up every day and went through his own drill work with the glove. It was no accident that he became the best ever.[6]

Like Ozzie, Tony Peña's strong defense would carry him through a long eighteen-year career that lasted a season beyond Smith's into 1997. While the Cardinals had surrendered a load of talent to acquire him from Pittsburgh at the beginning of 1987 season, they had nonetheless appeared to make the correct choice between Peña and Lance Parrish; although overcoming his back troubles and playing five more years as a starter and then four more as a reserve player, Parrish never regained the dominant form he displayed in Detroit.

Oquendo finally got his chance behind the plate in 1988, appearing in one inning as a catcher in a late-season game against the Mets at Busch Stadium—which meant he had appeared at all nine positions over the course of the year (including four innings of pitching). With the departure of Herr to Minnesota, Oquendo earned the starting second baseman job before embarking on a distinguished coaching career with the Cardinals, while Tom Lawless remained on the roster as a utility player for two more seasons before entering the coaching profession himself.

As with many championship teams, the deterioration of the pitching staff may have most rapidly accelerated the Cardinals' regression as the 1980s closed. The veteran mainstays Cox and Tudor would never regain their dominant form and were finished in St. Louis before the 1988 schedule had concluded. On August 16 Tudor was sent to the World Series–bound Dodgers for Pedro Guerrero, while Cox suffered through another injury-plagued season, pitching in only thirteen games at the age of twenty-eight before missing the next two years. A week before the Tudor trade, Cox would last only three innings against Montreal at Busch Stadium in what would be his final appearance as a Cardinal before resurfacing with other teams and pitching sparingly through 1995. Like Tudor with the 1988 Dodgers, Cox would appear in another World Series in 1993 with the Blue Jays after a brief stint with the Pirates and their trip to the NLCS in 1992. Ricky Horton, meanwhile, had been dealt, along with Lance Johnson, to the Chicago White Sox for pitcher José DeLeón earlier in the season and would join Tudor in Los Angeles later in 1988 to help the Dodgers triumph in the NLCS that autumn against the Mets.

In the cyclical nature of team sports, however, the personnel vacuum that had emerged on the Cardinals also permitted others to step into leadership roles. Coming to the fore on the mound was Magrane, who finished third in the 1987 National League Rookie of the Year voting behind Benito Santiago and Mike Dunne before leading the National League in ERA in 1988 (2.18) despite winning only 5 games and losing 9—giving him the distinction of the fewest victories by an ERA titlist in a nonstrike season. In 1989 Magrane finished fourth in the Cy Young voting with an 18–9 record, a 2.91 ERA, and just 5 home runs permitted in 235 innings. However, like Cox, he would miss nearly two full years of his prime with injury problems (1991 and most of the 1992 season) at approximately the same time Todd Worrell would miss two years as well (1990 and 1991) with a rotator cuff tear and Tommy John surgery. Also missing two full years would be Greg Mathews, forced to sit out all of 1989 and 1991 before finishing his playing days with the Phillies in 1992.

As had occurred with Ken Dayley the previous winter, Bob Forsch was released by the Cardinals in December 1987 but re-signed in January as planned. After posting 9 more wins for St. Louis in 30 appearances, Forsch became yet another trade-deadline casualty in late 1988, as he was dealt to Houston for Denny Walling, bringing down the final curtain on a Cardinals' career that lasted over twenty years since being drafted by the team in June 1968. By the time Busch Stadium II closed in 2005, Forsch had thrown the only two no-hitters in the history of the ballpark and was also the only Cardinals pitcher in history to author two such games (in 1978 and 1983).

Though parts of the machine were fading away as the 1990s approached, the respect would last. "It was the whole Cardinal culture that made them good," Mookie Wilson said in 2023. "They were similar to us, but they played according to their huge ballpark. It was a great rivalry, and I think we challenged each other in different ways. It wasn't just one player on the Cardinals you had to worry about; it was the entire team. And you didn't want to get into a close game with them. If it was close you were in trouble because they could steal a run at any time."[7]

Wilson's teammate Roger McDowell agreed; in characterizing the Mets, McDowell sounded like he was describing a Herzog-built team:

> I think we matched up very well against them. There were a lot
> of quality players on that team who were able to fuse together
> and not have the egos to say, "I'm not getting enough at-bats" or
> "I'm not getting enough innings." We just wanted to win. And if

you look on the other side, it was much the same way with the Cardinals. We didn't care about who got the credit; at the end of the day, we put up a W instead of an L.[8]

A myth that Herzog and the Cardinals of the 1980s have tried to dispel over the years was the notion that all of their success came from stolen bases. Whereas stolen bases had indeed peaked all around baseball in 1987, the Cardinals—though still posting them in large numbers—were on a downward trend in that category by the time they captured the National League pennant that season, and their totals would fall off precipitously as the team evolved to a different brand of offense by 1990:

Table 1

Season	Cardinals Stolen Bases	Total NL Stolen Bases	Total AL Stolen Bases
1982	200	1,782	1,394
1983	207	1,786	1,539
1984	220	1,728	1,304
1985	314	1,636	1,461
1986	262	1,842	1,470
1987	248	1,851	1,734
1988	234	1,789	1,512
1989	155	1,529	1,587

The game was shifting to one of power and has largely remained there. The 1,824 home runs hit in the National League in 1987 was a new record that was far beyond the previous mark of 1,683 hit in 1970, and over 300 more than had been hit in 1986.

THE CONNECTIONS BETWEEN THOSE WHO PLAYED FOR THE St. Louis Cardinals in 1987 remain strong to this day, as John Morris affirms. "I have greater memories of the people I got to be around every day than I do of the actual games. They were such amazing players but better people. It just made walking into that clubhouse every day so enjoyable. Everyone loved being there. It never felt like it was work."[9] Whether it was the clubhouse, the bus on the way to the airport, or anywhere else they found themselves sequestered together, the fellowship was always strong. "What I miss about the game is the camaraderie with the guys," Magrane said in 2024. "As I used to say, 'You're in the most exclusive men's club.' You can't buy or unduly influence your way into it; you're strictly there on merit. You've got a lot of alpha dogs in that locker room, and the ribbing will forever be in my memory and hard to replace. The Cardinal family, and the memories, connect with each other better than any organization."[10]

Morris agreed, as he continued with his recollections:

Willie McGee is one of my dearest friends. We just connected the first day we met. One day I was just playing around with him, doing an imitation of his batting stance and his running style. I didn't realize that there were ten other guys watching me, including Whitey. I was so shocked when I heard this laughter in the background. I turned around, and I was really embarrassed about what I was doing—and then I looked at Willie, and he was laughing his butt off. So, a few weeks later, Whitey came up to me and said, "Your job is to keep Willie laughing."[11]

Like Morris, Magrane is among the infinite number of those who cherish McGee's character. "I still admire Willie—not only for his ability, but for his grace. You're not supposed to run back to the dugout when you strike out, because it shows weakness to the other team. But Willie did it; both of his parents were pastors at his church, and Willie ran back to the dugout out of humility because he was embarrassed."[12]

But perhaps one of the most vivid tales of the personal bond among the 1987 Cardinals is also told by Morris, and the impact that Terry Pendleton in particular has had on his life:

Terry was such a wonderful teammate. I remember years later, he had a big impression on my family when my mom finally passed. He always stayed in touch with her. In late 1991 I had just seen Terry in Philadelphia. He asked me, "How's your mom doing?" And I said, "She's not doing well, Terry—she's in a coma, and I don't know how much longer she's got." He said, "Well I'm going to call her tomorrow at the house," because the Braves [Pendleton's new team] were going to New York. I said, "Don't even bother—she won't pick up, and she won't be able to talk to you." So, he goes to New York and doesn't tell me what he's about to do. He calls the house anyway. The phone is right next to the bed, and my brother Andrew picks it up. He says, "This is Andy; Morris residence." And Terry goes, "Hi, this is Terry Pendleton with the Atlanta Braves. Is Grace available?" And Andy yells out, "Terry Pendleton—how the hell are ya!" And my mom snaps out of her coma and says, "Is that Terry?" My brother hands her the phone. She says, "Oh hi, Terry, how are you doing? It's so nice to hear your voice. How's my son John doing? Oh, that's good to hear. It's so nice talking to you. Gotta go—bye." She hands the phone to my brother and falls back into her coma. That was the last person she ever spoke to. She died a week later.

That is why Terry has always been so endearing to me and such a close friend.[13]

BEARING WITNESS TO THE ENTIRE CARDINALS' MILIEU SINCE the glory days of the '80s is Horton, who returned to the team for two final seasons in 1989 and 1990, made his home in St. Louis, involved himself in numerous civic and philanthropic pursuits in the city and region, and is heard nightly during the hot Missouri summers on KMOX as a Cardinals broadcaster. "In 1987 you've got the Terry Pendleton home run on September 11. You've got the Tommy Herr "Seat Cushion Night" home run in April. Those two occurrences are iconic. You stop a Cardinal fan anywhere, and they'll remember those two moments in time." Yet to Horton, the season in which the Redbirds overcame and accomplished so much is an afterthought in the minds of many. "It is almost as if the 1987 team still clamors for respect. Oddly, when people talk about the Cardinals of the eighties, no one really talks about 1987 very much. It's almost as if '87 was the second half of the 1985 story."[14]

Finishing just one game short in both 1985 and 1987 did make for a somewhat-incomplete culmination of an otherwise exciting decade for St. Louis baseball. Nevertheless, it was a decade and style of play that Herzog and his team had gifted to the city, its fans, and to the sport itself, a brand of baseball that would become synonymous with his first name and had electrified the game with unparalleled motion, anticipation, and excitement.

Trying to define Whiteyball exactly is as difficult as corralling Willie McGee in going from first to third. But McDowell expressed it as well as anyone, illustrating that the mental pressure that Herzog's teams put on the opposition was just as powerful as the physical effect:

> I've always thought that baseball has a heartbeat. Data and analytics is a great tool, but it can't measure the heartbeat and the level of anxiety that you have when Vince Coleman is at first base and you know he's going to run. It is an anxiety level that you can't understand unless you've been there. Every team today has the same analytics, but at the end of the day, the teams that win are the ones with the best players.

> At Dodger Stadium, it is a hundred-some feet from home plate to the backstop. We had a pitcher in the bullpen—I won't say his name—who would not throw his breaking ball with a man on third base in Dodger Stadium because he was afraid of it bouncing and going to the backstop. You can't put that in the computer.[15]

THE DEATH OF GUSSIE BUSCH IN 1989 PRECEDED HERZOG'S resignation in the middle of the 1990 season with the Cardinals in last place. But by then, the impact of his teams had already been burned into the sport's memory—like the basepaths that his men had scorched on the turf of Busch Stadium, night after night.

"When the history of baseball in the 1980s is written, one club will stand out as a complete anomaly—a team that was not only different from others, but also a mystery to itself," penned Thomas Boswell.

"Herzog teams can be counted on to be tight-knit, extremely cocky and a tad paranoid on the subject of not getting enough credit. To be a Herzog Cardinal is to be a blunt, buck-stops-here type."[16]

Notes

1. Met with Disaster

1. Herzog and Horrigan, *White Rat*, 184.
2. Mike Smith, Eye Openers, *St. Louis Post-Dispatch*, September 12, 1987.
3. Herzog and Horrigan, *White Rat*, 184–85.
4. Herzog and Horrigan, *White Rat*, 184–85.
5. Jerry Stack, Eye Openers, *St. Louis Post-Dispatch*, March 18, 1987.
6. John Sonderegger, "KC Is Cards' Little Big Horn," *St. Louis Post-Dispatch*, October 28, 1985.
7. Rick Hummel, "Birds Get Heath, Deal Andujar," *St. Louis Post-Dispatch*, December 11, 1985.
8. Herzog and Horrigan, *White Rat*, 186.
9. Herzog and Horrigan, *White Rat*, 206.
10. Rick Hummel, "Porter, Cedeno Stack Up as 1986 Discards," *St. Louis Post-Dispatch*, October 30, 1985.
11. Howard Johnson, in discussion with the author, December 13, 2023.
12. Herzog and Horrigan, *White Rat*, 188–89.
13. Rick Hummel, "No Relief," *St. Louis Post-Dispatch*, February 25, 1987.
14. Bob Verdi, "Does Steinbrenner Have Laryngitis or What?" *The Sporting News*, May 26, 1986, 4.
15. Herzog and Horrigan, *White Rat*, 188–89, 192.
16. Herzog and Horrigan, *White Rat*, 194, 197.
17. Herzog and Horrigan, *White Rat*, 198.
18. Herzog and Horrigan, *White Rat*, 189, 199.
19. Herzog and Horrigan, *White Rat*, 200.
20. Rick Hummel, "Cards Win, Dare to Hope Again," *St. Louis Post-Dispatch*, June 23, 1986.

21. Rick Hummel, "Cardinals Help Cure LA's Pena," *St. Louis Post-Dispatch*, July 8, 1986.

22. Herzog and Horrigan, *White Rat*, 188–89.

23. Ross Newhan, "Hailed and Hated," *Los Angeles Times*, August 18, 1986.

24. Herzog and Horrigan, *White Rat*, 206.

25. Joseph Durso, "Aguilera Pitches Impressively but Mets Drop Spring Opener," *New York Times*, March 8, 1987.

26. Mike Tully, "Hal Lanier Represents the Revenge of Whitey Herzog," United Press International, *New York Times*, October 6, 1986.

27. Herzog and Horrigan, *White Rat*, 208–9.

2. Seeking Answers

1. Barto, "1986 Winter Meetings," 186.

2. Herzog and Horrigan, *White Rat*, 210.

3. "Couple of Beers Were a Good Buy for Duffy," *Los Angeles Times*, December 12, 1986.

4. Bruce Keidan, "Sales Hit Standstill at This Thrift Shop," *Pittsburgh Post-Gazette*, December 10, 1986.

5. Rick Hummel, "Clark: Parrish a 'Steal' for Phils," *St. Louis Post-Dispatch*, March 15, 1987.

6. Rick Hummel, "Herzog: Can the Mets Get Much Better?" *St. Louis Post-Dispatch*, December 14, 1986.

7. Murray Chass, "Willing Herzog Can't Strike Any Deals," *New York Times*, December 10, 1986.

8. Dave Anderson, "Can Mets Outbid Cards?," *New York Times*, November 2, 1986.

9. Robert Thomas, "Gooden, Mets' Star, Is Arrested after Fight with Tampa Police," *New York Times*, December 15, 1986.

10. Joe Ostermeier, "Cards Pose Questions, Decisions for Herzog," *Belleville (IL) News-Democrat*, March 22, 1987.

11. Hummel, "Can Mets Get Much Better?"

12. Rick Hummel, "Cards' Fast Start Impresses Herzog," *St. Louis Post-Dispatch*, March 11, 1987.

13. Rick Hummel, "New Hulk," *St. Louis Post-Dispatch*, March 3, 1987.

14. Rick Hummel, "Wish List," *St. Louis Post-Dispatch*, February 22, 1987.

15. Rick Hummel, "Clark Hopes Frequent Injuries, Clubhouse Friction Are History," *St. Louis Post-Dispatch*, February 22, 1987.

16. Rick Hummel, "Clark: Thumb Is OK," *St. Louis Post-Dispatch*, March 1, 1987.

17. "Slimmed-Down Herr Has High Hopes for Season," *Belleville (IL) News-Democrat*, March 2, 1987.

18. Rick Hummel, "Cards' Dunne Slowed by Auto Accident," *St. Louis Post-Dispatch*, February 27, 1987.

19. John Morris, in discussion with the author, November 3, 2023.

20. Hummel, "Cards' Dunne Slowed."

21. Joe Magrane, in discussion with the author, February 15, 2024.

22. Rick Hummel, "Magrane Starter in Camp Opener," *St. Louis Post-Dispatch*, February 26, 1987.

23. Magrane, discussion.

24. Rick Hummel, "Cox Seeks to Double Salary," *St. Louis Post-Dispatch*, January 21, 1987.

25. Bill Conlin, N. L. Beat, *The Sporting News*, April 6, 1987, 26.

26. Mike Smith, Eye Openers, *St. Louis Post-Dispatch*, February 24, 1987.

27. Rick Hummel, "Wins in Spring Not Worthless to 13-4 Cards," *St. Louis Post-Dispatch*, March 25, 1987.

28. Hummel, "New Hulk."

29. Herzog and Horrigan, *White Rat*, 209.

30. Rick Hummel, "Pendleton Renewed at Same Pay," *St. Louis Post-Dispatch*, March 5, 1987.

31. Rick Hummel, "Lindeman Poses Nice Problem for Cards," *St. Louis Post-Dispatch*, March 29, 1987.

32. Tom Herr, interview by Joe Garagiola, *National League Championship Series*, aired October 6, 1987, on NBC, https://www.youtube.com/watch?v=aEfJt8fz6fk.

33. Kevin Horrigan, "Life on Fringe Is One of Uncertainty," *St. Louis Post-Dispatch*, March 18, 1987.

34. José Oquendo, interview by Joe Garagiola, *National League Championship Series*, aired October 9, 1987, on NBC, https://www.youtube.com/watch?v=6jNI7GzH3hg.

35. Rick Hummel, "Oquendo Eyes All Positions," *St. Louis Post-Dispatch*, June 4, 1987.

36. Rick Hummel, "Cards Bolster Bullpen in Trade," *St. Louis Post-Dispatch*, December 23, 1986.

37. Rick Hummel, "Surprising Cardinals Hitting Almost .270," *St. Louis Post-Dispatch*, March 16, 1987.

38. Joe Ostermeier, "Cards Pose Questions, Decisions for Herzog," *Belleville (IL) News-Democrat*, March 22, 1987.

39. Rick Hummel, "Tudor Sounds Off, Wants Magrane in Pen," *St. Louis Post-Dispatch*, March 27, 1987.

40. N. L. East, *The Sporting News*, February 2, 1987, 42.

41. Ricky Horton, in discussion with the author, November 1, 2023.

42. National League, *Chicago Tribune*, March 30, 1987.

43. Rick Hummel, "McGee Has Knack for Driving in Runs," *The Sporting News*, July 6, 1987, 13.

44. "McDowell's Hernia Surgery Will Sideline Him Six Weeks," *Cincinnati Post*, March 31, 1987.

45. Rick Hummel, "A Flash or a Flash in the Pan?" *The Sporting News*, April 20, 1987, 22.

46. John Sonderegger, "Royals Turn Attention from Howser to Baseball," *St. Louis Post-Dispatch*, March 23, 1987.

47. Sonderegger, "Royals Turn Attention."

48. Rick Hummel, "Cards Swap 3 for Pirates' Pena," *St. Louis Post-Dispatch*, April 2, 1987.

49. Hummel, "Cards Swap 3."

50. Marian Uhlman, "Parrish's Back Means Pain and Risk," *Philadelphia Inquirer*, March 12, 1987.

51. Hummel, "Cards Swap 3."

52. Rick Hummel, "Tudor: 'Where's the Beef?'" *St. Louis Post-Dispatch*, April 5, 1987.

53. Rick Hummel, "Maxvill: Time Will Tell if Cards Erred on Parrish," *St. Louis Post-Dispatch*, April 8, 1987.

54. Hummel, "Cards Swap 3."

55. Bob Hertzel, "Goodbyes Emotional for Pena," *Pittsburgh Press*, April 2, 1987.

56. Kevin Horrigan, "Oh, Muffin! What's Going on in Sports?" *St. Louis Post-Dispatch*, March 4, 1987.

57. Mike Smith, Eye Openers, *St. Louis Post-Dispatch*, March 25, 1987.

58. Hummel, "Can Mets Get Much Better?"

59. Mike Smith, Eye Openers, *St. Louis Post-Dispatch*, March 24, 1987.

60. Jack Lang, "Mets Hoping Strawberry Can Get Act Together," *The Sporting News*, April 6, 1987, 20.

61. "Gooden Tells of Cocaine Use," *New York Times*, June 26, 1987.

62. Jack Lang, "Did Gooden Want to Get Caught?" *The Sporting News*, April 13, 1987, 24.

63. Rick Hummel, "Lefties Are All Right with Herzog," *St. Louis Post-Dispatch*, March 22, 1987.

64. Tom Wheatley, "Cards' Attitude Pleases Forsch," *St. Louis Post-Dispatch*, April 7, 1987.

65. Hummel, "Wins in Spring Not Worthless."

66. Bob Verdi, "Whitey's Fork Pops Mets' Balloon," *Chicago Tribune*, March 31, 1987.

3. The First Showdown

1. Rick Hummel, "Loss of Gooden Won't Do In Mets, Say Cards," *St. Louis Post-Dispatch*, April 5, 1987.

2. Hummel, "New Hulk."

3. Kevin Horrigan, "Dawson Has a K-Need to Play in Chicago," *St. Louis Post-Dispatch*, April 9, 1987.

4. Jim Lindeman, in discussion with the author, November 28, 2023.

5. Horrigan, "Dawson Has K-Need."

6. Kevin Horrigan, "Lindeman Box Score: 1 Big Hit, 1 Great Throw and 28 Passes," *St. Louis Post-Dispatch*, April 8, 1987.

7. Tom Wheatley, "Herzog 'Enjoys Managing at Wrigley the Worst,'" *St. Louis Post-Dispatch*, June 14, 1987.

8. United Press International, "Cubs in the Shadows at Lightless Wrigley," *St. Louis Post-Dispatch*, June 14, 1987.

9. Rick Hummel, "Herzog Airs Views on Campanis Case," *St. Louis Post-Dispatch*, April 10, 1987.

10. Rick Hummel, "Fans Give Pena Warm Greeting," *St. Louis Post-Dispatch*, April 11, 1987.

11. Rick Hummel, "Impatient," *St. Louis Post-Dispatch*, April 15, 1987.

12. "Now Is the Season of Phillies' Discontent," *St. Louis Post-Dispatch*, April 19, 1987.

13. Hummel, "Can Mets Get Much Better?"

14. Tom Wheatley, "Figuring Out the 'White Rat' Is Simple Task," *St. Louis Post-Dispatch*, April 25, 1987.

15. Joseph Durso, "Mets' Bats Are Finally Meek," *New York Times*, April 18, 1987.

16. Rick Hummel, "Cox Marvels at Cards' Saturday Night Special," *St. Louis Post-Dispatch*, April 20, 1987.

17. Roger McDowell, in discussion with the author, December 13, 2023.

18. Joseph Durso, "Herr Slams Mets in 10th," *New York Times*, April 19, 1987.

19. Hummel, "Cox Marvels."

20. Durso, "Herr Slams Mets."

21. Joseph Durso, "Yanks Win Two; Mets Fall Again," *New York Times*, April 20, 1987.

22. Durso, "Yanks Win Two; Mets Fall."

23. "A Bad Break for Cards," *The Sporting News*, April 27, 1987, 30.

24. Durso, "Yanks Win Two; Mets Fall."

25. Rick Hummel, "Landrum Slowly Getting Used to Dodger Blue," *St. Louis Post-Dispatch*, July 23, 1987.

26. Rick Hummel, "Crippled Cards Limp Past Cubs," *St. Louis Post-Dispatch*, April 24, 1987.

27. Horton, discussion.

28. Tom Wheatley, "Horton Is the Thinking-Man's Reliever," *St. Louis Post-Dispatch*, May 3, 1987.

29. Rick Hummel, "Cards Spelling Relief with Different Letters," *The Sporting News*, May 11, 1987, 22.

30. Rick Hummel, "Worrell Worrying Cards," *The Sporting News*, May 18, 1987, 18.

31. Morris, discussion.

32. Rick Hummel, "Cardinals Turn Tables on '86 Champs," *St. Louis Post-Dispatch*, April 27, 1987.

4. Powering Through

1. John Sonderegger, "Lasorda: Luck of the '85 Cards Went Bad," *St. Louis Post-Dispatch*, March 25, 1987.

2. Rick Hummel, "Magrane's Shutout Halts Cards' Skid," *St. Louis Post-Dispatch*, May 7, 1987.

3. Rick Hummel, "Flake," *St. Louis Post-Dispatch*, May 12, 1987.

4. Rick Hummel, Cardinals Notebook, *St. Louis Post-Dispatch*, May 14, 1987.

5. Rick Hummel, "Dayley's Pitching Status Hinges on Exam," *St. Louis Post-Dispatch*, May 12, 1987.

6. N. L. East, *The Sporting News*, May 25, 1987, 14.

7. Lindeman, discussion.

8. Rick Hummel, "Demotion Surprises Mathews," *St. Louis Post-Dispatch*, May 13. 1987.

9. Michael Sokolove, "Charlton Assumes the Early Lead in Competition for Pitching Staff," *Cincinnati Post*, March 14, 1987.

10. N. L. East, *The Sporting News*, May 25, 1987, 24.

11. N. L. East, *The Sporting News*, June 1, 1987, 19.

12. Rick Hummel, "Pagnozzi Sent to Louisville," *St. Louis Post-Dispatch*, May 22, 1987.

13. N. L. East, *The Sporting News*, May 11, 1987, 23.

14. Rick Hummel, "Lindeman to Make Stop in Louisville," *St. Louis Post-Dispatch*, May 26, 1987.

15. Horton, discussion.

16. N. L. East, *The Sporting News*, May 11, 1987, 23.

17. N. L. East, *The Sporting News*, May 18, 1987, 19.

18. Rick Hummel, "Cardinals Winning, but Hurting," *St. Louis Post-Dispatch*, May 30, 1987.

19. Hummel, "Cardinals Winning."

20. Rick Hummel, "Right Fielder Pena Prefers Catching," *St. Louis Post-Dispatch*, May 31, 1987.

21. Hummel, "Pagnozzi Sent to Louisville."

22. Bob Verdi, "Even Reagan Is Thrilled That Caray's Back," *The Sporting News*, June 1, 1987, 5.

23. Rick Hummel, "Cardinals Want to Keep LaPoint," *St. Louis Post-Dispatch*, June 28, 1987.

24. Peter Alfano, "Gooden Makes a Rousing Return as Crowd Roars," *New York Times*, June 6, 1987.

25. Frank Dolson, "Schmidt Made Some Big Plays for Parrish," *Philadelphia Inquirer*, March 15, 1987.

26. National League, *Chicago Tribune*, March 13, 1987.

27. Rick Hummel, "Coleman's Thievery Impresses Parrish," *St. Louis Post-Dispatch*, June 10, 1987.

28. Rick Hummel, "Herzog Defends Pena's Throwing," *St. Louis Post-Dispatch*, June 22, 1987.

29. Rick Hummel, "After Slow Start, Van Slyke Back in Groove," *St. Louis Post-Dispatch*, June 15, 1987.

30. Rick Hummel, Cards Notebook, *St. Louis Post-Dispatch*, June 14, 1987.

31. Dave Luecking, "Howser's Death Hits Home for John Morris," *St. Louis Post-Dispatch*, June 18, 1987.

32. Rick Hummel, "Cards Are a Threat to Win NL East, Schmidt Says," *St. Louis Post-Dispatch*, June 25, 1987.

33. Rick Hummel, "Clark, Pena Talks on Collision Course," *St. Louis Post-Dispatch*, June 28, 1987.

34. Rick Hummel, "Tudor's Therapy: Cards' Offense," *St. Louis Post-Dispatch*, June 14, 1987.

35. Joseph Durso, "Cards Knock Mets 7½ Out," *New York Times*, June 30 1987.

36. Rick Hummel, Cardinals Notebook, *St. Louis Post-Dispatch*, July 1, 1987.

37. Joseph Durso, "Mets Pour It On after Rain Lets Up," *New York Times*, July 2, 1987.

38. Sam McManis, "Rain Not Only Saves Dodgers, It Washes Away Clark's Homer," *Los Angeles Times*, July 7, 1987.

39. Rick Hummel, "Rain Washes Out Magrane's Trip Home," *St. Louis Post-Dispatch*, July 8, 1987.

40. Magrane, discussion.

41. Rick Hummel, "Marshall Returns, Guerrero Out," *St. Louis Post-Dispatch*, July 7, 1987.

42. Tom Wheatley, "Early Birds," *St. Louis Post-Dispatch*, July 9, 1987.

43. Wheatley, "Early Birds."

44. Wheatley, "Early Birds."

45. Rick Hummel, "Would a Gold Glove Fit Pendleton?" *The Sporting News*, July 27, 1987, 27.

46. Rick Hummel, "Andujar Back to Cards? Don't Bet on It," *St. Louis Post-Dispatch*, July 19, 1987.

47. "Johnson Awaiting the Call," *St. Louis Post-Dispatch*, July 7, 1987.

48. Rick Hummel, "Tudor Target: Aug. 5 Return," *St. Louis Post-Dispatch*, July 17, 1987.

49. Rick Hummel, "Clark: No Harm Meant," *St. Louis Post-Dispatch*, July 12, 1987.

5. All Hands on Deck

1. Rick Hummel, "Trying Times," *St. Louis Post-Dispatch*, July 16, 1987.

2. Rick Hummel, "Mathews Steps into Void, Hands Padres 4–3 Defeat," *St. Louis Post-Dispatch*, July 19, 1987.

3. N. L. East, *The Sporting News*, August 3, 1987, 23.

4. Rick Hummel, "Cards Fall to Padres in 10," *St. Louis Post-Dispatch*, July 19, 1987.

5. Rick Hummel, "Lindeman Still Seeking Old Swing, Confidence," *St. Louis Post-Dispatch*, July 22, 1987.

6. Rick Hummel, "Caution," *St. Louis Post-Dispatch*, August 2, 1987.

7. Jack Buck, Hall of Fame induction speech, National Baseball Hall of Fame and Museum, July 26, 1987, Cooperstown NY, 2:45, https://www.youtube.com/watch?v=0r3FVeHIqBo.

8. Rick Hummel, "Buck at Bat," *St. Louis Post-Dispatch*, July 26, 1987.

9. Hummel, "Andujar Back to Cards?"

10. Joseph Durso, "Cards Lose Game and Clark," *New York Times*, July 30, 1987.

11. Joseph Durso, "Mets Down Cards with Late Rallies," *New York Times*, July 29, 1987.

12. McDowell, discussion.

13. Johnson, discussion.

14. Joseph Durso, "Gooden Helps Mets Sweep, 5–3," *New York Times*, July 31, 1987.

15. Rick Hummel, "NL East Dominating West," *St. Louis Post-Dispatch*, August 16, 1987.

16. Rick Hummel, "League Ignores Cheating, Herzog Says," *St. Louis Post-Dispatch*, August 1, 1987.

17. Rick Hummel, Cards Notebook, *St. Louis Post-Dispatch*, August 3, 1987.

18. Rick Hummel, "Cards Notebook," *St. Louis Post-Dispatch*, August 12, 1987.

19. Mike Smith, Eye Openers, *St. Louis Post-Dispatch*, August 1, 1987.

20. Rick Hummel, "Collusion Ruling Won't Change Cards' Policy," *St. Louis Post-Dispatch*, September 20, 1987.

21. John Sonderegger, "Astroturf: 130," *St. Louis Post-Dispatch*, August 3, 1987.

22. Magrane, discussion.

23. Rick Hummel, Cards Notebook, *St. Louis Post-Dispatch*, August 2, 1987.

24. Rick Hummel, Cards Notebook, *St. Louis Post-Dispatch*, August 4, 1987.

25. Rick Hummel, "Steve Who?," *St. Louis Post-Dispatch*, August 9, 1987.

26. Rick Hummel, Cards Notebook, *St. Louis Post-Dispatch*, August 8, 1987.

27. Rick Hummel, "Targets," *St. Louis Post-Dispatch*, August 23, 1987.

28. "Baseball Pops Cork on Bat Theory for Homers," *Washington Post*, August 16, 1987.

29. Ricky Horton, interview by Jim Palmer, *1987 World Series*, aired October 17, 1987, on ABC, https://www.youtube.com/watch?v=cD9-0b_w9Bw.

30. Rick Hummel, Cards Notebook, *St. Louis Post-Dispatch*, August 7, 1987.

31. Rick Hummel, "Forsch Blanks Bucs for 10th Victory," *St. Louis Post-Dispatch*, August 11, 1987.

32. Rick Hummel, Cards Notebook, *St. Louis Post-Dispatch*, August 14, 1987.

33. Patrick Reusse, "Brew Chief: Former MLB Ump and St. Paul Native Tim Tschida Goes from behind the Plate to behind the Bar," *Minneapolis Star-Tribune*, August 25, 2020, https://www.startribune.com/brew-chief-former-mlb-ump-and-st-paul-native-tim-tschida-goes-from-behind-the-plate-to-behind-the-ba/572195662/.

34. Rick Hummel, "Schmidt's Two Homers Power Phils 5–2," *St. Louis Post-Dispatch*, August 16, 1987.

35. Hummel, "NL East Dominating West."

36. Hummel, "NL East Dominating West."

37. Rick Hummel, Cards Notebook, *St. Louis Post-Dispatch*, August 19, 1987.

38. Mike Smith, Eye Openers, *St. Louis Post-Dispatch*, August 20, 1987.

39. Rick Hummel, "Reuschel Deal Rankles Clark," *St. Louis Post-Dispatch*, August 22, 1987.

40. Rick Hummel, Cards Notes, *St. Louis Post-Dispatch*, August 23, 1987.

41. Rick Hummel, "Pirating of Dunne Made Trade for Pittsburgh," *St. Louis Post-Dispatch*, August 30, 1987.

6. Down Goes Jack

1. N. L. East, *The Sporting News*, September 21, 1987, 17.

2. N. L. East, *The Sporting News*, September 14, 1987, 19.

3. Herzog and Pitts, *You're Missin' a Great Game*, 160.

4. "Mets Beat Phils after Watching Cards Lose," *New York Newsday*, September 10, 1987.

5. Mike Smith, Eye Openers, *St. Louis Post-Dispatch*, September 10, 1987.

6. John Sonderegger and Rick Hummel, "Cards Sign Pena to Two-Year Pact," *St. Louis Post-Dispatch*, September 12, 1987.

7. Mike Smith, Eye Openers, *St. Louis Post-Dispatch*, September 29, 1987.

8. Rick Hummel, "Cards' Rally Shocks Mets," *St. Louis Post-Dispatch*, September 12, 1987.

9. Joseph Durso, "Mets, One Out from Victory, Are Stunned by Cards," *New York Times*, September 12, 1987.

10. John Sonderegger, "Several Mets Praise Their Conquerors," *St. Louis Post-Dispatch*, September 13, 1987.

11. Sonderegger, "Several Mets Praise Their Conquerors."

12. Rick Hummel, "Cards Have Picked Up Pena for Most of the Season," *The Sporting News*, September 14, 1987, 20.

13. Joseph Durso, "Darling Is Lost for Rest of Season," *New York Times*, September 13, 1987.

14. Johnson, discussion.

15. Rick Hummel, Cards Notebook, *St. Louis Post-Dispatch*, September 15, 1987.

16. Morris, discussion.

17. Mike Smith, Eye Openers, *St. Louis Post-Dispatch*, September 22, 1987.

18. N. L. East, *The Sporting News*, October 5, 1987, 19.

19. Dave Dorr, "Up 3½," *St. Louis Post-Dispatch*, September 23, 1987.

20. N. L. East, *The Sporting News*, October 5, 1987, 19.

21. Rick Hummel, Cards Notebook, *St. Louis Post-Dispatch*, September 28, 1987.

22. Rick Hummel, "Herzog Has Three Favorites for MVP," *St. Louis Post-Dispatch*, September 6, 1987.

23. Rick Hummel, "Cards Hold On to Win 5–3," *St. Louis Post-Dispatch*, September 27, 1987.

24. John Sonderegger, "Pirates Rip Gooden, Mets," *St. Louis Post-Dispatch*, September 27, 1987.

25. Hummel, "Cards Hold On."

26. Buck, "Expos at Cardinals."

27. Magrane, discussion.

28. Rick Hummel, "Cards Sweep; Magic No. 2," *St. Louis Post-Dispatch*, September 30, 1987.

29. Rick Hummel, "Clark Gets His Rips—at Big Red," *St. Louis Post-Dispatch*, October 1, 1987.

30. Brenda Slover, interview by St. Louis National Baseball Club, *That's a Winner*, directed by Tom Uhlis (1987; Saint Louis: St. Louis National Baseball Club), https://www.youtube.com/watch?v=OB9JMb4Tr00.

31. Joseph Durso, "Mets' Pitchers Begin the Slide," *New York Times*, October 3, 1987.

32. Joseph Durso, "Mets' Victory Leads to 2d Spot," *New York Times*, October 5, 1987.

33. Whitey Herzog, interview by St. Louis National Baseball Club, *That's a Winner*, directed by Tom Uhlis (1987; Saint Louis: St. Louis National Baseball Club), https://www.youtube.com/watch?v=OB9JMb4Tr00.

34. Rick Hummel, "A Wild Ride," *St. Louis Post-Dispatch*, October 17, 1987.

35. N. L. East, *The Sporting News*, September 21, 1987, 17.

7. A Giant Fight

1. Dave Luecking, "Youngblood Takes Shot at Coleman," *St. Louis Post-Dispatch*, October 13, 1987.

2. Wilson, "St. Louis Cardinal San Francisco Giant Brawl."

3. Rick Hummel, "Herzog Hopes That Cox Can Pitch Friday's Game," *St. Louis Post-Dispatch*, October 7, 1987.

4. Anne Tobik, Eye Openers, *St. Louis Post-Dispatch*, October 8, 1987.

5. Rick Hummel, "Playoff Clubs Sticking With 24-Man Rosters," *St. Louis Post-Dispatch*, September 27, 1987.

6. Hummel, "Herzog Hopes."

7. Rick Hummel, "Mathews' Arm, Bat Lift Cards," *St. Louis Post-Dispatch*, October 7, 1987.

8. Dave Luecking, "Flu Makes Lindeman Questionable Today," *St. Louis Post-Dispatch*, October 7, 1987.

9. Tom Uhlenbrock and Bill Smith, "Cold Bats, Day Numb Fans, but Pennant Fever Still Hot," *St. Louis Post-Dispatch*, October 8, 1987.

10. Dave Luecking, "No Love Lost between Cardinals, Giants' Leonard," *St. Louis Post-Dispatch*, October 8, 1987.

11. Kevin Horrigan, "Dravecky Does His Job with a Religious Zeal," *St. Louis Post-Dispatch*, October 8, 1987.

12. John Sonderegger, "Cards Mostly Try to Ignore Giants' Taunts," *St. Louis Post-Dispatch*, October 9, 1987.

13. Rick Hummel, "Lawless Starts at 3rd for Hobbled Pendleton," *St. Louis Post-Dispatch*, October 10, 1987.

14. Mike Smith, "Cardinals Crumple, Drop Game 2 to Giants, 5–0," *St. Louis Post-Dispatch*, October 8, 1987.

15. Candy Maldonado, interview by Vin Scully, *National League Championship Series*, aired October 10, 1987 on NBC, https://www.youtube.com/watch?v=E9Z5xdS73Q0.

16. Lindeman, discussion.

17. Ellen Futterman, "'It's Just a Temporary Setback,' Cards' Fan Says," *St. Louis Post-Dispatch*, October 11, 1987.

18. Rick Hummel, "Leonard's Homer Followed Vow of Revenge," *St. Louis Post-Dispatch*, October 11, 1987.

19. Mike Smith, "Comeback," *St. Louis Post-Dispatch*, October 10, 1987.

20. Dave Luecking, Eye Openers, *St. Louis Post-Dispatch*, October 10, 1987.

21. Horton, discussion.

22. Hummel, "Leonard's Homer Followed Vow."

23. Rick Hummel, "Cards' Grounders Fuel for Giants' DP Machine," *St. Louis Post-Dispatch*, October 11, 1987.

24. John Sonderegger, "'Arrogant' Cards Fan Krukow's Fire," *St. Louis Post-Dispatch*, October 10, 1987.

25. Scully, *National League Championship Series*, October 10, 1987.

26. Jeffrey Leonard, interview by Vin Scully, *National League Championship Series*, aired October 10, 1987, on NBC, https://www.youtube.com/watch?v=E9Z5xdS73Q0.

27. Rick Hummel and John Sonderegger, "Cox, Hammaker to Pitch in Pennant-Clincher," *St. Louis Post-Dispatch*, October 14, 1987.

28. Kevin Horrigan, "Whooosh! Ill Wind Blows Away Cards," *St. Louis Post-Dispatch*, October 12, 1987.

29. Luecking, "Youngblood Takes Shot."

30. Kathleen Nelson, Eye Openers, *St. Louis Post-Dispatch*, October 13, 1987.

31. John Tudor, interview by Joe Garagiola, *National League Championship Series*, aired October 13, 1987, on NBC, https://www.youtube.com/watch?v=z-v4hAg2oNY.

32. Mike Smith, "Tudor Gets 'Rocky' Reception," *St. Louis Post-Dispatch*, October 14, 1987.

33. Scully, *National League Championship Series*, October 10, 1987.

34. Scully, *National League Championship Series*, October 14, 1987.

35. Ozzie Smith, interview by Jay Randolph, *National League Championship Series*, aired October 14, 1987, on NBC, https://www.youtube.com/watch?v=ptPowVSmDXA; and Tom Wheatley, "Smallest Cardinals Stand Tall in Conquest of Giants," *St. Louis Post-Dispatch*, October 16, 1987.

36. Wheatley, "Smallest Cardinals Stand Tall."

37. John Sonderegger, "Champs!" *St. Louis Post-Dispatch*, October 15, 1987.

38. Rick Hummel, "Cox Expected to Start Game Five," *St. Louis Post-Dispatch*, October 22, 1987.

8. Battle on the Mississippi

1. McCarver, *1987 World Series*, October 17, 1987.

2. Bill Smith, "Twins Fans Crazy over Homer Hankies," *St. Louis Post-Dispatch*, October 16, 1987.

3. Lindeman, discussion.

4. Rick Hummel, John Sonderegger, and Dave Luecking, World Series Notes, *St. Louis Post-Dispatch*, October 18, 1987.

5. Dave Luecking, "Best Pitcher Was Best Man," *St. Louis Post-Dispatch*, October 16, 1987.

6. Hummel, Sonderegger, and Luecking, World Series Notes, October 18, 1987.

7. Rick Hummel, World Series Notes, *St. Louis Post-Dispatch*, October 17, 1987.

8. Rick Hummel, "Twins Slam Redbirds 10–1," *St. Louis Post-Dispatch*, October 18, 1987.

9. McCarver, *1987 World Series*, October 17, 1987.

10. Magrane, discussion.

11. Dave Luecking, "Home Runs Fail to Faze Blyleven," *St. Louis Post-Dispatch*, October 18, 1987.

12. Magrane, discussion.

13. Rick Hummel and Dave Luecking, Cards Notes, *St. Louis Post-Dispatch*, October 19, 1987.

14. Kevin Horrigan, "Herzog Relaxes on Day Off, Holds Court in Downtown Bar," *St. Louis Post-Dispatch*, October 20, 1987.

15. Tom Wheatley, "Lawless Act Receives Mixed Reviews," *St. Louis Post-Dispatch*, October 23, 1987.

16. Rick Hummel, Cards Notes, *St. Louis Post-Dispatch*, October 21, 1987.

17. John Sonderegger, "Ozzie Assails Media," *St. Louis Post-Dispatch*, October 22, 1987.

18. Mike Smith, "Cards to Twins: Let's Dome It Again," *St. Louis Post-Dispatch*, October 22, 1987.

19. Rick Hummel and Dave Luecking, Cards Notes, *St. Louis Post-Dispatch*, October 23, 1987.

20. Horton, discussion.

21. Dave Luecking, "McGee Critical of Metrodome," *St. Louis Post-Dispatch*, October 25, 1987.

22. Dave Luecking, "Hrbek's Slam Was Knockout Punch," *St. Louis Post-Dispatch*, October 26, 1987.

23. Steve Lake, interview by Tim McCarver, *1987 World Series*, aired October 25, 1987, on ABC, https://www.youtube.com/watch?v=7aQdU1L6CIA.

24. Mike Smith, "Cox in the Thick of Downfall," *St. Louis Post-Dispatch*, October 26, 1987.

25. Mike Smith, "Cards' Catalysts Can't Get Going," *St. Louis Post-Dispatch*, October 26, 1987.

26. Smith, "Cards' Catalysts."

27. Dave Luecking, "Cox Couldn't Get Third Clincher of '87," *St. Louis Post-Dispatch*, October 26, 1987.

Epilogue

1. Rick Hummel, "Giants Belt Cards 5–0," *St. Louis Post-Dispatch*, July 25, 1988.

2. Rick Hummel, "Herr's Head Spinning after Trade," *St. Louis Post-Dispatch*, April 23, 1988.

3. Rick Hummel, "Cards Deal Herr for Brunansky," *St. Louis Post-Dispatch*, April 23, 1988.

4. Lindeman, discussion.

5. Horton, discussion.

6. Magrane, discussion.

7. Mookie Wilson, in discussion with the author, December 14, 2023.

8. McDowell, discussion.

9. Morris, discussion.

10. Magrane, discussion.

11. Morris, discussion.

12. Magrane, discussion.

13. Morris, discussion.

14. Horton, discussion.

15. McDowell, discussion.

16. Thomas Boswell, "Cardinals' 1890s Style Working Well in the 1980s," *Miami Herald*, July 7, 1987.

Bibliography

Barto, Jeff. "1986 Winter Meetings: A Rigged Market: Collusion II." In *Baseball's Business: The Winter Meetings: 1958–2016*, vol. 2, edited by Steve Weingarden and Bill Nowlin, 183–90. Cooperstown NY: Society for American Baseball Research, 2017.

Buck, Jack. "Expos at Cardinals," *Cardinal Baseball*, WGEN-FM, September 29, 1987, doubleheader. https://www.youtube.com/watch?v=3tst9_wgXMc.

Herzog, Whitey, and Kevin Horrigan. *White Rat: A Life in Baseball*. New York: Harper and Row, 1987.

Herzog, Whitey, and Jonathan Pitts. *You're Missin' a Great Game*. New York: Simon and Schuster, 2007.

McCarver, Tim. *1987 World Series*. Aired October 17, 1987, on ABC. https://www.youtube.com/watch?v=cD9-ob_w9Bw.

Scully, Vin. *National League Championship Series*. Aired October 10, 1987, on NBC. https://www.youtube.com/watch?v=E9Z5xdS73Qo.

———. *National League Championship Series*. Aired October 14, 1987, on NBC. https://www.youtube.com/watch?v=ptP0wVSmDXA.

Wilson, Ken. "St. Louis Cardinal San Francisco Giant Brawl '86." KSDK-TV, Saint Louis, July 22, 1986, video, 10:00. https://www.youtube.com/watch?v=mtsdJIEu2uk&t=9s.

Newspapers Utilized

Belleville (IL) News-Democrat
Chicago Tribune
Cincinnati Post
Los Angeles Times
Miami Herald
Minneapolis Star-Tribune
New York Newsday
New York Times
Philadelphia Inquirer
Pittsburgh Post-Gazette
Pittsburgh Press
St. Louis Globe-Democrat
St. Louis Post-Dispatch
The Sporting News
Washington Post

Index

Busch Stadium (*cont.*)
95, 100; three-millionth fan in 1987,
120, 126, 127, 129–30, 139, 140–42, 149,
151, 155, 157–59, 163, 170, 175, 177, 178
Bush, Randy, 148
Butera, Sal, 152

California Angels, 111
Candelaria, John, 111
Candlestick Park (San Francisco), 131–
32, 134–35, 137–38, 143, 146, 150, 157
Caray, Harry, 44; return after 1987
stroke, 68–69
Carew, Rod, 30, 154
Carlton, Steve, 25–26, 157, 166
Carter, Gary, 9–11, 20, 26, 39, 44, 47, 48,
58, 69, 96, 109
Cashen, Frank, 39–40
Cedeno, Cesar, 107, 117
Chicago Bears, 173
Chicago Cubs, 14, 16, 28, 40, 44–47,
57, 64, 67–68, 71, 73, 75, 88, 95, 96,
99–100, 107, 112–14, 115–17, 136, 164
Chicago White Sox, 15, 25, 30, 74
Cincinnati Reds, 2, 11, 29–30, 64–65, 71,
85, 96, 101, 102–3, 148, 155
Clark, Jack, 2, 11–13, 19, 21–25, 27–29,
33, 67–68, 71–73, 80, 94–95; ankle
injury, 106–7, 108, 113, 115–16, 128–29,
131, 174–75, 176; consecutive NL game
walk record, 98, 100–101, 102–3
Clark, Will, 130–31, 173–74
Cole, Alex, 82
Coleman, Vince, 7, 11, 15, 21–22, 24–25,
47–48, 51–52, 54–55, 59–60, 62, 78,
85–86, 90, 93, 98, 102–3, 106, 108;
leaving the Cardinals, 176, 182; one
hundredth stolen base of 1987, 110,
117, 119, 122, 123, 125–26, 128, 136,
144, 153–55, 157, 160, 162, 163–64, 165,
167–68
College World Series, in 1984, 26
Concepcion, Onix, 3
Cone, David, 40, 121
Conroy, Tim, 8–10, 13, 32–33, 57, 97
Cooper, Cecil, 30
Cooper, Mort, 121
Cox, Danny, 13, 33, 43, 56, 62, 76, 77, 87,

92, 94, 96–98, 110, 112, 116, 118; pitching 1987 division-clinching game, 119,
121, 126–27, 130, 135–36, 142–44, 155–
56, 163–64, 167–69, 170–71, 177–78;
broken foot in July 1987, 81, 126, 142
Craig, Roger, 81, 83, 88, 93, 102, 125–27,
129–32, 136, 139, 140, 142
Cuellar, Mike, 40

Darling, Ron, 34, 39, 108, 110, 121, 151–
52, 175
Daulton, Darren, 115
Davis, Charles "Chili," 140, 144
Davis, Eric, 60, 64–65, 68, 73, 85, 87
Dawley, Bill, 30–31, 47, 62, 80, 86, 92,
96, 97, 120
Dawson, Andre, 18, 44–46, 87, 95–96,
107, 116, 176
Dayett, Brian, 46
Dayley, Ken, 1, 14, 21, 31–33, 66, 73, 75,
79–80, 83, 86, 87, 91, 94, 109, 115; leav-
ing the Cardinals, 176, 178; returning
after injury, 121–22, 129, 141–42, 162,
164, 166
Dean, Jay "Dizzy," 4, 118, 139
Dean, Paul, 118
Deer, Rob, 99
Deleon, Jose, 177
Denkinger, Don, 2–3, 5–6, 9
Detroit Tigers, 2, 14, 18, 27, 70, 120, 147,
151–52, 157, 177
DiPino, Frank, 116
Ditka, Mike, 173
Dodger Stadium (Los Angeles), 63, 87,
182
Dominican Baseball League, 49
Dravecky, Dave, 101, 129–31, 138, 139,
142
Driessen, Dan, 71, 107, 108–9, 117, 119,
127–29, 133, 135, 138, 155
Duncan, Mariano, 88
Dunne, Mike, 35, 69, 112, 177
Dunston, Shawon, 113
Durham, Leon, 46, 113
Dykstra, Lenny, 38

Engel, Bob, 140

Fairmount Park (Collinsville IL), 158